Security Entrepreneurs

Security Entrepreneurs

Performing Protection in Post-Cold War Europe

Alexandra Gheciu

OXFORD
UNIVERSITY PRESS

OXFORD

UNIVERSITY PRESS

Great Clarendon Street, Oxford, OX2 6DP,
United Kingdom

Oxford University Press is a department of the University of Oxford.
It furthers the University's objective of excellence in research, scholarship,
and education by publishing worldwide. Oxford is a registered trade mark of
Oxford University Press in the UK and in certain other countries

© Alexandra Gheciu 2018

First Edition published in 2018
Impression: 1

Published in the United States of America by Oxford University Press
198 Madison Avenue, New York, NY 10016, United States of America

British Library Cataloguing in Publication Data

Data available

Library of Congress Control Number: 2017958464

ISBN 978–0–19–881306–4

Printed and bound by
CPI Group (UK) Ltd, Croydon, CR0 4YY

Acknowledgments

It is often said that writing a book is a lonely process. Yet, my experience in researching and writing this book was a very different one. It was my privilege to benefit from the generous support, advice, and guidance of a large number of individuals. I am extremely grateful to all of them.

My intellectual journey was profoundly shaped by what I learned during extended trips to the UK, Belgium, Bulgaria, Romania, Serbia, and Bosnia. In each of those countries I benefited enormously from meetings with large numbers of academics and practitioners who shared with me their impressive knowledge and expertise. In the course of my fieldwork, I was fortunate enough to be hosted by several institutions that conduct groundbreaking research in the field of security: the Centre for the Study of Democracy (CSD) in Sofia, the Belgrade Centre for Security Policy (BCSP), and the Centre for Security Studies (CSS) in Sarajevo. For their warm hospitality and generous support I am extremely grateful to Philip Gounev and his colleagues at the CSD; Sonja Stojanović Gajić, Predrag Petrović, and the entire team of the BCSP; as well as Denis Hadzović and his colleagues at the CSS. All of them kindly welcomed me to their institutions, offered valuable advice and information, and helped me set up large numbers of interviews. I really can't thank them enough.

I am also deeply grateful to many other academics and practitioners based in Eastern Europe, who carved time out of their busy schedules to hold long meetings with me and help me understand key aspects of security commercialization in that part of the world. Particular thanks go to Jasmin Ahić, Vlado Azinović, Gabriel Badea, Dimitar Bechev, Tobias Flessenkemper, Mihai Prisacariu, as well as to managers of local and global private security companies (G4S and Securitas) operating in Bulgaria, Romania, Serbia, and Bosnia, and to Robert Juhos (G4S's Regional Managing Director for Central/Eastern Europe). I am equally grateful to many East European managers/directors of businesses that employ private security companies, as well as to representatives of NGOs and members of think tanks, journalists, and government officials who agreed to meet with me and helped me gain a broader perspective of the dynamics of post-1989 transformations in Eastern Europe. This book could not have been completed without their help.

In addition, I would like to thank Hilde de Clerck and her team at the Confederation of European Security Services (CoESS), as well as many UN, NATO, and EU officials working in the Balkans who kindly participated in long meetings with me. They all provided valuable information and generous guidance, and helped me locate important data for this project. For all that, I am truly in their debt.

Over the past five years, various aspects of research related to this book were presented at conferences, seminars, and workshops in Ottawa, Turin, London, Paris, Ithaca (NY), and Washington, DC, as well as at several ISA Conventions. I would like to thank the organizers and the participants in those conferences and workshops for a series of questions and comments that helped me sharpen my analysis.

At the University of Ottawa, I have a huge debt of gratitude to Michael Williams and Srdjan Vucetic, who were so kind as to read the first draft of the manuscript and provided extremely helpful comments and suggestions. Chris Leite deserves special thanks for his terrific research assistance. Many more friends, colleagues, and family members offered advice, support, and comments on various aspects of my project—and patiently endured long conversations about this book. They all have my heartfelt gratitude.

This list of acknowledgments would not be complete without my deep thanks to the reviewers at Oxford University Press for their extremely valuable comments, and to Dominic Byatt, Olivia Wells, Sarah Parker, and the entire OUP team for their enthusiasm and wonderful support for this project.

Last but certainly not least, I gratefully acknowledge the financial support provided by the Social Sciences and Humanities Research Council of Canada for research leading to this book.

I could not have researched and completed this book without the unfailing support of so many individuals and institutions. Of course, the final product is entirely my responsibility.

Contents

1

The Reconstitution of Security Provision after the Cold War

A quarter of century after the collapse of communism, there is no simple answer to the question of who provides every day, non-military security in East European polities—or in what ways they do so. This matters because the complicated, complex practices of security governance and provision enacted in those countries have a profound impact on the (re)constitution of key state institutions, blur the boundary between public/private domains, and shape—while also being shaped by—the participation of those countries in European practices of governance and in global economic and political circuits. Questions about the evolving nature and implications of security provision sit side by side with issues of state capacities and growing inequalities at a time when many people in Eastern Europe demand more protection from what they perceive as a growing number of dangers, yet also feel that their states are unable or unwilling to provide adequate security. More broadly, developments in Eastern Europe are linked to current debates about the extent to which the protection of EU residents is best achieved via a move toward closer European integration and a greater degree of security "harmonization," or, conversely, more reliance on national-level institutions and arrangements.

Focusing on four East European polities—Bosnia, Serbia, Bulgaria, and Romania—this book examines the dynamics and implications of processes of commercialization of security that have occurred following the collapse of communist regimes. These processes have been central to post-communist liberalization, and have profoundly shaped those states and their integration into European institutional structures and global economic and political circuits. They have also affected the behavior and power of regional and global actors (e.g. European institutions, regional and global corporations) in Eastern Europe. Several aspects of security commercialization are particularly important. To begin with, private actors—specifically private security companies (PSCs)—have been reconstituted as partial agents of public power. As such, they have come to be systematically involved in security governance and provision—helping to (re)define and implement the "rules of the game" in the field of security, as they are now empowered to protect citizens and their property and also to contribute to the maintenance of public order. Today, public officials across Eastern Europe admit that their (often cash-strapped) state agencies would find it extremely difficult to "behave like a state" without the aid of the private security industry. In the words of a senior official from the Bulgarian Ministry of Interior: "the truth is that we just don't have the resources to be everywhere at once and do everything that we are supposed to do to protect our population. The state needs a 'little brother', and that can only come from the private sector."[1]

In addition, under the influence of neo-liberal norms, a potent commercial logic has come to permeate public security institutions—leading to a situation in which cost-cutting has become a key concern for police forces and other governmental agencies. In several instances, ministries of interior and police forces have not only devolved important responsibilities to private actors but have also started to offer commercial services to private customers— sometimes in direct competition with private security providers. In some cases, the private security function seems to be privileged over the public one, as the police have devoted more attention and resources to their commercial operations than to the public security provision. There is evidence that in some parts of Eastern Europe the police often warn the population that they lack the resources to adequately protect the property of individuals and businesses, and actively encourage them to hire a security company run by policemen or their families. This has led to a redefinition of the relationship between the state and its population—now cast in the dual role of citizens and paying customers—in ways that defy conventional wisdom about the role of the state, and pose particularly difficult normative challenges in societies with weak democratic traditions.

More broadly, as the next chapters demonstrate, processes of security commercialization in Eastern Europe have led to the emergence of complex, hybrid networks of security providers that transcend domestic/international and public/private boundaries, and behave, in many ways, as entrepreneurs. The concept of entrepreneurs in the field of security is not new. A particularly influential statement of the role of entrepreneurship in the reconstitution of security following the collapse of communist regimes can be found in Vadim Volkov's book on the role of violence in creating the institutions of a new market economy in Russia in the 1990s (Volkov 2002). As we shall see, countries of the former Eastern bloc have, like Russia, experienced aspects of violent entrepreneurship in the process of commercializing security provision. Yet, to focus only on violence would be to oversimplify the dynamics of entrepreneurship that have emerged in post-communist Europe. In this book, the terms entrepreneurs and entrepreneurship refer to a broader set of practices, involving not only the use of coercion but also, and increasingly, productive power (Barnett and Duvall 2005a and 2005b) mobilized by networks of public/private actors in the name of participating in the protection of public order via the production of "responsible" citizens. Linked to this, we can think of the participants in the field of security as "norm entrepreneurs," in the sense that they have been involved in redefining the norms of security in post-communist Europe (Finnemore and Sikkink 1998). In all those entrepreneurship practices, the private security industry has mobilized various forms of capital to both cooperate and compete with public agencies as they (re)define the rules of the game in the provision of a key public good, security. Interestingly, there is an important performative dimension involved in the practices through which private actors—in this case private security companies—cast themselves in public roles and seek broad recognition as competent agents of public power. In essence, PSCs do not simply carry out functions of protection conventionally attributed to the state; they literally *perform* those practices.

Why examine post-communist states? There is something particularly interesting about the dynamics and consequences of practices through which polities that had previously defined their identity around a firm state control over the provision of (in)security embraced but also manipulated liberal ideas concerning state/society relations after 1989. During the Cold War, Central/ East European states were governed by highly repressive regimes that defined their missions around communist ideals—as such, they had very large and complex state agencies aimed at ensuring "domestic order," systematically monitoring the entire population and quickly silencing any actual or potential dissidents. The contrast between that situation, characterized by a quasi-absolute state monopoly in the field of security, and the present situation (in which the police and the military have been significantly downsized and in which PSCs are increasingly prominent security actors) is striking. Across the former Eastern bloc, PSCs have come to perform functions that range from the protection of people, private property, and public spaces to securing critical infrastructure, transporting valuables, gathering intelligence, helping to run prisons, and managing crowds at cultural and sporting events (Caparini and Marenin 2005). Yet, to cast this change as a mere shift from the predominance of the public domain to the triumph of the private arena would be misleading. Rather, in those states the security of persons and property is provided by hybrid networks of actors, which both reflect and contribute to broader transformations of domestic and transnational practices in the field of security. To further complicate matters, in some instances networks of security providers not only transcend the public/private boundary but also blur the licit/illicit divide. Thus, particularly in the first years of post-communism transition, many of the networks of professionals involved in security provision had links to organized crime. In recent years, those links have become weaker and more subtle—but have not vanished altogether.

In recent years, several excellent works have been published on the subject of security commodification in the neo-liberal age (Abrahamsen and Leander 2015; Abrahamsen and Williams 2007, 2008, 2011; Avant 2005, 2006, 2016; Avant and Haufler 2014, 2018; Ayling et al. 2009; Berndtsson 2012; Dunigan and Petersohn 2015; Eichler 2015; Haufler 1997, 2007, 2010; Krahmann 2003, 2007, 2010; Leander 2004, 2005, 2010, 2013; Leander and Van Munster 2007). The increasingly rich academic literature in this area also includes a series of important analyses of security privatization in former communist countries (e.g. Volkov 2002; Caparini and Marenin 2005; Gounev 2007; Tzvetkova 2008; Ganev 2009; Petrović 2010; Bureš 2015). Through their case studies, those works shed valuable light on the transformations in security provision that occurred in individual states from the former Eastern bloc. In many ways, this book builds on those studies—expanding the analysis in several ways, both conceptually and empirically. Thus, this book focuses on several countries, examines the interplay between global/regional/national/local dynamics, and explores the links among politics/security/economics in the reconstitution of the field of security. Conceptually, the book draws on multiple disciplines, combining various analytical tools in an effort to better understand the complexity and deep implications of a new political economy of security provision that defies conventional categories, breaks down traditional divides, and complicates moral thinking about the nature and relative merits of actors involved in providing a key public good.

The nature and impact of commercialization of security in East European polities is profound and, in itself, deserves more attention than it has received so far. But the processes and practices examined in this book transcend the boundaries of those polities. A study of East European commercialization of security also sheds new light on aspects of the evolution of the European Union (EU) and the wider structures of European policing and security that have been insufficiently examined until now. The reconstitution of the field of security—as a key aspect of the reconstruction of states in post-communist Europe—is inextricably linked, but not reducible, to European integration and enlargement, as well as to processes of globalization. As the next chapters show, we cannot understand the changing nature of security provision in Eastern Europe unless we take into account the reforms conducted as part of the EU accession negotiations (or, in the case of Bosnia, within the framework of the international administration in which the EU plays a key role). More broadly, we need to understand how processes of liberalization in those countries have facilitated the influx of multinational corporations demanding Western standards of protection—and of global PSCs claiming to provide those standards. Far from confining their activities to the private sector, those global actors have forged alliances with a series of local players, and have also become involved in efforts to reshape the institutional and legal fabrics of their host societies.

At first glance, it might be tempting to conclude—given the massive resources commanded by global PSCs, as well as the power exercised by the EU in accession negotiations, not to mention within the framework of the international administration in Bosnia—that East European polities had no choice but to comply with the demands and prescriptions of international actors. Yet, this would be an oversimplification of the evolution of security provision in former communist polities. A careful analysis of the evolution of those countries reveals that, far from being the passive recipients of Western-prescribed norms and institutions, national and local actors have exercised significant forms of power in shaping the logics of security provision in the post-communist era. By exploring the dynamics and consequences of those exercises of power, this book builds on recent critiques of the literature that ignore or marginalize the agency of national/local actors in the processes of dissemination of international norms.[2] Linked to this, the analysis developed in the following chapters sheds light on the fluidity of security provision arrangements in the former Eastern bloc. Even a quarter century after the collapse of communism, the domain of security in each of the four East European countries continues to be the site of transformation via power-filled practices through which various actors and networks cooperate and compete, mobilizing—and seeking recognition for—diverse types of material and non-material resources or forms of capital.[3]

By examining these complex sets of practices, I seek to contribute to the effort to map an analytic terrain for the study of globalization that includes but is not limited to a focus on growing interdependence and global institutions (Avant et al. 2010; Sassen 2006, 2008). This book builds on several excellent studies of the interplay between global, regional, and local dynamics in practices of security provision (Abrahamsen and Williams 2011; Abrahamsen and Leander 2015; Brodeur 2010; Bureš 2015; Gould 2017; Johnston 2000; van Steden and de Waard 2013). In particular, it builds on Abrahamsen and Williams's sophisticated analysis of global security assemblages—defined as transnational structures and networks "in which a range of different actors and normativities interact, cooperate and compete to produce new institutions, practices and forms of deterritorialized security governance" (Abrahamsen and Williams 2011: 90).

More broadly, I suggest that recent developments in the field of security in Eastern Europe can be seen as a reflection of what a series of scholars call "glocalization." Glocalization refers to a situation in which, far from being disconnected from the local, global processes are local in each of their points

(Latour 1993). This means that wherever globalization has effects, those effects will depend on the particular setting or context in which they occur (Robertson 1992; Swyngedouw 1997, 2004). Proponents of glocalization have long argued that globalization dynamics are always reinterpreted locally, leading to an interpenetration of the local and global scales that creates context-dependent outcomes (Robertson 1992; Swingedouw 1997, 2004). As Saskia Sassen has cogently argued, "[T]he fact that a process or entity is located within the territory of a sovereign state does not necessarily mean that it is a national process or entity; it might be a localization of the global or a denationalized instance of the national" (Sassen 2006: 2). Under these circumstances, studying the global "entails not only a focus on what is explicitly global in scale. It also calls for a focus on locally scaled practices and conditions articulated with global dynamics...And it calls for a focus on the multiplication of cross-border connections among subnational localities where certain conditions recur" (Sassen 2006: 7). Processes that are localized in national and subnational settings can be part of globalization by inserting those localities in global economic, social, or political processes. Often, they involve transboundary networks and entities connecting diverse local or national processes and actors. Applying this conceptualization to security practices carried out in Eastern Europe, I show that countries emerging from the collapse of the communist bloc have been deeply shaped—albeit in different ways—by processes of "glocalization."

In the following chapters, we shall see that the nature, functions, and power exercised by security providers in many ex-communist states cannot be understood in abstraction from the global rise of neo-liberal ideas and practices, and, in more concrete terms, the growing presence in those countries of global corporations—including multinational private security companies (PSCs). Indeed, to grasp the growing role played by private actors in the provision of security in East European polities, one needs to take into account the broader context of international normative transformations within which processes of post-communist transition were taking place. Those normative transformations became particularly important when East European elites embarked upon ambitious processes of moving closer/seeking accession to the EU and integrating their polities into global economic circuits (particularly by opening their doors to foreign capital). In that context, countries from the former Eastern bloc became more open to international influences, including the influence of prevailing norms of commodification of security that became globally dominant in the 1990s.

As Abrahamsen and Williams have persuasively argued, the neo-liberal focus on the roll-back of the state and efficient governance has facilitated the growth of the private security sector (Abrahamsen and Williams 2011). As the neo-liberal logic came to prevail in many areas of life in countries around the world, the security sector, too, came under pressure to embrace "new managerialism" strategies for cost efficiency. Neo-liberal norms have served to legitimize both the outsourcing of functions that were previously seen as falling within the purview of the state and the partial commodification of security—leading to a situation in which, at least within certain limits, security becomes a service to be bought in the marketplace and a commodity capable of being exported as a set of technical capabilities, knowledge, and skills (Avant 2005, 2016; Brodeur 1983, 2010; Button 2007; de Waard 1999; Dupont et al. 2003; Dupont 2014; Joachim and Schneiker 2014; Loader 1999, 2000; Sklansky 2006; Westermeyer 2013). The adoption of neo-liberal policies and practices, with their focus on the alleged efficiency and rationality of the market, led to a growing acceptance of private security corporations as legitimate providers of security. In contrast to the conventional view that only certain (state) actors had the authority to provide security, the neo-liberal logic suggests that non-state actors that have the necessary material and symbolic capital (expertise, knowledge, prestige) could compete with public actors— albeit within certain limits—in various areas in the field of security. Against the background of those changes, public–private partnerships in the protection of citizens and their property have also proliferated, and community-based forms of policing have gained new prominence in many countries around the world. More broadly, post-Keynesian policing has become increasingly detached from imageries of public dependency on police expertise and has moved toward a more contractual neo-liberal imagery. In this emergent discourse, the community appears as a "network of agentive, expert and independent actors who enter partnerships with the police" (O'Malley and Palmer 1996: 138).

It is in the context of these neo-liberal transformations that private actors, especially private security companies, have come to operate as a third sector of security provision, working alongside the police and punitive institutions of the state. Interestingly, private security actors have come to play important roles not only in the provision of security as related to physical dangers such as robbery, but also in the identification and management of risk. It could thus be argued that private security in Eastern Europe, as in so many other countries, reflects the rise to prominence of a logic of risk-management, articulating—and seeking to implement—a vision of a polity in which societies manage many of their risks via individual consumer choices (Abrahamsen and Williams 2011; Beck 1992, 1999, 2002; Coker 2009; Ericson and Haggerty 1997; Gheciu 2008; Krahmann 2010).

The private security industry promises to minimize the risk to private clients that doubt the capabilities, skills, and will of government agencies to protect them against a multitude of dangers and risks. At the same time, PSCs seek an ever greater involvement in partnerships with public agencies, arguing that they have the skills, knowledge, expertise, and material capabilities to effectively address not only immediate physical threats but also the diverse national and transnational risks (including financial and cyber risks) of the twenty-first century (Krahmann 2010). For their part, state agencies now "seek to build broader alliances, enlisting the governmental powers of private actors, and shaping them to the ends of crime control" (Garland 2001: 124). As private actors become systematically involved in the provision of security, they are both aided by and further reinforce a culture of responsibilization of individuals and businesses, which focuses on educating social actors on how to minimize the risk of becoming victims of various forms of insecurity. The notion involved here is that individuals and communities have both the ability and the duty to contribute to their own security by behaving in a "rational," "responsible" way—most notably by engaging the services of a private security company to prevent violence against them and their property.

As we shall see, in all ex-communist states individuals and businesses have been systematically targeted by education campaigns—and in some cases have witnessed the adoption of new legislation that imposes duties of "responsible" behavior in the field of security. The focus on risk-management and responsibilization of individuals and communities is reflected in new discourses on security and also inscribed in important pieces of legislation. For instance, recent legislation introduced in countries like Bulgaria and Romania extends to PSCs the function of preventive policing. In a world of risk-management, the focus is on establishing "risk profiles," by using categories developed by experts and data gathered from a multitude of public and private sources, and then formulating strategies for managing those risk factors (Valverde and Mopas 2006).

While global and regional actors and dynamics have played powerful roles in redefining security provision in ex-communist Europe, one cannot forget the ways in which those dynamics were also affected by local conditions. The analysis developed in the next chapters illustrates the multiple ways in which localities are productive in shaping their articulation with global dynamics, rather than simply being the powerless victims of the global. This enables us to contest the idea that globalization homogenizes place and that it subsumes the local. For instance, it is revealing that, in the initial years of post-communist transition, even the most powerful global security corporations were unable to gain access to East European markets. Their problem was that, for all their material resources and globally recognized expertise, they lacked the specific material capabilities and non-material capital that was valued in those markets.[4] The irony of that situation was that, even as East European polities were officially embracing liberalization, adopting norms of security privatization as part of the effort to gain admission to Western institutions and to integrate into global economic circuits, in practice international security companies were virtually excluded from those markets. It was only by acquiring some of that specific local capital—and in some instances making normatively problematic compromises—that those global players were able to acquire powerful positions in the field of security.

To fully grasp the impact of the multitude of local, national and global ideas, practices, and actors it is necessary to conceptualize the space of the political as going beyond conventional dichotomies of national/international and public/private (Abrahamsen and Williams 2011). It is only by doing so that we can understand, for instance, the emergence of a transnational space of political mobilization, in which national private security providers and local NGOs have forged alliances with global corporations and regional profesional associations to promote legislative changes and seek more labor protections in their countries. In a similar vein, it is only by transcending conventional wisdom about neat boundaries that we can study the emergence of hybrid networks of security providers that defy the distinction between public/ private domains and engage in a broad spectrum of activities—including, in some instances, by participating in the illicit economy, nationally and internationally. Those hybrid networks have become powerful actors in many ex-communist states, where they combine—often in problematic ways—the logics of public good provision and pursuit of private profit (Best and Gheciu 2014).

It would be impossible, within a single book, to examine the dynamics of transition in all ex-communist states. Therefore, in an effort to give a broader overview of the new logics of security provision in that region, I have focused on countries that have had particularly interesting—and also different—trajectories post-1989. By including ex-communist polities with different trajectories, the book hopes to enable the readers to gain a better understanding of the diverse sets of practices—and their implications—through which national, regional, and global actors participate in security provision and governance. Two of the countries examined here, Bulgaria and Romania, are now members of the EU, but are widely regarded as the most problematic of the new members—in part precisely because they emerged from particularly repressive communist regimes. At the heart of those regimes were extremely powerful state security institutions. The contrast between that situation and the current security landscape, in which private security companies occupy very prominent positions, is particularly sharp. It thus invites questions about the specific practices through which such transformations were possible, and the challenges associated with those practices.

An analysis of the evolution of security practices in countries like Romania and Bulgaria also enables us to shed new light on the dynamics and consequences of processes of European integration and enlargement. It is worth recalling that, when they joined the Union in 2007, Romania and Bulgaria were regarded as having so much work to do in the areas of judicial reform, corruption, and organized crime that EU officials decided to impose on them a special supervision mechanism (the "Cooperation and Verification Mechanism"). Even today Romania and Bulgaria continue to be assessed under the special verification scheme, as the EU is still applying pressure on Bucharest and Sofia to improve their judicial and administrative systems. This mechanism has had a significant impact on the measures taken by the Romanian and Bulgarian governments—including steps aimed at excluding organized crime from the field of security—but has not been uncontroversial. While the Romanian and Bulgarian governments have been keen to put an end to this mechanism and thus gain more autonomy from Brussels, many NGOs from those countries have expressed continued support for the verification scheme, arguing that in the absence of monitoring from Brussels key reforms would be delayed or abandoned. Given the special nature of the relationship between the EU and these two countries, an analysis of the ways in which Brussels has interacted with Bucharest and Sofia can help us gain a better understanding of the nature but also limits of EU power in (re)shaping candidate states.

In addition, this study also examines the transformation of security provision in two very different countries: Bosnia and Herzegovina, and Serbia. Their inclusion enables us to study the added complications of transforming practices of security provision in countries that, on top of communist legacies, have also had to deal with the consequences of violent conflict. Among the countries emerging from the collapse of Yugoslavia, Bosnia and Serbia are especially interesting case studies because, while they share powerful legacies (the Yugoslav communist regime and the history of recent conflict), they are also different in important ways. Above all, while Serbia emerged from the Yugoslav wars as an independent state, Bosnia continues to be under an international administration—though the nature and power of that administration has changed significantly in recent years. Therefore, processes of reform of security provision in those two polities have been significantly different in terms of the actors engaged in the reform process, and the social, economic, and political contexts in which those actors have had to operate. Particularly important for our purposes is the fact that, through the direct intervention of international administrators, legislative reform could be achieved much faster in Bosnia compared to Serbia. In spite of that difference, however, in both countries the persistence of attitudes and various (material and non-material) resources inherited from their violent past has had a profound impact on attempts to reform security governance and provision.

The analysis developed in this book is based on research in the four ex-communist polities and at European institutions in Brussels as well as the London headquarters of a leading multinational PSC that has come to occupy a prominent position in Eastern Europe, G4S. It covers, broadly speaking, the first quarter of a century following the collapse of communism in Eastern Europe. It traces transformations in the field of security that started, albeit with some significant problems, in the early 1990s in Bulgaria and Romania, and—in the cases of Serbia and Bosnia—after the end of the Yugoslav wars. It then examines the evolution of practices of security provision in the context of growing integration into European institutional structures and insertion of those polities into global circuits, focusing on events that occurred up until 2015. The analysis of this long period of time is needed in order to capture key developments in the evolution of practices of security governance and provision at both the national and the European levels. This includes the start of a rapid process of commercialization of security in post-1989 Eastern Europe; the professionalization of the private security industry and its reconstitution as agent of public power especially in the 2000s and early 2010s, as well as European-level debates and contestations over the roles of PSCs, which led to the adoption, in 2014, of significant new EU "rules of the game" that help shape the field of security. Given that the focus is on some twenty-five years of numerous transformations in four different countries, it would be impossible to pay attention to each and every change in the field of security. Instead, the aim of this book is to shed light on some of the most fundamental aspects of post-communist transformations in the field of everyday, non-military security provision, exploring the ways in which these transformations are linked to a multifaceted process of commercialization. My aim is to give readers a better sense of the complex, fluid new political economy of security provision in several former communist states, and to help them understand how practices of security provision and governance are connected to—but not simply determined by—other fields and to broader developments at the European and global levels.

In an effort to minimize the danger of bias, I adopted the strategy of triangulation, combining different qualitative methods (interviews, participant observation, literature review, and content and discourse analysis of relevant documents), and drawing on multiple data sources. Thus, the book draws on some 120 formal, semi-structured interviews and numerous additional informal meetings in each of the countries included in the study. In each country, I interviewed senior staff members of the main global and local PSCs, representatives of professional associations of the private security industry, government officials (including those involved in regulating the private security industry), NGO representatives, EU officials, public and private clients of the security industry, and investigative journalists. I also spent time at sites guarded by private security actors in Eastern Europe—both private clients, especially financial institutions, and public institutions, such as schools, government buildings, parks, and cultural venues—observing the interactions between PSCs, state security actors, and the local population. This material was supplemented by a study of official documents related to the commercialization of security. This included key pieces of legislation concerning the role and powers of PSCs as well as their relationship to the police and other public institutions; official national and EU reports and statements on the partnership between public actors and PSCs in the provision of security; and reports by NGOs and investigative journalists concerning the dynamics of—and challenges associated with—the commercialization of security. Finally, I also studied the texts and images present in the promotional material circulated by global and local private security companies, including printed material (newsletters, posters, etc.) but also images disseminated via video clips, pictures, and reports posted on the websites of PSCs and their professional associations. This material—studied in conjunction with informational and promotional material published by national governments and EU institutions—was important in helping me to gain a broader perspective of how all these different actors represent themselves, perform particular roles, and depict their relationships to other players involved in security provision in Europe.

As the next chapters reveal, the relationships that emerge between public and private actors involved in security provision are complex and often fluid. As a corollary to this, any of the alliances between various security providers identified here may well be fundamentally transformed (if not terminated) in the future. Therefore, it has to be said that this book's findings are specific to these case studies—and do not claim to enable any predictions regarding future security arrangements. However, the analysis developed here offers a new conceptualization of post-1989 dynamics and implications of security governance and provision in those countries, and of the links between those dynamics and broader processes of European integration and globalization. More broadly, it suggests ways in which one can draw on bodies of literature associated with different disciplines to capture the various forms of power as well as the challenges and normative dilemmas associated with the reconstitution of practices of security in the contemporary era. I suggest that this type of conceptual framework could be applied to explore dynamics, challenges, and dilemmas of security provision in various regions and at different times.

Toward New Forms of Public Power in Post-Communist Europe

Post-communist processes of commercialization of security have led to a fundamental reshaping of public power in Eastern Europe. Following a neo-liberal logic, at the heart of those processes of commercialization of security has been the mobilization of private actors, specifically private security companies (PSCs), in the performance of functions traditionally associated with the state. It might be tempting to conceptualize the proliferation of PSCs following the collapse of communism as the expression of the growth of the private sector at the expense of the public domain of governance (Börzel and Risse 2005). Yet, this would be an oversimplification of the rise and growing power of the private security industry. Instead, what was involved in those countries was the reconstitution of private actors as agents empowered to perform public power.

What, then, do we mean by public power? To understand this, we need to place our discussion within the framework of liberal thinking about political legitimacy. Central to liberal political thought and practice are norms of political legitimacy that are concerned with the problem of constituting and controlling the exercise of power within the social order "in a manner that simultaneously empowers institutions to perform valued collective functions, and prevents powerful institutions from degenerating into tyranny."[5] A fundamental purpose served by liberal norms of political legitimacy is to set out the nature of the public goods/values and purposes that should be upheld by political institutions, and to prescribe institutional forms capable of upholding these public liberal values both by enabling a series of political actors to perform protective functions, and by constraining the abuse of their power. In light of these social goals of political legitimacy norms, the subject of those norms can be conceptualized as public power: the power that must be institutionally enabled to serve some public liberal values or goods, and institutionally restrained in order to protect those public liberal values/goods from a potential abuse of power.[6]

On this logic, particular agents or institutional forms of public power can be deemed legitimate to the extent that they protect/promote those values/goods that are recognized as valuable by a liberal polity. These include the basic individual rights and freedoms that are the heart of liberal thought, but also a series of collective goods—above all, security. Conventional wisdom about modern polities has long tended to equate public power with the state, but the liberal logic of public power as concerned with protecting liberal values/goods suggests that public power can be identified in any existing powers wielded not only by states but also by non-state political actors that are in a position to promote those values/goods.[7]

A particularly interesting illustration of the process of investing non-state actors with the right to exercise public power can be found in the context of post-communist transitions in Europe. Against the background of the new normative environment discussed above, East Europeans have adopted policies and practices that, far from casting commercial, profit-driven security corporations in opposition to the state, have in effect constructed some of those actors as agents engaged in the exercise of public power. As we shall see, new legislation and institutional arrangements have been adopted that both empower private actors—particularly private security companies—to perform security functions and, in recognition of the influence that such actors can exercise, seek to prevent them from abusing their power.

The contemporary proliferation of PSCs raises important and complex questions regarding their role in—and potential impact on—democratic societies. It is worth noting that today the private security industry is one of the most important economic sectors in each of the countries studied in this book. For instance, by 2010 the private security industry had a yearly turnover of approximately 29 million euros in Bosnia, 311 million euros in Bulgaria, 153 million euros in Serbia, and 497 million euros in Romania (CoESS 2011, 2013b). A further illustration of the importance of the private security industry can be found in the ratio between private security agents/the population. In three of the four countries examined in this book, by 2011 that ratio was higher than that between the police/the population: in Bulgaria, the private security/population ratio was 1/132, compared to the police/population ratio of 1/155. In Romania, the PSC/population ration of 1/229 was higher than the police/population ratio of 1/1,050, and in Serbia the PSC/population ratio of 1/146 was also higher than the police/population ratio of 1/218 (CoESS 2011). Of the four countries, it was only in Bosnia that the PSC/population ratio was lower than that between the police/population: 1/2,295, compared to 1/217 for the police. This difference is hardly surprising given the special political situation in Bosnia. Furthermore, as we shall see, the fact that fewer PSCs were operating in Bosnia compared to other East European polities has not prevented the private security industry from playing a powerful role in that country.

The PSCs' empowerment as agents of public power in Eastern Europe and elsewhere can appear as a problematic departure from that quintessential modern principle, involving a systematic weakening of the state and an unavoidable dilution of what Benedict Anderson (1983) called the imagined horizontal community of citizens.[8] This book suggests that such fears of societal polarization are to some degree well founded. Indeed, in the Western Balkans as well as in Romania and Bulgaria the partial privatization of security has contributed, in part, to an accentuation of the divide between those who can afford to pay private security and those who cannot. This problem is often stressed by critics of neo-liberalism, who regard the privatization of what is widely regarded as the core function of the state, security, as an alarming indicator and source of a decline of the state. This is a serious concern, which cannot and should not be ignored. As the next chapters show, the consequences of the "violent entrepreneurship"[9] of some private security companies that emerged in the Balkans in the 1990s provide a potent reminder of the possible dangers involved in rapid security privatization.

Yet, this is not the whole story of the transformation of security provision in the context of privatization. To capture the more nuanced relationship between security and the state, we need to recognize that the power to provide public goods—including security—may be differently constituted in different settings (Best and Gheciu 2014). In fact, in some instances the ways in which private security companies have worked with specific segments of government bureaucracy raise the possibility that they may reinforce/extend the structures of the state instead of undermining them. For instance, in many East European states cash-strapped police forces often rely on private security companies to help them protect critical infrastructure. In such instances, PSCs can be seen to help enact or perform the state in the eyes of its citizens, making the state more visible and tangible—and arguably also more effective in daily life.

At times, however, the dynamics of public/private cooperation have been more problematic. For instance, there have been situations in which individuals with prominent positions within the state enlisted the services of PSCs in an effort to bypass laws and accountability norms and perform functions (e.g. illegal surveillance of their competitors) that cannot be carried out by state agencies. In other words, we should not assume that the ever increasing prominence of private security actors will necessarily aid in the construction of democratic, transparent, accountable institutions. On the contrary: in some instances it may well reinforce the coercive capacities of already abusive state actors. But the important point is that we cannot simply conceptualize commercial security actors as either a source of support or a threat to formal state institutions. The ways in which private security relates to state institutions is context-dependent and can thus alter radically over time.

Thinking about Security Commercialization from Different Perspectives

A central claim in this book is that it is only by employing a multidisciplinary approach that we can capture the complexity of processes of security commercialization in Eastern Europe. In developing such an approach, I draw on different bodies of literature from the fields of political science, sociology, anthropology, and criminology, and seek to contribute to the recent literature on the reconstitution of the public domain in global governance and the new logics of public/private interactions (e.g. Abrahamsen and Williams 2011; Avant et al. 2010; Best and Gheciu 2014; Hall and Biersteker 2002). The next chapters examine the nature and practices of hybrid networks of actors that defy conventional boundaries between domestic/international, public/private, and security/economics and that exercise significant forms of coercive and productive power in post-communist Europe. As we shall see, the actors who exercise public power and participate in the provision of a key public good—security—do not always act in a manner consistent with the logic conventionally attributed to public entities. In this context the book seeks to capture not simply the outsourcing of security provision but also, more broadly, changes in the nature of public agencies and in the logics that they enact. Thus, the emergence of complex links between state agencies, private security, and in some instances organized crime have facilitated practices of security that cannot be understood as long as we use conventional International Relations categories.

In essence, we can understand developments in post-communist Europe as reflecting the reconstitution of political space and the emergence of a new political economy of security, in which new actors are empowered, the public function of security provision is redefined, new alliances emerge, and new capabilities are valorized.[10] In this context, in sharp contrast to the Weberian model, the state is only one of a number of actors or nodes involved in the governance and provision of security (Shearing and Wood 2003a; Wood and Dupont 2006). In today's world, security is also the responsibility of individuals, local communities, corporations, and private security companies, all of whom participate—with various degrees of influence—in "hybrid security structures" (Johnston 1992; Bigo 2006; Loader 2005; Amoore 2007; Abrahamsen and Williams 2011; Avant and Haufler 2014).[11] An analysis of the plurality and hybridity of security actors is linked to another important aspect of contemporary security provision: we cannot conceptualize the transformation of the field of security in static terms. In other words, it would be misleading to think about the field of security in terms of a stable geometry of arrangements of security provision. Analyses that interpret the evolution of security as involving a form of stability—be it in terms of the prominence of private actors at the expense of public ones or vice versa (as many IR accounts do)—fail to take into account the dynamic nature of contemporary security provision. As the next chapters show, we should not underestimate the persistent fluidity and complex, power-filled practices through which the public and private actors are redefined and relationships among them are (re)articulated.

The refusal to assume, a priori, the existence of a particular, fixed model of security provision also enables us to understand that the process of blurring boundaries involves not just the dilution of borders between the global, regional, and national in the context of glocalization, but also the partial dissolution of the boundary between the licit and illicit domains of activity. By examining the blurring of the licit/illicit boundary, this book builds on analyses developed by criminologists, political geographers, and critical IR scholars. As Tim Hall (2013), among others, has pointed out, the illicit should not be seen as a discrete ontological realm. Rather, the licit and illicit are intertwined in complex ways, in various regions and through social, economic, and political practices (Galeotti 2005; Hobbs 2001). To understand the emergence of links between licit/illicit domains we need to cast our minds back to the early days of post-communist transition, and shed light on the flawed processes of privatization that occurred in many East European states. To capture those problems it is useful to draw on classical sociological accounts, particularly Max Weber's work. As discussed in Chapter 2, the first years of post-communism witnessed the rise of what Weber called "political capitalism."[12] Weber's fears (particularly the "iron cage") and his hopes (concerning the "taming" of bureaucracy via the establishment of horizontal and vertical accountability) have been the subject of countless scholarly interpretations. Less well known, however, are his fears of a different possible scenario: the corruption of the civil service, leading to a de-bureaucratization of the state. According to Weber, unusual circumstances could lead to a situation in which politically oriented practices of profit-making become prominent. Political capitalism, in other words, is associated with predatory profits from politically connected people, and the distortion or breakdown of rule-enforcement mechanisms and decision-making processes that are at the heart of the public domain. As politically connected entrepreneurs gain "unlimited and uncontrolled command over the state," the core institutions of the state are emasculated, fractured administrative apparatuses become too weak to exercise any significant control over their environment, and the distinction between state/non-state agencies becomes blurred.[13] It was in the context of the rise of political capitalism that the field of security in many East European polities witnessed the emergence of networks of security providers that transcended the licit/illicit boundaries.[14]

In analyzing the blurring of licit/illicit boundaries in Eastern Europe, however, it is important to keep in mind that this process was affected not only by domestic processes (often linked to flawed privatizations) but also by global dynamics. In recent years, a series of criminologists and political scientists have highlighted the fact that licit economic activities constitute only some dimensions of globalization (Galeotti 2005; Wilson 2009). Therefore, by limiting investigations and not acknowledging the presence of the illicit, we fail to capture globalization in all its complexities—and we also fail to capture the ways in which perfectly legitimate actors often participate in illicit circuits. For instance, contrary to conventional wisdom, states have always—and in complex ways—been implicated in illicit aspects of globalization—including in the area of (in)security provision (Andreas 2011). In fact—ironically—states and key international organizations (the UN and NATO) were implicated in the growth of illicit economic activities in the Balkans following the Yugoslav wars—most notably via their involvement in sex trade/human trafficking in Bosnia. Even in East European polities that did not suffer from conflict, one of the most problematic developments following the collapse of communism was the emergence of powerful links between certain state security institutions, private security companies, and organized crime. Understanding how such developments have affected the dynamics of security provision and have reshaped relations between the state and its citizens enables us to capture one of the most interesting (yet under-analyzed) aspects of post-communist transition. In some extreme cases, illicit actors, including organized criminal groups, have acted as proxy agents of governance, extending informal governance in areas where the state presence is weak or inefficient. This is what happened, for example, in the 1990s in some of the provincial towns and Black Sea resorts in Bulgaria, where organized criminal groups played more important and powerful roles as (in)security providers than the police, thereby undermining the credibility of the state. Over time, the relationship between the licit/illicit has evolved. Particularly in the context of growing European integration, some of the most violent practices associated with the illicit economy have vanished or have become marginalized. Yet, certain links between political actors/business/white-collar crime/transnational organized crime persist in parts of Eastern Europe, complicating—and raising difficult questions about—contemporary practices of security governance and provision.

Performing Protection in Post-Communist Europe

In a broader perspective, by examining processes of contestation involved in the redefinition of norms and practices of security provision, this book invites us to think about security provision from an unusual angle: that of security as a performative practice. In particular, the pluralization of the field of security has been accompanied by efforts by the private security industry—as actors that have not been conventionally regarded as providers of security—to gain recognition as legitimate, effective participants in the protection of both private individuals and public spaces, and thus to secure lucrative contracts with both private clients and public agencies. In that context, PSCs have sought to effectively perform a multitude of security tasks traditionally attributed to the state, but also to "act out" their roles as they seek to persuade multiple audiences that it is normal for them to be key players in the twenty-first century's security environment.

To understand the performative aspect of security provision, I draw on performance studies, including the constructivist works of International Relations (IR) scholars like Emanuel Adler (2005, 2010) and Erik Ringmar (2012, 2014, 2017) and sociologists like Jeffrey Alexander (Alexander et al. 2006; Alexander 2011), the literature on authority in the age of mediatization by public policy scholars (Hajer 2009), and studies of staging techniques developed by students of dramaturgy and performance studies (Schechner 2002, 2015). Those works—which were often developed in dialogue with one another—help us decipher the ways in which the private security industry has used particular scripts as well as various "stage props" to construct chains of meaning that legitimize their proposed courses of action.[15]

Within the field of International Relations, the analysis of security performances can be seen as part of a larger constructivist effort to return to symbolic interactionism in order to understand the production of social order. While symbolic interactionist scholars (especially Herbert Mead) have long been a source of inspiration for constructivists, their key insights into social interactions often appear to have been forgotten in conventional constructivist accounts. As Lawson and Shilliam put it, "[i]n IR, many constructivists appear to have ignored—either by accident or design—what symbolic interactionists have been arguing for the past century or more" (Lawson and Shilliam 2010: 80). In particular, the problem is that conventional constructivists conceptualized the self as individualistic. However, for symbolic interactionism, the self is first and foremost a social phenomenon, not an individualist or psychological one (Mead 1913). In fact, this may be one of the key assumptions that all symbolic interactionists share. Mead's fundamental argument about consciousness was that it arose out of constant shifts and role-taking, of seeing things from the point of view of the other(s). For symbolic interactionism, the self is highly complex, fragile, and always in the making. This sophisticated conception of the social self was never fully imported into IR constructivism. One of the major critiques raised against the first generation of constructivism was exactly the way it translated symbolic interactionism into IR by turning the state into a unitary actor (Weldes 1999). This approach makes it difficult to grasp the multiple, evolving fractures and fissures within states, as well as the practices through which various public and private, and domestic and international, actors collaborate but also compete in the (re)constitution of states and, more broadly, in the production and reproduction of international order.

It is by returning to the symbolic interactionist view of the self as a fragile phenomenon, always in the making through multiple social interactions— and by building on the recent constructivist literature that applies this view to the sphere of international politics—that we can better grasp the dynamics and implications of contemporary practices of security provision in Europe. Particularly important for our purposes is the recent constructivist literature that focuses on the performative dimension of the practices through which social selves are constructed and, in turn, help (re)shape international order (Adler 2010; Ringmar 2012, 2017). Focusing on the performative aspect of social practices, I suggest that we can understand how security is literally performed in everyday life by actors who engage in strategic action in part by conforming to key aspects of the accepted scripts regarding the roles of security providers in post-Cold War Europe and in part by contesting certain rules of the game in the field of security.

It is useful to conceptualize practices in which private security actors both share and contest the prevailing "rules of the game" as staged performances. Through those practices, representatives of the private security industry remind their audiences of how society works, and which rules and shared ideas enable and constrain their actions (Ringmar 2012). As Ringmar has pointed out, in performances social actors use particular vocabularies to assemble scripts through which they seek to obtain recognition from their audiences (2012: 7). Scripts provide individuals and groups with roles and goals, "with instructions for how to act and for how to go on" (2012: 7). They tell us who we are and how we are related to various others in the international arena, and how people in "our" society should interact with one another.

By conceptualizing security practices as staged activities, we can gain a better understanding of how private actors have taken advantage of a changing security environment—marked by the commodification of security and pluralization of security providers—to enact performances through which they seek recognition by multiple audiences of their authority as legitimate, efficient security providers in the twenty-first century. Those audiences include public authorities at both the national and international level, but also private clients—be they individual citizens or corporations, both East European and international. All those actors have been the target of PSC attempts to convince them that it is normal for the private security industry to perform increasingly important roles as providers of public as well as private security. While in the new field of security there is a shared understanding that private actors will play important roles, there continue to be significant debates and contestations among field participants over the precise definitions and boundaries of those roles. In that context, representatives of the private security industry both cooperate and compete with public actors as they enact their roles as partial agents of public power and enact multiple practices of protection.

To understand how PSCs stage performances aimed at enhancing their roles and power in the field of security, it is also useful to draw on studies of performativity produced by public policy and dramaturgy scholars. As one of the pioneers of the field of performance studies, Richard Schechner, has argued, at the simplest level, a performance may be defined as all the activity of a given participant on a given occasion which serves to influence in any way any of the other participants (Schechner 2002: 23). From this perspective, performances only exist as actions, interactions, and relationships; therefore, to treat any work or product as "performance" means to investigate what the object does, how it interacts with other objects or beings, and how it relates to other objects or beings (2002: 24). Importantly, Schechner argues that we can understand all human activity as "performance" (2002: 25). To study a form of behavior as "performance" means to analyze it in terms of doing, behaving, and showing (2002: 32; Kirshenblatt-Gimblett 1999: 1–2). Thus, to perform is first to execute, to carry out to completion, to discharge a duty—in our case, to discharge a duty of protection of citizens and their property and of maintaining domestic order. Second, to perform is to behave in everyday life in a manner that conforms with the habits, customs, laws, and etiquette that prevail in a given society at a particular moment in time. To perform in this sense is to provide protection in a way that is deemed appropriate, considering the habitus or dominant dispositions in the field of security in post-communist East European polities. Third, to perform is to show. Thus, when doing and behaving are displayed, when they are shown, when participants are invited to exercise discernment, evaluation, and appreciation, security practices move toward the theatrical or the spectacular—they become representations that mobilize particular discursive and stage "props" aimed at generating the positive evaluation of specific audiences.

In our case, we shall see that the PSCs' use of the spectacular has involved their effective mobilization of a multitude of material and non-material resources in order to enhance their position and power in the field of security. Indeed, PSCs have proven adept at using scripts or discourses sanctioned by states and international organizations in the context of the affirmation of neo-liberal norms to "stage perform" as trustworthy security providers. The private security industry's quest to secure greater recognition often involves a combination of speech acts and various "stage props" or "means of symbolic production."[16] These include practical, visually potent displays of material capabilities, expertise, and experience in a variety of security provision scenarios (ranging from displays of their ability to protect critical infrastructure and public institutions to instances of caring for vulnerable members of the public during cultural and sporting events). Staging practices seek to establish a connection between the audience and the actors, and thus to create conditions for projecting particular sets of meanings from the performers to the audience (Alexander 2011: 53–5). In other words, the objective is to get audiences to regard actors that enact security practices as genuine, honest, and trustworthy, and to interpret their performances as natural.

In an effort to convince audiences to accept the performed meanings, the private security actors enact scripts that often involve good/bad binaries. In general, they cast themselves as sources of protection—similar to, and in some ways better than, the state—and radically different from, and opposed to, individuals and groups that represent a threat or risk to the security and well-being of individuals, their property, and their community. This type of representation has become particularly important in recent years, as PSCs have come under pressure from both national authorities and international actors (especially the EU) to distance themselves from the lawless behavior that had been widespread among private security providers in the first years of post-communism. In that context, as we shall see, performances of virtuous protection are important not only as part of an effort to gain legitimacy in the eyes of multiple audiences, but also as a way for members of the private security industry to (re)-imagine themselves as participants in an ethical community, involved in the important function of provision of protection by legal and efficient means, transcending the stigma of private security as "dirty work."[17]

Overview of the Book

To understand contemporary practices of security provision in the former Eastern bloc, we need to start with a genealogical analysis, exploring the reconstitution of East European polities in the early days of post-communism, and analyzing the impact of those transformations on the field of security. In particular, we need to understand the peculiar dynamics and consequences of the flawed privatization processes that occurred in Eastern Europe in the 1990s. Those dynamics are the subject of Chapter 2, which sheds light on a phenomenon that can be explained through the prism of Max Weber's concepts of political capitalism and de-bureaucratization of the state.[18] That phenomenon had a profound influence on processes of security commercialization in the early days of post-communism, and continues to shape the ways in which security is performed in that part of the world even today.

In the early years of post-communist transition, many East European states—including the countries examined in this book—were dominated by ex-communist elites whose primary concern was to maintain their power and privileges in the new era. What took place in those years was the rise of political capitalism through a de-bureaucratization of the state as a result of massive, abusive transfer of state assets into the hands of the ex-communist nomenclature. Particularly relevant was the privatization of security-related ministries, which involved the transfer of the communist state's coercive and information-gathering capabilities into assets that were placed under the control of networks of (ex-communist) political and economic entrepreneurs. Many of those entrepreneurs—who often retained connections to key individuals within state structures—established private security companies, invoking global norms of security commodification to cast themselves as legitimate security providers who were contributing to the liberalization of their countries. In other words, what former communist polities witnessed was not a process of replacing states with markets but, rather, "a merger of the state with quasi-markets" (Los 2003; Los and Zybertowicz 2000), both of which are constituted and controlled by state/corporate/criminal organized interests. As substantial assets shifted from the state to private control, newly (re)created public institutions in charge of providing security were left without the resources needed to fulfill their mandates. This further reinforced the power of newly created PSCs, both because many people and businesses came to rely on their services (since they did not trust the cash-strapped, often corrupt police forces), and because public agencies did not have enough resources to monitor and restrain the power of PSCs.

In many instances, PSCs took advantage of the legal and institutional weaknesses in ex-communist states to engage in what would normally be considered criminal practices, including protection rackets and illegal surveillance of their clients' competitors.[19] In the course of those practices, they systematically used the material resources as well as non-material capital, particularly the expertise and skills (including in the use of violent, illegal techniques of "protection") inherited from the communist era. In a social context in which those skills and expertise were highly valued, domestic security providers clearly dominated the market, limiting or excluding the operation of global security companies—despite the latter's superior material capabilities and international reputation. Ironically, while in the early years of post-communism there was a limited influx of European and global actors in the legitimate business of security provision, a different type of internationalization was taking place. What was occurring in that context was an illicit internationalization, involving the participation of security providers from ex-communist states into international networks of organized crime.

Drawing on Los's sociological account of the quasi merger of states and markets, on Bourdieu's concepts of field, habitus, capital, and strategies, and on the recent literature on global security assemblages (Abrahamsen and Williams 2006, 2011), Chapters 3, 4, and 5 examine the evolution of security provision after the early years of post-communism. As we shall see, in recent years East European polities have become more closely integrated into the European field of security, and started to move away from some of the most problematic, violent dynamics of the early days of post-communism. Processes of integration into the EU and insertion into global economic flows have played important—albeit not unlimited—roles in pushing East European polities to adopt new legislative frameworks governing private security, and to deal with some of the most obvious abuses inherited from their problematic post-communist transitions. Practices of inclusion of East European polities in the European field of security have also entailed the growing participation of security providers based in those countries in transversal networks of European security professionals—especially via integration of the national associations of PSCs into the Confederation of European Security Services (CoESS). CoESS has served as a forum for transnational mobilization through which the private security industry has advocated for more rights for security workers in their national arenas, has pushed their national governments for better legislation, and has also started to participate in efforts to reshape

European security governance. Yet, in spite of all these changes, certain actors, attitudes, and forms of non-material capital inherited from the communist past persist and continue to affect the ways in which security is performed.

Chapter 3 places the analysis of developments in Eastern Europe in a broader international context, examining how the transformation of the field of security has been shaped by processes of European integration as well as globalization—especially through the influx into Eastern Europe of multinational corporations, including global security companies. In particular, as each of the countries examined in this book embarked upon processes of European integration, they came to be deeply affected by EU legislation and specific accession/partnership conditionality, including in the field of security.

We noted above that at the heart of the reconstruction of public power in the field of security in Eastern Europe has been the reconstitution of private security companies as partial agents of public power. This has continued—indeed, in many ways has accelerated—in the context of Europeanization and growing integration into global circuits. Consequently, many PSCs, both international and national, have come to be increasingly recognized as legitimate participants in the provision of public security. What *is* different from the early years of post-communism is the definition of desirable attributes and types of resources associated with legitimate participation in the provision of public security. New legislation and institutional reforms have presented powerful incentives for many national private security providers to restructure themselves and seek to distance themselves from some of the abusive practices of the early days of post-communism.

In many ways, the process of European integration has served to reinforce global norms and dynamics in Eastern Europe. For instance, in the process of preparing their countries for accession to the EU, countries like Bulgaria and Romania have come under pressure to liberalize their economies—in part by opening up their security markets to international competition, including multinational PSCs. The process of European integration has also translated into greater EU pressure on East European countries to strengthen the rule of law and fight corruption and organized crime—including in the field of security. In that context, East European governments have adopted a series of legislative measures that have addressed, or at least minimized, some of the abuses associated with security provision in the first years of post-communism.[20] In a broader perspective, the process of European integration has enhanced the credibility of East Europeans in the eyes of international business, leading to a growing influx of global corporations—especially financial institutions—into countries like Bulgaria and Romania. In turn, this development has further reinforced the position of global PSCs: as many of the international banks and multinational corporations required Western

standards of security provision, upon arriving in Eastern Europe they generally hired global, rather than national, PSCs—at least for some of their
operations.

Under these circumstances, by the mid-2000s, international actors had
come to occupy far more important positions in the field of security than
they had held in the early years of post-communism. Particularly important,
as Chapter 3 shows, has been the connection between the development of the
banking sector (especially via the influx of international banks) and the
growing presence and power of global PSCs in Eastern Europe. In addition,
the chapter explores the ways in which dynamics of Europeanization and
globalization have generated new opportunities for reshaping the field of
security for a series of domestic actors engaged in performing security. For
instance, via the involvement of PSCs from former communist states in the
Confederation of European Security Services (CoESS), which represents a
powerful corporatist professional alliance at the European level, the private
security industry has sought to enhance its legitimacy and power in the
national arenas, and has sought to secure more rights and protections for
security workers in their countries.

Chapter 4 continues the exploration of practices of insertion of East European
polities in the European field of security. Here, the focus is on the bigger
picture of European security governance. Specifically, the chapter explores
practices through which private security actors—including, increasingly,
PSCs from former communist countries—seek to enhance their power and
enact more prominent roles in European security governance. In recent years,
one of the most interesting developments in the European field of security
has been the growing mobilization of the private security industry—again,
especially within the framework of CoESS—in an effort to enhance its role in
security governance and provision. One of the key aims of these campaigns
has been to contest what the private industry perceives as a move by European
institutions to maintain and reproduce a clear hierarchy between public and
private security providers. In particular, the industry has sought to challenge
specific aspects of the conventional definition upheld by public actors—
namely, those aspects that marginalize or exclude PSCs from certain areas of
security provision.

In essence, while PSCs collaborate extensively with EU officials and public
institutions, they are also engaged in what could be called battles with them
over the definition of the "rules of the game" of security provision and, more
broadly, over the restructuring of the field of security. Thus, on the one hand,
one could point to a shared sense between EU officials and PSCs that a partial
commodification of security is both acceptable and desirable, that the principle of market efficiency is also relevant in the sphere of security, and that in a
complex world of multiple risks and reduced budgets private actors need to

play significant roles—in partnership with public institutions—in security provision. All these ideas are largely uncontested by public and private security actors alike. On the other hand, however, what is being struggled over is the limit of expansion of the right of private security actors to be recognized as legitimate producers of knowledge about dangers/risks and solutions to address those risks, and legitimate participants in the implementation of those solutions. To this end, strategies are mobilized in order to accumulate enough capital to support and enhance PSCs' positions in the contemporary era, and to challenge definitions of security according to which the private industry can only play limited roles in certain sensitive areas of security governance and provision.

More broadly, significant processes of contestation have also occurred over the definition of the meaning of European integration in the field of security. For instance, CoESS has systematically sought to enhance the power of PSCs by contesting the particular vision of harmonization of private security services prescribed by the European Commission. Most notably, CoESS has opposed the application of the Services Directive to the private security sector, arguing that, given the very different national standards and national legislation regulating private security services, it would lead to a premature and deeply flawed harmonization of security across Europe. In adopting that position, CoESS has cast itself—and has sought the EU officials' recognition—as the sector's representative and, hence, as an authoritative source of knowledge about the logic of EU integration, the needs of the European security sector, and the best way to address those needs. Furthermore, in an effort to protect the credibility of the private security sector, CoESS—as the organization that portrays itself as the voice of European private security services—has been keen to not only secure a privileged position for PSCs in the protection of critical infrastructure, but also to act as a gatekeeper, denying recognition and seeking to exclude from the domain of private security providers those companies that fail to live up to the standards of professionalism as defined by the Confederation.

Building upon the analysis of international developments in Chapter 4, Chapter 5 returns to recent developments in the national arenas of Bulgaria, Bosnia, Romania, and Serbia. The chapter seeks to understand the fluidity and complex mix of practices that have resulted from the growing insertion of those polities into the European field of security in combination with the persistence of some old actors, attitudes, and non-material resources inherited from the communist past. By examining practices of security provision that result from the intersection of European and global factors and actors with national players and local dynamics, the chapter seeks to give readers a better sense of what "glocalization" actually looks like in specific settings, at a given moment in time. The chapter shows that, in parallel to EU-level dynamics of cooperation and contestation between the private security industry and European public institutions, in each of the four polities examined in the book PSCs cooperate with state officials, but also engage in practices of contestation over the "rules of the game" of security provision. In the context of those contestations, all sides mobilize a variety of material and non-material resources and seek to cooperate with a variety of actors in order to enhance their power. The result is a fluid and complicated political economy of security provision, in which new alliances are forged while others are reconstituted or terminated, and competing logics of security provision coexist—often in a problematic way.

Finally, Chapter 6 places the analysis developed in this book in a broader normative perspective, focusing on a series of challenges and dilemmas associated with the transformation in the logic of security provision examined in the previous chapters. It pays special attention to the ways in which the particular dynamics of commercialization of security provision have involved departures from principles of transparency and democratic accountability, and the problems associated with such departures in countries with long histories of anti-democratic governance. Furthermore, we explore some of the dangers involved in the creation of exclusive communities of security— that is, communities of paying customers, who expect not only PSCs but also state agencies involved in commercial security provision to devote more attention and resources to them, at the expense of services provided to the general public. Such developments could further weaken an already fragile idea of a "horizontal community" of citizens, and—particularly in countries that have recently emerged from conflict, such as Bosnia—could endanger social stability. In its concluding pages, the chapter reflects on the difficulties of promoting liberal-democratic standards of "good governance" in contexts in which (in)security is performed by hybrid networks of security professionals that blur the boundaries between licit/illicit activities. In particular, the fact that a series of PSCs with links to illicit networks continue to play powerful roles in Eastern Europe—and, indeed, appear to have increased their power in a situation in which the global financial crisis has strengthened the "gray economy" in the region—poses serious challenges to the legitimacy and credibility of the state as provider of that key public good, security.

While in many ways PSCs have come to play prominent roles in all the countries examined in this book, we should not assume that their roles and power are now carved in stone. On the contrary, in Romania as in Bulgaria, Serbia, and Bosnia the field of security remains very fluid and dominated by power-filled practices. This dynamism and related power-filled practices— which are both affected by and, in turn, shape other social fields (particularly the economic field)—are dominant features of the contemporary logic of security provision. Under these circumstances, it is impossible to predict what security provision in those countries will look like in another twenty-five years. What is both possible and highly important, however, is to understand what has happened in the previous quarter of century, how a new political economy of security provision has emerged and constantly evolves, and how that has a profound impact not only on East European polities but also on processes of European integration and globalization that transcend the boundaries of the former communist bloc. This is what this book sets out to do.

Notes

1. Interview conducted in Sofia, June 15, 2012.
2. See in particular the Special Issue on "Norm Diffusion, Contestation and Localisation in the Western Balkans," *Journal of International Relations and Development*, 18(3), July 2015: 249–382. Also relevant are: Acharya 2004; Flockhart 2006; Mac Ginty 2010; Millar et al. 2013; Noutcheva 2009; Perdan 2008.
3. My focus is on non-military, everyday security provision to individuals and businesses, though the phenomenon of commodification of security has also affected the military aspects of security provision (see, for instance, Percy 2007; Singer 2004, 2008; Leander 2013; Leander and Van Munster 2007).
4. I use the concept of capital in a Bourdieusian way: capital refers to the resources that actors can mobilize in order to act successfully in a given field of activity. More on this in the next chapters.
5. Macdonald 2008: 548.
6. Macdonald 2008: 548.
7. Macdonald 2010.
8. In addressing this, I am building on a body of literature that challenges conventional understandings of the role of the state. For a particularly interesting analysis see Abrahamsen and Williams 2011. See also Sklansky 2006 and Loader and Walker 2007.
9. I borrow this term from Vadim Volkov (2002).
10. In employing the phrase "new political economy of security," I follow Adam White (2012). The phrase helps us understand how both the economic context and the political context shape the conduct of contemporary security providers.
11. This is similar to the analysis of "nodal governance" in the field of security (Wood and Shearing 2006; Loader and Walker 2007). The broad context in which nodal security governance emerges is the diversification and fragmentation of the security field (Krahmann 2007). As a corollary to this, the nodal security literature suggests that the various nodes can be seen as sites of knowledge, capacity, and resources that function as governance providers (Johnston 2006: 34). For the most part, advocates of this approach do not grant conceptual priority to any particular node. Instead, the particular nature of governance and the contribution of the various nodes to it are regarded as open questions, to be answered via careful empirical investigations (Shearing and Wood 2003b: 404).

12. See Ganev 2009.
13. Weber 1994: 104.
14. As noted above, there are certain similarities between the phenomena that occurred in Eastern Europe in the early 1990s and the violent privatization of security that occurred in post-communist Russia (Volkov 2002). Yet—again, as noted above and as examined in the next chapters—violence was only one aspect of a much more complex set of processes of security privatization.
15. For other interesting accounts of the role of performances in social life, see, for example, Bell 1997; Carlson 2004; Denzin 2008; Jeffrey 2012.
16. I draw here on Hajer's and Alexander's analyses of the ways in which actors mobilize "dramaturgical tools" to get audiences to see things in a certain light. These include discursive tools (such as metaphors or story-telling) as well as "stock practices" (or routinized ways of acting) to create historic chains of meaning that seek to legitimize their proposed courses of action. See Hajer 2009; Alexander et al. 2006; Alexander 2011.
17. In discussing the ways in which actors employ performances as a way to collectively (re)imagine their identity, I draw on Ringmar 2017. On the nature of—and efforts to transcend—the stigma related to the private security industry, see also Herbst 2013; Löfstrand et al. 2016; and Thumala et al. 2011.
18. Weber 1994: 104.
19. Weber 1994: 104.
20. Yet, one should not assume that the EU and, more broadly, the international community has always had a positive impact on the evolution of East European polities. For instance, as we shall see, in post-Dayton Bosnia the presence of the EU and global actors has facilitated illicit activities, and strengthened links between the licit economy and organized crime. We shall revisit this issue in the next chapters.

2

The State–Market–Crime Nexus in the Early Days of Post-Communism

To understand the key characteristics and challenges of security provision in contemporary Eastern Europe, we need to engage in a genealogical analysis, exploring the origins of new practices of security in the early years of post-communist transition. As the next chapters demonstrate, transformations that took place at that point in time continue to have a major impact on the field of security in East European polities. In particular, though contemporary security arrangements in those states differ in many ways from those of the 1990s, one cannot understand the identity, practices, and power of some of the key contemporary security providers unless one pays close attention to what happened in Eastern Europe immediately after 1989. Especially significant were the ways in which in countries like Bulgaria, Serbia, and Romania, as well as in other ex-communist states, processes of liberalization entailed the weakening of state structures and the empowerment of particular networks of individuals, who came to operate (and exercise significant power) both in the public and in the private domains. In the 1990s, individuals that had occupied powerful public positions under the communist regimes (or at least had been connected to powerful state officials in those states) emerged as key "liberal" security providers. In that context they cast themselves as actors who were in a particularly strong position to protect private persons and wealth, as well as to participate in the provision of public order, and, more broadly, contribute to a successful and "virtuous" post-communist transition.

Paradoxes of Liberalization in Eastern Europe

There are few regions in the world where the rise of private security has been as dramatic as it has been in Eastern Europe. Prior to the collapse of communist regimes, the Eastern bloc countries were dominated by particularly powerful and repressive security apparatuses, which exercised overwhelming control over all areas of security provision. The idea that private actors could play any significant roles in the provision of security in a manner that was independent of party-controlled state structures was inconceivable. Yet, just a few short years after the fall of communism many East European countries had apparently liberalized their security field, and were allowing private actors to play key roles in the provision of both public and private security. In the new environment, private security companies were able to perform a variety of functions, ranging from the protection of individuals and their property to the provision of security for various private and public companies (including financial institutions, schools, and various ministries), the transport of cash and valuable items, and even crowd control during cultural and sporting events. More recently, as noted in Chapter 1, PSCs also became involved in new risk-management activities. In essence, by the mid-2000s, the private security sector had witnessed tremendous growth in many ex-communist states. It is revealing that in Bulgaria, for instance, about 9 percent of all employed males were engaged in a private security-related activity, while in Romania more than 1,000 private security companies were active, employing around 38,000 people (Page et al. 2005; Gounev 2007). In Serbia and Bosnia, too, private security companies have come to be a powerful presence in the field of security. By 2005, more than 3,000 PSCs were operating in Serbia, employing tens of thousands of people. In Bosnia, PSCs also became important players in the field of security—although the official number for the same period was significantly smaller, at just forty private security companies. It should be noted, however, that a series of reliable reports have suggested that the number of unregistered entities acting as private security providers was much higher.[1] Under these circumstances, it is particularly interesting to ask how such a massive transformation was legitimized, what were its key features, and what were some of its implications.

One might be inclined to assume that the legislative and institutional changes carried out in the 1990s and 2000s led to the emergence of a powerful private security domain governed by the laws of the market—in other words, generated a set of institutions and security practices that are diametrically opposed to those that prevailed under communism. Yet, a closer glance reveals that some of the key security actors associated with the old (communist) regime were able to perpetuate important privileges and power even after the collapse of communism, and strategically employed the discourse and practices of liberalization to legitimize their (re)constitution as powerful public and private security providers in the new era.

At first glance—particularly considering the rapid proliferation of PSCs in the former communist bloc—one might be tempted to conclude that, by embarking on processes of security privatization, East European countries moved away from what could be called a republican model of security governance (involving centralized government and an undisputed monopoly of the state on the provision of security), and embraced instead a liberal model of fragmented governance, characterized by the distribution of security provision functions among multiple public and private providers (Krahmann 2010). However, to explain the evolution of Bulgarian, Serbian, Bosnian, or Romanian security arrangements in terms of that distinction would be to lose sight of the complex interpenetration of what might, on the surface, appear as distinct public and private domains. The supposedly different logics of public good provision and profit-seeking have come to be intertwined in complicated, normatively problematic ways as certain state agencies operate as quasi-private companies, offering commercial security services to paying customers, while private security companies seek recognition as agencies involved in the provision of public security.

It might be tempting to interpret processes of liberalization in former communist states as the expression of a phenomenon of nomenclature privatization. This refers to a process whereby individuals who had occupied positions of political power in the communist era took advantage of economic liberalization—often conducted at the advice of Western governments and financial institutions—by appropriating significant state resources for themselves (Windolf 1998). This line of argument sheds important light on the problems and paradoxes of liberalization in post-communist countries. The problem, however, is that it relies on an image of conversion of power involving a migration of assets from one distinct, clearly defined domain (the state, as the public domain) to another distinct domain (the economic domain, now governed by the market and private property rights), where the old political players (re)emerge as powerful entrepreneurs. This image tends to obscure the important links between the entrepreneurial behavior and the reconfiguration of arrangements through which public power came to be exercised in Eastern Europe (Los 2003; Los and Zybertowicz 2000).

To understand the emergence of an environment in which politically oriented modes of profit-making could flourish, it is useful to draw on Max Weber's concept of political capitalism. It is well known that Weber drew attention to the problems associated with the rise of a unitary bureaucracy. Beyond that, however, it is less known that he also expressed concern about another potential scenario, which could be called the rise of political capitalism (Ganev 2009: 654). According to the second scenario, far from giving the state additional strength, the merger of bureaucracies makes it possible for politically connected profit seekers to gain "unlimited and uncontrollable command over the state" (Weber 1994: 104). The result is not a domineering state but an emasculated or de-bureaucratized one. In essence, Leviathan is reduced to a collection of fractured administrative apparatuses that are unable to control their environment. The erosion of boundaries between state/non-state bodies in a modern polity generates dysfunctionality in the infrastructure of governance from the perspective of an idealized unitary state, though it may be very functional—if unstable and often conflictual—for those benefiting from it. As a corollary to this, the rule-enforcement function of the state is severely compromised, and the decision-making processes that are the foundation of the public domain are undermined by the power exercised by political entrepreneurs (Ganev 2009: 657).

A series of important transformations that took place in Eastern Europe immediately after 1989 can be understood as reflecting the logic of Weber's political capitalism. The collapse of communism gave rise to a series of privilege-centered polities where *de facto* control over assets (including security-related capabilities) was asserted via fragmented, personalized enforcement mechanisms. The borders between the state and the private domain were porous and open to transgression by profit-seeking political entrepreneurs, while the de-bureaucratization of the public domain reduced the ability of the state to perform functions conventionally associated with modern sovereignty.

Building on Weber's conception of emasculation of the state, we can interpret developments in post-1989 Eastern Europe as a partial reversal of the process of construction of modern states depicted in the influential work of Charles Tilly (Tilly 1992; Ganev 2007). For Tilly (1992), an understanding of historical processes affecting state structures requires a study of elite strategies in a particular historical environment, an account of the interplay between those strategies and particular socio-economic structures, and an analysis of the emergence of a coherent institutional framework of governance. One of Tilly's key insights is that European processes of state formation involved elites creating webs of institutions designed to channel resources to the treasury. Importantly, those elites were forced to negotiate the terms of their predatory projects with mobilized social groups, resulting in the establishment of robust state structures.

A very different type of scenario unfolded in the (re)construction of states after the anti-communist revolutions in Eastern Europe. Thus, in countries like Bulgaria, Bosnia, Serbia, and Romania elites with links to the previous regimes deliberately set out to weaken existing public agencies in order to extract resources from the state (Ganev 2009; Gounev 2007). In a situation in which there was little civil society mobilization, in the early and mid-1990s those elites did not have to contend with societal counterparts, or face constraints associated with the enforcement of rules—as should happen in a liberal-democratic polity.[2] In essence, Bulgarian, Serbian, Bosnian, and Romanian elites were able to carry out processes of liberalization in a way that entailed the perpetuation of their power and privileges in a situation in which most citizens were almost exclusively focused on adapting to (and in many instances surviving in) the new socio-economic context—and, in the cases of Bosnia and Serbia, recovering from years of violent conflict. Moreover, there was a widespread perception among most individuals in Eastern Europe that security-related arrangements could not be altered by ordinary citizens; hence, to even attempt to exercise influence in that area was futile.[3] Consequently, key decisions regarding the evolution of private security after 1989 were made and implemented at the elite level, without any significant consultation with (much less control by) civil society actors.

Not surprisingly, the profound changes in state structures in the early years of post-communist transitions had a substantial impact on the field of security in East European polities. To shed light on those developments, and especially to understand how old players were able to (re)emerge as powerful actors in the post-communist field of security, it is useful to draw on the sociology of Pierre Bourdieu—particularly his concepts of fields, capital, and habitus.

Reproducing Old Ways of Doing Things in the New Age of Liberalism

To understand the persistence of old ways of acting after 1989, it is useful to draw on key categories developed by French sociologist Pierre Bourdieu.[4] In so doing, I am building upon the work of scholars who have already applied various Bourdieu-an concepts to IR (Abrahamsen and Williams 2011; Adler-Nissen 2013; Leander 2011; Mérand and Pouliot 2008; Williams 2007). What is especially important, in the context of the present study, is that Bourdieu's approach enables us to develop an analysis that escapes the agency/structure dichotomy (Leander 2011). Consequently, we can explore both the strategic behavior of actors involved in security provision in Bulgaria, Romania, Bosnia, and Serbia and the ways in which those strategies are shaped by the social context in which actors operate. Particularly relevant for our purposes are Bourdieu's concepts of field, capital, and strategies (Bourdieu and Wacquant 1992; Bourdieu 1998).

As a series of scholars have explained, for Bourdieu, a field is analogous to a game in that it is a socially constructed, historically specific domain of activity that is governed by a specific set of rules (Bourdieu 1990; Leander 2011; Williams 2007). Within a given social field, as actors perform multiple social practices, they mobilize different forms of capital. While those forms of capital are specific to particular social fields, under certain circumstances they can also be converted across fields (Williams 2012: 314). Fields are social constructs that are constituted, sustained, and reproduced by the willingness of agents to participate in them, play by the "rules of the game" that prevail in each field, and believe in the value of playing that game (Bourdieu and Wacquant 1992: 19). Participants in a given field share an often unarticulated understanding of the rules of the game, and a common sense of what is at stake within that field (Leander 2008: 15). To understand how actors come to share such a "common sense" one needs to focus on the role of "habitus." Habitus is acquired by actors through the occupation of particular social positions and inclines them to perceive the world—and act within that world—in particular ways. In other words, habitus is the product of socialization of individuals into particular ways of seeing, feeling, and behaving, and is "at once a system of models for the production of practices and a system of models for the perception and appreciation of practice" (Bourdieu 1990: 131). The structured dispositions associated with the habitus are relatively stable, as they operate at the semi-conscious level, where it is difficult to reflect on and modify them. Nonetheless, one should not assume that a given habitus is immutable (Williams 2007: 27).

It is also important to keep in mind that the logics of specific social fields are shaped by the logics of other fields—particularly the state, as a meta-field (Leander 2008: 16). Beyond meta-transformations, fields also change as a result of internal struggles. Thus, while actors share a sense of what is at stake in the game in each field, they are also engaged in permanent competitions with other actors as they seek to advance their positions within that field. In other words, fields can be seen as battlegrounds (Leander 2008: 17), in which the positional struggles in which the players are engaged compel them to work to enhance the value of the capital that they possess. The concept of capital refers to the resources that actors can mobilize in order to act successfully in a given field, and in particular to exercise symbolic power. From Bourdieu's perspective, fields are loci of symbolic as well as institutional and material power: "the power to constitute the given by stating it, to act upon the world by acting upon the representation of the world" (Bourdieu and Wacquant 1992: 116). On this logic,

> There are many different forms of capital: not only "economic capital" in the strict sense (i.e. material wealth in the form of money, stocks, and shares) but also cultural capital (i.e. knowledge, skill, and other cultural acquisitions, as exemplified by educational or technical qualifications), symbolic capital (i.e. accumulated prestige or honour), and so on.   (Thompson cited by Williams 2007: 32)

Bourdieu accords special importance to symbolic capital because, as Guzzini has explained, capital "is never only in material or ideational resources but in the recognition it encounters in agents." In short, symbolic capital is the form that any capital will take if it is recognized—that is, "perceived through those very conceptual categories which are, however, themselves the effect of the distribution of capitals in the field" (Guzzini 2013: 81).

Actors who inhabit a given field participate both in struggles over the distribution of currently recognized forms of capital and in struggles to enhance their position by changing the structures of valorization within the field. Interestingly, layers can—and often do—seek to change the relative value attributed to specific forms of capital "through discrediting the form of capital upon which the force of their opponents rests" (Bourdieu and Wacquant 1992: 99), and increasing the value of the forms of capital that they possess. Furthermore, players can also import capital from other fields, and can attempt to influence the overall understanding of the rules of the game and the stakes involved in an effort to (re)structure the field to their advantage. While concepts like interests and strategies occupy prominent positions in Bourdieu's work, they do not have the same meanings they have in game theory accounts of strategic behavior (Bourdieu 1998: 81). According to Bourdieu, interests and strategies are always socially constructed within specific fields and are, as such, "at once a condition of the functioning of the field ... in so far as it is 'what gets people moving,' what makes them get together, compete and struggle with each other, and a product of the way in which the field functions" (Williams 2012: 314).

In the context of our analysis, it is useful to conceptualize strategies in a Bourdieusian way—that is, as involving more than rational calculation and asocial choices. From this perspective, the nature and quality of strategies available to actors is determined in part by the social context in which those actors operate (Lamaison 1986: 113). The practice of strategy involves competent moves that are needed to reproduce one's advantage in a social game. In order to be able to formulate effective strategies, actors must have a certain "feel for the game" (Lamaison 1986: 111). The notion involved here is that if actors do not understand a certain social game, they will not be able to play it in an advantageous manner. The ability to effectively play any given social "game" thus depends on an investment in it and an understanding of what is at stake and what is the repertoire of potential strategies.

An analysis that draws on Bourdieu-an concepts enables us to shed light on the ways in which the field of security is being (re)constituted and struggled over in post-communist states, in part through practices enacted in other fields. Linked to this, a focus on the complexities of social practices and the multiple relations between material, cultural, and symbolic factors allows an exploration of the ways in which capital can be converted and exported across fields, and how any given social field can be influenced by developments in other fields. Specifically, despite significant differences in their recent past and contemporary circumstances, in all the East European polities examined here security privatization was legitimized and profoundly affected by processes of liberalization that transcended the field of security. In particular, processes of transition to a market economy that were carried out in the 1990s sought to change the "categories of vision and division" (Guzzini 2013: 87) in multiple fields including the field of security. This resulted in a significant empowering of commercial actors, endowing them with epistemic power and inscribing it in a new doxa that authorizes the arguments and capital of commercial actors (Leander 2005, 2011). Specifically in our case, doxic transformations in the field of security in East European countries empowered private security professionals, authorizing them to participate in the provision of security functions traditionally attributed to the state.

In describing the early 1990s in Eastern Europe, we can speak of a partial interpenetration between the economic and security fields. This, in a situation in which networks of private security professionals with close links to the state were able to transfer into the security field capital acquired as a result of transformations in the economic field (particularly the rapid and flawed privatization of state assets). One of the consequences of this partial interpenetration was that the logic typically associated with the economic field (financial gain) became almost as important to security providers as the logic of security provision.

To understand this development, we need to place it within the framework of broader transformations that occurred in East European polities in the 1990s, and in particular the emergence of a complex state–corporate–crime nexus. This involved a partial merger between changing state agencies and new, controlled markets, in which both are influenced by state/corporate/criminal organized interests. Consequently, the state was simultaneously weakened and reinforced, undermined and augmented, via the quasi marketization of corruption and security. In many East European states, as communism was collapsing, old (state and party-based) power networks started to engage in the privatization and marketization of various aspects of the state.[5] In fact, as Los has cogently argued, in many of those polities a hidden privatization of the state was already under way before the communist system's breakdown: behind the façade of official state structures, power was exercised by networks of privatized, clientelistic, bureaucratic relationships (Los 2003). Under these circumstances, when the option of *de jure* privatization of state assets became viable—following the collapse of communism—the nomenclature/police networks were able to institutionalize and legitimize their influence via massive and rapid transfers of public assets to themselves and their families or friends (Handleman 1994; Los 2003).

In the early years of post-communist transition, many East European polities adopted legislation aimed at legalizing what had previously been seen as illegal and an unacceptable violation of communist ideology. Those laws legitimized the massive transfer of state assets to members of the nomenclature, and in effect legalized the shadow economy that was already controlled by the communist party/police/state bureaucracy networks (Gheciu 2014).

The political elites' support for—and often direct involvement in—the corrupt enrichment schemes as well as the lack of reasonable standards of public conduct on the part of the new elites fuelled a widespread perception that under capitalism the values of honesty and integrity were not applicable. Corruption came to be conceptualized as a market phenomenon, meaning that political influence was yet another commodity that could be purchased (Los 1998). A rapid commercialization of government via corruption was just one of the consequences of that evolution. In other words, following the collapse of communism, many former communist polities did not simply experience a process of replacing states with markets. Rather, as Los has argued, they underwent a "merger of the state with quasi-markets, both of which are constituted and controlled by state/corporate/criminal organized interests" (Los 2003: 161).

Not surprisingly, those transformations of the state and public power had significant impacts on the field of security in East European polities. In a situation of transition—at least in principle—toward a democratic state, many functions of the former communist state could no longer be carried out in the same form. At the same time, however, the police/nomenclature networks were keen to preserve the power of the former police/security sector as a way to enable them to protect their interests and enhance their positions in the new context. Consequently, in most post-communist states, a substantial proportion of the former police state apparatus was turned into a powerful private security industry (Coulloudon 1997; Los and Zybertowicz 2000; Shelley 1995; Volkov 2002). Furthermore, the private security industry has had a profound impact on practices of economic competition in both legal and illegal markets. In the early years of post-communism, private security employees had access to superior weapons, sensitive information, and sophisticated surveillance equipment. The private firms were, for the most part, run and staffed by former members of state security agencies and, in some cases, by former state-sponsored athletes (especially those involved in martial arts). The ex-state security agents brought with them secret knowledge, skills, material capabilities, as well as the willingness to use political connections and often resort to violence. From its birth, this new industry was intertwined with ex-communist power networks as well as with various national and international networks involved in organized crime and various types of shady business operations (Los and Zybertowicz 2000; Nikolov 1997; Wedel 2003).

On the licit side, starting in the 1990s the private security industry came to be systematically involved in performing functions traditionally associated with the state, including law enforcement, administration of justice, conflict resolution, and protection of goods and people (Los 2003: 153). Yet, the involvement of PSCs in the provision of security did not end there. Particularly interesting from our perspective is the fact that, in parallel to their licit functions, many security companies also became involved in the illicit side of security. During that time, the licit and illicit sides of security provision became partly intertwined, as PSCs offered legal but also criminal services to both legal and criminal actors. Many of those companies were often involved in illegal debt collection, extortion, kidnapping, criminal rackets, secret surveillance, illegal arms trade, and contacts with organized crime (Tayler 2001). In some instances, registered private security companies served as fronts for criminal groups' intelligence and protection operations or had ties to private armies run by criminal syndicates. At the same time, PSCs often provided key services to state officials (for instance via the illegal surveillance of their opponents and/or the protection of their illegally acquired wealth), thereby blurring the boundary between the state and private security.

A phenomenon that can be seen as "network corruption" acquired the status of smart market strategy and became one of the defining factors of the new society (Los 2003: 157), involving a form of collectivization and high-level organization of corruption practices by strategically placed powerful networks. Those networks were able to define the rules of the game, and established a controlled market, turning government services into a commodity that could be bought on the market.

To put this in a broader perspective: it is useful to conceptualize the actors who took advantage of their privileged status and access to assets inherited from the communist era as entrepreneurs both in the most obvious sense of the word and in a larger, more systemic way. In the most immediate sense, the emerging security entrepreneurs acted to turn the provision of security into a lucrative business, seeking to persuade a variety of potential clients that they could effectively "perform" functions of protection traditionally associated with the state, and protect them from their rivals, if need be. In a broader sense, those actors played the role of norm entrepreneurs as they sought to take advantage of processes of liberalization to redefine the "rules of the game" of security provision so as to further empower themselves, pushing even further the boundaries of state functions that could and should be devolved to the private sector.

The Old Nomenclature as Entrepreneurs

Contrary to what one might have expected, in the early years of post-communist transitions some of the most important reforms involving the restructuring of the state in Bulgaria and Romania were not carried out by neo-liberal politicians (Gounev 2007: 15). Instead, in those early days—in Bucharest as well as in Sofia—it was mainly former nomenclature members (or their friends and families) who, in the name of reform, initiated many of the changes that eventually led to the emergence of complex, hybrid networks of security providers. Particularly significant was the privatization of power ministries, involving the transfer of the communist state's coercive and information-gathering capabilities into privately controlled assets that were at the disposal of strategically placed networks of political and economic entrepreneurs and their new companies.[6] Processes of privatization of power ministries were legitimized by reference to the neo-liberal discourse of commodification of security. Thus, in interactions with EU officials and international financial institutions and Western governments, Bulgarian and Romanian elites were able to portray a deeply problematic process of privatization as a legitimate development by characterizing it as a reform that was needed in order to reduce the role of the state, and adopt principles of market rationality in the field of security.[7]

In Bulgaria, the government of Andrei Lukanov (who had been a high-ranking member of the communist nomenclature) broke up various units within the Ministry of Interior and the security services that were primarily charged with overseeing the conduct of managers of state property (Ganev 2007: 48). Lukanov initiated the exodus of a large wave of state security officials, and ensured that, after several reorganizations of the security services, former cadres could eventually re-emerge as private protection agencies. When they left office, those individuals took with them their know-how as well as a series of incriminating documents. Their departure meant that newly appointed officials had to rebuild investigative mechanisms from scratch—including mechanisms that should have been used to prevent the abuse of power by former state employees. To further complicate matters, the new public agencies did not receive the financial or human resources needed to perform their functions. For their part, many of the officials who retained prominent positions within the state (and thus had access to public resources) were also busy reinventing themselves as private entrepreneurs, looking for lucrative business opportunities, often in partnership with networks of trusted former colleagues and friends who were now private citizens.

Following the accession to power of a new (for the first time, non-communist) government in 1992, the reform of the security apparatus became a priority—paradoxically building on some of the developments that had been initiated by the communist elites. For instance, one of the measures taken by the new Bulgarian government was to fire all the staff in the Ministry of Interior that were over forty years old, on the grounds that those individuals had been too deeply socialized into communist thinking to be of use in the new era.[8] The desire to purge the Ministry of Interior of officials who had been responsible for abuses under communism may have been perfectly reasonable, but the way in which this action was carried out meant that virtually overnight an additional contingent of

12,000 individuals joined the ranks of those who were no longer employed by the state. At the same time, those individuals were still part of a tight community of security professionals, retained connections to a few key individuals within the state, and had substantial expertise and experience (albeit, in some ways, deeply problematic communist experience) in the field of security. Furthermore, Bulgaria had a large number of professional athletes (especially those associated with the martial arts), who had lost the support traditionally provided by the communist government, and were looking for a new employer. Those individuals had a very narrow set of skills that could help them in the job market. They did, however, have close connections with security providers, and even influence in political circles.[9]

Following the persistent lobbying by all those individuals who were searching for a new role in the field of security, and also in response to the EU insistence that Sofia should accelerate liberalization reforms, the Bulgarian government decided to open the field of security to private actors. It is interesting to note that Bulgaria was one of the first former communist countries to relinquish state monopoly on force (Gounev 2007). The legislation that was introduced in the early 1990s to regulate the budding private security sector was quite loose, with very few conditions imposed upon those who wanted to set up such firms. It was only with the 1994 *Ordinance no.14 for the Issuance of Permits for Guarding of Sites and Private Individuals by Physical and Legal Persons* that the government set some minimal rules concerning the establishment and functioning of PSCs. For instance, the Ordinance stipulated that a PSC could not be registered if one of the owners or its employees had criminal records, were under investigation, or had not paid taxes (Gounev 2007).

In the absence of a solid legal and institutional framework, the partial privatization of security led to a situation where the field of security came to be dominated by a peculiar type of complex, hybrid networks of private security entrepreneurs and state officials. Those actors, with a shared communist past, were united by common ways of looking at the world—and practical dispositions for acting in that world—and also had a strong interest in continuing to exercise power in the field of security.[10] One can conceptualize them as members of a community of practice, sharing a stock of inter-subjective understandings as well as practical dispositions inherited from their communist past. Thus, they shared a common worldview, which included communist-style ideas regarding the privileged position that security agents should play in society, as well as practical knowledge, including expertise in—and dispositions to use—techniques of surveillance and intimidation of targeted segments of the population that they came to use in the post-communist context.[11]

It is interesting to note that even in the early days of post-communism, there were concerns that PSCs were becoming too powerful, and thus a possible source of threat to the authority of the state. In Bulgaria, for instance, in the mid-1990s then Chief Army Prosecutor General Yotsev referred to private security companies as a threat to the state because of their "military subordination, iron discipline, high-quality communication devices, ultra-modern cars, and weapons that the police did not have" (Tzvetkova 2008: 333). Under those circumstances, the Bulgarian authorities sought to reform the relationship between public/private security providers, in part by impos-ing a series of new conditions on the creation and operation of PSCs, and shutting down some of the companies that were seen as particularly guilty of abusive behavior (e.g. via their systematic involvement in violent criminal acts). This translated into the adoption of legislation that was designed to prevent PSCs from committing abuses, for instance, by making it more diffi-cult for private security companies to obtain licenses, limiting the PSCs' access to weapons, requiring PSC personnel to undergo specialized training, etc. Yet, those changes were limited in scope and in their application. Following the promulgation of Regulation 14 in 1994, the government refused to license many security firms suspected of criminal activity (Gounev 2007; Tzvetkova 2008). Yet, while the Bulgarian government sought to push out of business certain PSCs, it continued to protect and promote the security companies owned by former policemen (Tzvetkova 2008). In short, the close connections between the state and the private security domain were maintained and even strengthened in the aftermath of the introduction of new rules in 1994.

Linked to that, while PSCs accused of criminal activity were pushed out of the official security business, they did not entirely disappear from the field of security. Thus, many of those companies re-emerged as insurance companies (Gounev 2007; Tzvetkova 2008; Vaglenov 2010). Those companies came to be known by the general public as "power insurers," as they engaged in "insur-ance" practices that were synonymous with protection racket: the "insurer" would leave a sticker on a car or venue, and the price for having the sticker would have to be paid. Refusal to comply could result in car theft or damage of property. In other words, the violent side of the provision of security to individuals and businesses continued and, in the mid-1990s at least, was tolerated by the state. As Stoytchev noted: "This went on from the local kiosks for newspapers and cigarettes to camping sites and beaches. Moreover, this was seemingly legal. There is a contract whereby the two sides have obligations" (cited in Tzvetkova 2008: 338).

Several aspects of this violent side of security provision practices are particu-larly relevant for our purposes. Above all, "power insurers" were able to exploit the post-communist government's new insistence on risk-management and responsibilization of citizens. As part of the process of liberalization, Bulgaria, (like other former communist countries, followed established liberal democ-racies in transferring part of the responsibility for protection to citizens themselves, adopting legislation that allowed the establishment of private insurers and encouraged individuals to take out policies provided by those private insurers. In this case, the new emphasis on self-protection translated into a mafia-like approach, one which was nevertheless treated by the state as a private issue rather than a matter of common concern. In essence, in the mid-1990s, governmental authorities and "power insurers" were *de facto* (if not *de jure*) working together to (re)define the (public) realm of common concern, and to cast matters that had previously fallen under the purview of the state (protection of individuals from criminal activities) as private issues simply because those matters were assumed to be governed by an implicit contract between the "protector" and the "protected."

Similar to Bulgaria, post-communist Romania also embarked on a process of legal transformation that facilitated the creation of hybrid networks of actors that defy conventional boundaries between the public and the private spheres. While the first (neo-communist) government that came to power after 1989 did not surrender the state's monopoly on force quite as quickly as the government in Sofia, Romania did experience processes that were very similar to post-communist changes in Bulgaria. Thus, in Bucharest, too, there was a systematic transfer of state-owned assets into the hands of the former nomenclature, many of whom were reinventing themselves as businessmen while also retaining positions of influence within the state (Prisacariu 2010). As a corollary to this, there was a weakening of public institutions and a proliferation of networks of a community of practice that shared conceptual and practical dispositions inherited from the communist regime, had access to substantial material resources, and had a shared interest in maintaining power in the post-communist context (Prisacariu 2010). In the first years of the post-communist era, the regime governing the creation of private security companies was very loose; it was only in the mid-1990s that the Romanians started to put in place a (loose) legal framework designed to govern private security companies. This fluid regime allowed private entrepreneurs, particularly former policemen and Securitate officers who were reinventing themselves as businessmen, to create private security companies without any significant constraints or controls by the new state agencies (Prisacariu 2010).

In essence, post-communist security practices in Bulgaria and Romania challenged conventional divides between public and private, and economic and security. As Bulgaria and Romania were embarking on market-based reforms in the early 1990s, they did not have the political, economic, and legal institutions in place to support market transactions and to protect property rights.[12] In that context, newly created PSCs were able to enhance their position in the field of security by effectively performing functions that were traditionally associated with the state. As noted in Chapter 1, it is useful to conceptualize performances as involving three dimensions: to execute or discharge a duty; to act in a manner that is consistent with prevailing laws, customs, and habits in a given society at a particular moment in time; and to show the effective performance of the first two dimensions to various audiences in an effort to gain their positive evaluation. In the cases of post-communist Bulgaria and Romania, newly created PSCs embarked on a systematic campaign to show to actual/potential clients, both individuals and businesses, that they could perform the function of protection better than the cash-strapped, often corrupt public agencies. Thus, what was particularly important to those companies in the early years of post-communism was not only to be able to effectively protect their clients, but also to *be seen* by actual and potential clients—and, more broadly, by the public at large—as effective providers of protection during a time of uncertainty and insecurity.

The efforts to gain the trust of their audience and secure recognition as effective security providers were facilitated by widespread public distrust in the police forces of East European polities. As Caparini and Marenin have argued, in the post-1989 context, all former socialist societies experienced an explosion of regular and organized crime—and in particular a growth in crime concerning private property (Caparini and Marenin 2005). There was also a persistent perception that the police were corrupt and inefficient, that they were serving the interests of the state or private interest, rather than those of the community.[13] In the 1990s, the general level of satisfaction with the police remained low across Central and Eastern Europe. For instance, in a 1996 survey, only 33 percent of Central and East European respondents were satisfied with the police (Caparini and Marenin 2005). The International Crime Victim Surveys revealed that in the 1990s, of all the major regions of the world, citizens in the countries in transition in Central and Eastern Europe felt the least safe, with only 46 percent indicating they felt safe in the street, while 53 percent claimed to feel unsafe or very unsafe. Furthermore, victims of crime in Central/Eastern Europe also remained unlikely to report crimes to the police: in 1996 only 32 percent of the victims reported crimes, a figure that increased only slightly to 34 percent in 2000.[14] Fearing that the police would not protect individuals and property from increasingly assertive criminals (including organized crime), and unable to count on the court system to settle disputes and collect debts, many Bulgarians and Romanians turned to PSCs to secure their assets. In Bulgaria, in particular, many PSCs were in effect "muscle for hire" firms that would use any method possible on behalf of their client (Vaglenov 2010). More broadly, in many instances the newly created PSCs were very useful in that they provided a façade of legitimacy to individuals who cast themselves as liberal security providers, while continuing to employ the expertise, techniques, and material assets inherited from the communist regime in the service of their clients.

Furthermore, while in many cases PSCs responded to the demand for extra security generated by the weakness of state structures, there were also companies that actively contributed to the production of that need for security. As noted above, they did so via a technique that has long been familiar to students of protection rackets: encouraging private citizens and business owners to hire them, on the grounds that Bulgaria and Romania were not "safe countries," while in practice contributing actively to that insecurity.[15] In Bulgaria, in particular, there is evidence that certain PSC owners even carried out criminal acts designed to persuade businessmen that it was safer to hire private security providers. They also provided for the enforcement of contracts between their clients in situations where the state was unable to do so.[16] In essence, private security firms—and the mafia-like activities in which some of those firms engaged in the 1990s—played key roles in the post-communist process of liberalization. Many of them became the "violent entrepreneurs"[17] that contributed to a significant rise in the level of criminality in post-communist Bulgaria, while also acting as powerful security providers in a situation in which state agencies were often too weak to effectively provide that basic public good. As such, PSCs were at once fundamentally linked to the state and a threat to the legitimacy of the state due to their ability to systematically engage in violent activities that escaped the control of public agencies.

In their effort to show their audiences that they could effectively perform security functions, newly created PSCs mobilized—and sought to enhance their possession of—various types of capital in an effort to gain strong positions—and be recognized as efficient, competent players in the evolving field of security.[18] While some of those forms of capital were inherited from the old regime, others were associated with—and legitimized by—the recent processes of liberalization. For instance, in Bulgaria as well as Romania, PSCs mobilized material assets—including money, light arms, and security-related technologies—that had become available to them through the above-mentioned flawed processes of privatization. In addition, security professionals sought to style—and display—their skills, knowledge expertise, and professional background as cultural capital in order to gain symbolic capital and thus to enhance their companies' prestige in the field of security. The cultural capital mobilized by prominent PSCs involved, in part, knowledge of techniques of intimidation and surveillance that were inherited from the old regime, and could now be put to effective use in the service of businesses and private individuals who needed to know more about their rivals.[19]

In addition, PSCs were able to draw on significant symbolic capital, including prestige that was to a large extent related to the PSCs' connections to influential ex-nomenclature actors within the state, combined with prestige associated with their ability to fulfill a new and important function: the protection of private property. The argument frequently put forward by PSCs in their advertising campaigns and in discussions with potential clients was centered on the skills and know-how they had acquired in many years of service in the security agencies. Communist governments may not have been very efficient in most areas of life, they argued, but they did know how to train their security services—and those skills and expertise were now available, for a reasonable cost, to the PSCs' customers. In the words of a former Bulgarian PSC director, "many businesses wanted to know exactly what their rivals were up to, and sought to use that information to pre-empt their moves and gain a stronger position in the Bulgarian market."[20] This meant that, in addition to their more visible functions of protection and debt collection, in some instances PSCs also became involved in the collection of sensitive information on behalf of their clients—and in some instances apparently acquired new, sophisticated technologies aimed at enhancing their capacity to engage in the surveillance of their clients' rivals. What was particularly problematic in that context was that some of the information collected by PSCs was used in illegal schemes. Thus, new states inherited substantial surveillance capabilities, and further expanded them via the development of the private security industry and the adoption of new surveillance and computing technologies. Furthermore, private security and organized crime networks have also been involved in gathering compromising information to use in blackmail schemes against government officials, businessmen, and other actors (Los 2003: 160).[21] What was involved in many ex-communist polities was the emergence of "surveillance assemblages" that combine the capabilities and traditions of the former police state and demands of state/corporate/organized crime networks (Los 2003: 160).[22]

All those forms of capital were systematically mobilized by PSC owners and directors/managers in Romania and Bulgaria as they sought to secure recognition as efficient, trustworthy security providers and to recruit clients—both private individuals/businesses and public institutions. To reach their existing and potential clients, they conducted individual meetings/consultations and also orchestrated public demonstrations of their presence in the security field. For instance, Romanian and Bulgarian PSCs sought to ensure a very visible presence on the premises of their clients and, more broadly, in the cities and towns where they were operating. Interviews with Romanian and Bulgarian owners of small businesses and investigative journalists revealed that private security guards appeared to be everywhere, making those individuals and businesses that had not hired a firm feel like outliers, who were not doing enough to protect themselves.[23] PSCs reportedly used their physical presence to convey the image that they were fully in control in the space they were protecting. That often involved displaying their people and cars as visibly as possible, with private security guards issuing instructions to people who were on their clients' premises and adopting an aggressive stance vis-à-vis individuals they classified as "risky"—particularly those who appeared to belong to lower socio-economic classes. In effect, through such practices, PSCs sought to enact a particular script about how security should be performed in the post-communist era. That script revolved around the idea that the private security industry could and should occupy a prominent position in the post-communist security landscape.

As Ringmar has noted, scripts provide individuals and groups with roles and goals, and with instructions for how to act and how to go on (Ringmar 2012: 7). The script tells us who we are and who others are, what relations are between us, and how people in our society are expected to interact with each other. Or, as Hajer put it, scripting refers to "efforts to create a setting by determining the characters in the play and providing cues for appropriate behavior" (Hajer 2009: 6). From this perspective, scripts are at the heart of social performances; in fact, "a performance concerns the way a script is staged and enacted. To the extent that the performance is successful, the audience identifies with the events that take place before them and recognizes the actors as convincing and thereby legitimate" (Ringmar 2012: 8). This approach is useful in enabling us to understand how, in a post-Cold War context in which old rules and norms had been disrupted, PSCs that had emerged in Romania and Bulgaria assembled and enacted a script that stressed the powerful role that the private security industry could and should play. In their script, PSCs cast themselves as having the skills and technology to play powerful roles in society: as a reliable, efficient partner of the state, but more effective than the state.

Within the PSCs' script, the key discursive strategy was to provide a clear, simple but potentially very powerful storyline, which highlighted the weaknesses of the law-enforcement agencies, and cast their companies as more effective security providers.[24] The discourse articulated by owners and directors of PSCs depicted law-enforcement agencies as inadequate, often corrupt, and generally unable or unwilling to fully and efficiently protect individuals and businesses.[25] Linked to this, there was the idea that "[the police and other public security institutions] continued to have a communist-style mentality," which fails to take into account the needs and priorities of individuals.

By contrast, PSCs presented themselves as "private actors responding to the logic of efficiency"—that is, agents that could be trusted to respond much more quickly to address the needs of their clients.[26] Under these circumstances, the only logical option available to individuals and businesses—according to the PSC script—was to hire a private security provider. In staging their scripts, PSCs combined this storyline of superior skills and higher commitment and reliability of the private security industry with a series of "theatre props" aimed at enhancing the effect of their discourse. In particular, several

PSCs—both in Romania and Bulgaria—sought to "stage" themselves as reliable, state-like actors by adopting recognizable uniforms that were in some ways similar to (but often made to look better designed than) the police, and patrolling in cars that looked like official vehicles. Interestingly, however, they also combined those state-like symbols with stage props designed to portray PSCs as actors that were more efficient than state agencies and, importantly, were not afraid to go beyond what the police were willing to do in protecting their clients.

For instance, reports from several sources suggest that PSCs often used—and publicly displayed—cars that were faster than regular police cars, or trucks for the transport of valuables that were better/more modern than those used by state agencies. Apparently, they also intimated in conversations with their clients that they would not be "shy" about removing "troublemakers" from properties owned by their clients. In interviews with the author, more than a dozen investigative journalists and small business owners who hired private security indicate that PSCs would often suggest to their clients that, while state agencies would waste time going through endless bureaucratic procedures and generally "drag their feet" in dealing with security risks, "we [PSCs] get things done."[27] The message often implied in those communications was that private security agents would not necessarily be constrained by each and every rule and administrative procedure in protecting the interests and safety of their clients. In practice, the employees of leading PSCs ensured that they were highly visible on the properties that they were guarding; they often drove cars that were obviously more expensive than the police, and frequently sought to make their presence seen not just by their clients but also by the public at large by stopping and questioning (often aggressively) individuals that were on/close to the properties of their clients and were seen by the security guards as a potential problem. For instance, there is significant anecdotal evidence that individuals belonging (or perceived as belonging) to the Roma ethnic minority were repeatedly and sometimes aggressively stopped and questioned by private security employees, in ways that possibly involved violations of their rights.[28] In essence, the image projected by PSCs in those first years of post-communism was one of power protectors, able and willing to use material and non-material capabilities superior to those of the police in protecting their clients.

This takes us to the third aspect of social performances. As we noted above, to perform is not only to carry out an action and to publicly show it, but also, in carrying out that act, to behave in a manner that conforms with the habits, customs, and laws that prevail in a given society at a particular moment in time—or, in Bourdieusian terms, to act according to the prevailing habitus. In the cases of both Romania and Bulgaria, PSCs that achieved prominent positions in the field of security immediately following the collapse of communism were able to draw on material and non-material forms of capital inherited from the communist past because the attitudes and rules of the game that prevailed in those societies had not fully changed. While some significant legislative and institutional changes had occurred, a much-needed, radical transformation was delayed and complicated by the fact that it was inserted in a security field in which prevailing perceptions and dispositions were still shaped by the communist past. In that context, PSCs both took advantage and sought to reproduce a peculiar mix of liberal/illiberal ideas and rules of the game. Thus, liberal ideas of security commercialization—which provided legitimacy to private security companies as actors that could perform state-like functions—were mixed with illiberal understandings of the methods/tools and techniques that could be employed by those actors. In particular, there was an inclination to accept illiberal practices of security provision and to value forms of capital that underpinned those practices.

In essence, there were no expectations—among elites or publics—that security actors had to be bound by clear rules of democratic accountability and respect for fundamental individual rights and freedoms. Security actors had a well-established violent reputation: the prevailing view of them was that they were effective in/expert at achieving their goals/protecting the subjects/ objects that they were tasked to protect—even if that meant applying techniques that were at the limit of—and inconsistent with—existing laws. In other words, security actors were seen as subjects that had significant material capital (in the form of technologies inherited from the communist regime) as well as cultural resources (derived from their expertise/training in effective, if anti-democratic institutions). Furthermore, the prevailing perception was that security agencies had significant social capital in the form of close connections with actors within the political apparatus, and were able to use those connections to protect their interests and the interests of their clients.[29] Linked to this, there was a widespread perception that they could, to a significant extent, get away with this due also to the connections with the police/state security services. In the early years of post-communism, that inclination to continue to accept illiberal practices and value-related forms of capital in effect sustained violent assemblages that blurred the public/private divide in the provision of insecurity, and in which PSCs played important roles.

The persistence of old perceptions in the field of security fuelled what could be seen as a paradoxical attitude: on the one hand, as noted above, there was widespread distrust in the police forces' ability and willingness to protect the public good. On the other hand, however, there was the view that if actors who were or had been associated with those services could be hired by individuals or companies, they would be effective—and would not be bound by substantial legal constraints—in protecting their clients. The resilience of those views and dispositions facilitated the perpetuation of illiberal practices, leading to what could be seen as a situation of complicity between security professionals, public officials, and even members of the general public, as those actors adhered to a form of "common sense" that was reproduced by their investment in the "game" of security. For instance, there is evidence that even members of the Romanian and Bulgarian public agencies accepted and reproduced practices such as racketeering, deemed as acceptable in the name of a larger good: security. They did so primarily by advising businesses and private individuals to hire PSCs that were known to have connections with the police, arguing that they would be particularly efficient security providers.[30]

Transforming Security Provision after the Yugoslav Conflicts

While Serbia's and Bosnia's post-communist transitions obviously followed different—more violent—trajectories, they do share significant similarities with Romania and Bulgaria. In particular, developments in both Serbia and Bosnia following the end of the Yugoslav wars demonstrate that the field of security is not a completely autonomous field with clearly demarcated borders. Rather, it is a field that has been significantly shaped by developments in other fields, particularly the economic field. In both cases there was a partial interpenetration between the economic and security fields in a situation in which networks of private security professionals with close links to the state were able to transfer into the security field capital acquired as a result of transformations in the economic field, particularly the problematic privatization of state assets. This has also led to a situation in which the logic typically associated with the economic field (financial gain) has become almost as important to security providers as the logic of security provision.

The process of liberalization of security in Bosnia needs to be understood in the context of the particular status of that country following the Yugoslav wars of the 1990s. Following the conclusion of the Dayton Accord in 1995, a complex international administration was established in Bosnia and Herzegovina, empowering international actors to perform functions that went far beyond conventional peacekeeping (Caplan 2005, 2012; Paris 2002, 2004; Gheciu 2005, 2011; Zaum 2007). Within the field of International Relations, the international administration became the subject of a passionate debate between those who regarded governance practices conducted by international administrators as relatively benign efforts at turning the country into a stable, Western-style liberal democracy (Ignatieff 2003), and those who perceived that type of international intervention as an unacceptable version of neo-colonialism (Chandler 2006).[31] While the debate between those two schools of thought continues, there can be little doubt that in post-Dayton Bosnia international actors came to perform a series of roles traditionally attributed to the sovereign state.[32] In the modern age, it is the prerogative of the state—which represents the culmination of a process of concentration of various forms of capital—to interfere in all fields, and to impose and enforce regulations "concerning organizations or the behaviour of individual agents" (Bourdieu 1998: 33). In Bosnia, the function of enforcing regulations came to be performed, in different fields and in many instances, by international administrators. Central to the international governance practices have been attempts to transform the security sector—in a situation in which that sector was widely regarded as vital to the stability of the country and of the entire region (Flessenkemper and Helly 2013).

What is fascinating, however, is that one key aspect of security sector transformation—the privatization of security—was almost completely overlooked by international administrators in the period following Dayton. In Bosnia, private security companies started to proliferate in the mid-1990s, in a situation in which the post-war transition to a market economy legitimized the involvement of private actors in security provision, and in which a lack of trust in public authorities generated demand for alternative security providers (Azinović et al. 2011: 54). On the "supply" side of the equation, various changes in the security sector facilitated the rise of private security. This included internationally sponsored reform processes that resulted in the dismissal of large numbers of policemen and soldiers who had participated in the Yugoslav conflict, and whose only skills and experience were in the area of (in)security provision (OCCRP 2010). In that context, many of those who had played key roles in Yugoslav security services—including individuals who had been involved in military and para-military activities during the conflicts of the 1990s—set up (or were hired by) private security companies. Factors such as the lack of a regulatory system to govern PSCs, the fluid security environment and presence of large numbers of weapons in Bosnia, as well as the military/paramilitary background of several PSC owners, combined to create an environment in which many private security companies acquired assets that had been under the control of public authorities and engaged in dubious practices and often in criminal activities, especially racketeering (Azinović et al. 2011; Ahić 2009).[33] As we shall see later in the book, the international administrators eventually became closely involved in efforts to reshape the process of security privatization—with mixed results. But in the first years of post-conflict transition the practices of private security companies largely escaped the control of the international administrators.

To grasp the growing importance of PSCs following the Bosnian war, one needs to examine the strategies and power of the security professionals that had emerged as owners or directors of PSCs but retained close links to key public officials. Those security professionals had access to significant forms of material and non-material capital, which enabled them to enhance their companies' positions in the field of security. Similar to the situations in Bulgaria and Romania, they mobilized those assets to persuade clients that they could perform security functions more effectively than public agencies—though at times, if necessary, they could also act in cooperation with key individuals within the state. For instance, PSC owners and directors were able to draw on the significant material capital controlled by their companies—particularly weapons inherited from the war, as well as money and technology acquired, in part, as a result of the PSCs' links to political parties, local bosses, and police and army officers (OCCRP 2010). In addition, those security professionals sought to style their skills, knowledge expertise, and professional background as cultural capital in order to gain symbolic capital—that is, to enhance their companies' prestige in the field of security. What is particularly interesting about this process is that owners/directors of PSCs were seeking to turn what was an apparent disadvantage into an advantage: they were claiming that the skills/expertise that they had acquired prior to or during the Yugoslav wars were highly useful specialized skills, which would ensure that their companies would effectively protect individuals and businesses. Factors that, in an established liberal democracy, would have been seen as a reason for disqualification—such as skills acquired through links with organizations accused of massive human rights violations during the wars—came to be invoked as an asset in post-Dayton Bosnia.[34]

PSC owners and directors/managers deployed all those forms of capital as they assembled and staged a script whose key storyline was similar to the storyline of PSCs in Bulgaria and Romania. Thus, they highlighted the weaknesses of the law-enforcement agencies, and cast their companies as more effective security providers. And—again, similar to practices conducted in Bulgaria and Romania—private security professionals engaged in a struggle to enhance the prestige and power of their companies vis-à-vis Bosnia's public institutions. According to the discourse articulated by owners and directors of PSCs, law-enforcement agencies were cast as inefficient, cash-strapped, and "stuck with old technologies." Consequently, according to this logic there was a serious gap in Bosnia's security provision arrangements that PSCs could fill.[35] PSC representatives also insisted that, as private actors, their companies were in a better position to respond to the logic of the market and the security needs of businesses and individuals than the "slow-moving" and "often corrupt" state agencies. In a similar vein, surveillance and intelligence-gathering skills acquired during or even before the Yugoslav wars were invoked to cast PSCs as effective security providers. The aim was to obtain lucrative contracts with businesses/political actors who were interested in surveillance practices targeting their rivals.[36]

It is also interesting to note that, similar to the Bulgarian and Romanian cases, PSCs sought to convince potential clients—and, more broadly, the public at large—that they had the ability to effectively perform security functions by systematically displaying their presence in the Bosnian security landscape. Thus, the employees of leading PSCs maintained a highly visible presence on the properties that they were guarding through the positioning of their employees in key locations, the display of modern technologies of security, and, as in the cases of Bulgaria and Romania, an aggressive stance vis-à-vis individuals belonging (or perceived as belonging) to the Roma ethnic minority.[37] Those strategies were apparently very effective: the private security industry grew rapidly in the 1990s, a situation in which both private individuals and business came to rely extensively on PSCs (Azinović et al. 2011: 55).

Problematic privatizations of security following the Yugoslav wars were not limited to Bosnia. Particularly interesting in this context is the case of Serbia. In the aftermath of the fall of the Milošević regime in 2000, Serbia joined other ex-Yugoslav states in efforts to carry out liberal-democratic reforms, and in so doing to prepare its "return" to Europe. However, in Serbia processes of liberalization and democratization—including in the security sector—took place without the type of direct international involvement that was characteristic of reform processes in polities like Bosnia and Kosovo. In Serbia, in contrast to many other East European countries, the first private security companies emerged in the late 1980s, following the adoption of the 1986 Law on the System of Social Self-Protection (Petrović and Milošević 2015). Interestingly, in the context of democratic reforms in what was then Yugoslavia, the 1990 Constitution put private ownership on equal footing with other forms of property, leading some police officers to set up security companies.

However, the start of the Yugoslav wars and international sanctions imposed in the 1990s meant that it was only after the removal from power of the autocratic regime of Slobodan Milošević that reforms could be resumed and gain significant momentum (Petrović and Milošević 2015: 84). As in many other polities, security came to be partly redefined as a commodity that could be sold and bought in the market. Serbian experts estimate that by 2010 there were some 3,000 private security companies, employing between 30,000 and 50,000 people and owning about 47,000 firearms in their country (Petrović 2010). Before going any further, it should be noted that it is difficult to obtain accurate data about the PSCs that operated in Serbia at that time because—in sharp contrast to most European countries, including other former Yugoslav republics—up until late 2013 there was no effective, comprehensive legal framework governing private security.[38] The fact that until very recently there were no licensing requirements and no background checks, and that even criminal gangs looking for a way to arm their members were able to establish PSCs, meant that the private security sector in Serbia experienced tremendous growth after 2000, and "operated based on the law of the jungle."[39]

Similar to the situation in Bosnia, transformations in the field of security were influenced by developments in the economic field—especially the flawed transition to a market economy. That transition enabled members of the communist nomenclature to illegally gain control over state assets and redefine themselves as entrepreneurs. In Serbia, the corrupt privatization process in the 1990s led to the emergence of what Petrović calls a "reserved domain" in the private security sector, which was excluded from systematic reforms and democratic oversight and in which there were strong, illegitimate links between owners of PSCs, political parties, and senior public officials (Petrović 2010). In short, Serbia witnessed the rise of powerful networks that included political figures, PSCs, and organized criminal groups, and that engaged in practices ranging from money laundering to targeted assassinations (Dojčinović 2010). At the heart of those networks were individuals who had close ties to Serbia's past—as members of the communist nomenclature who were able to take advantage of corrupt privatization processes to gain control over state assets and often set up private security companies while at the same time retaining close links to (and preferential treatment from) powerful individuals within the state (Petrović 2010; Dojčinović 2010). It is also worth noting that in the 1990s they played important roles in the protection of opposition parties. Once in power, these praetorian guards benefited from a reserved domain that was exempted from systematic reforms and democratic oversight. Under these circumstances, it is hardly surprising that influential players in Serbia's field of security were against the adoption of liberal-democratic norms, which are associated with demands for transparency and accountability that would have been detrimental to their business. As Davidović has explained, there were:

> strong lobbies in the private security industry and political parties, which hamper the adoption of the law [on PSCs] as the status quo makes it possible for them to supply privileged companies with favourable business deals, and the companies, in turn, show immense gratitude by the end of each month.
>
> (Davidović quoted by Petrović 2010: 18)

Just as in the case of Bosnia, Serbian actors with links to the country's problematic past were able to mobilize material and cultural forms of capital to secure recognition and prestige as effective security providers. Thus, owners and managers of PSCs that emerged as dominant in the early years of transition had ties to political parties and were able to transfer into the field of security assets obtained in the economic field, particularly as a result of corrupt privatization processes (Dojčinović 2010; Petrović 2010). Furthermore, those private security professionals were able to style as cultural capital their specialized expertise, knowledge, and skills in the use of techniques of surveillance and intimidation. Ex-security service officers who came to occupy managerial positions in PSCs had learned those skills during the communist era or during the Yugoslav wars, and in post-Milošević Serbia deployed them against the real or perceived rivals of their clients. As a Belgrade-based security expert put it, "the most powerful of these private agencies know all there is to know about how to conduct surveillance operations, just as they know how to intimidate their clients' opponents. They learned these skills during the Yugoslav wars, or in some cases even before the war."[40] In addition, the fact that the directors and managers of many PSCs shared the same educational and professional background as individuals that continued to occupy key positions within the state security apparatus also constituted an important source of capital. In many instances, those connections meant that the owners and managers of PSCs were able to gain access to sensitive information that could be used to gain an unfair advantage over rival companies, and/or to engage in illegal practices of surveillance and extortion (Petrović 2010: 18–19).

It is also interesting to note that, similar to the other East European polities examined above, in Serbia, too, there was a systematic effort on the part of leading PSCs to not simply perform in the sense of carrying out a variety of security functions, but also to publicly, visibly stage that performance. Here, too, PSCs maintained a visible presence on the properties that they were guarding, displayed their superior technology (e.g. modern systems of electronic surveillance), and hassled or excluded from the properties owned by their clients not just individuals caught in the act of committing/attempting to commit a crime but also those that, although not guilty of any transgression of the law, were seen by the security guards as people who didn't "belong" there—especially because of their socio-economic status. For instance, there appears to have been a systematic effort to keep out the homeless, and those suspected of belonging to particular ethnic groups (e.g. the Roma were, again, particularly targeted).[41]

Through such performances of protection, leading PSCs in Serbia were able to recruit many clients and play powerful roles not only in the provision of physical-technical security to individuals and their property, but also, as in the case of Bosnia, in intelligence services. Companies involved in intelligence services often called themselves detective agencies, but their activities went beyond the usual activities of detecting marital infidelity and searching for missing persons to include counter-espionage and secret recordings targeting their clients' rivals, electronic surveillance, investigation of court data, etc. (Petrović 2010: 20).[42] This situation was especially problematic as it occurred in a country with a heavy legacy of anti-democratic practices and human rights violations. Particularly given the absence of a legislative framework able to curb the activities of private security companies, there was deep concern about the involvement of PSCs in abusive practices, in which individuals and companies were subject to extensive, illegal surveillance, in clear violation of basic liberal principles of respect for the rule of law and human rights.

As in the cases of Romania and Bulgaria, to understand the problems associated with security privatization in the former Yugoslav republics, one needs to pay attention not only to the forms of capital possessed by PSCs, but also to the way in which they were able to perform security functions in a manner consistent with the prevailing habitus in their security field. In both Bosnia and Serbia, central to the persisting habitus was a disposition to accept illiberal security practices and to value forms of capital linked to those practices. In particular, the fact that security providers had been involved in (anti-democratic) military or police organizations during and/or before the Yugoslav wars, and, consequently, possessed particular skills associated with that background (intelligence-gathering as well as coercive techniques, including surveillance without accountability and illegal forms of coercion) was not regarded as a reason for de-legitimation. On the contrary, such skills and experience constituted a source of cultural capital.[43] The prevailing view was that such actors, by virtue of their expertise and experience, would be able to effectively protect and promote the interests of their clients—even if that was achieved via illegal actions.

Given the absence of an effective, comprehensive regulatory framework governing private security, by high levels of crime and weak—often corrupt—law-enforcement agencies (Petrović 2010; Jovanović 2013), both security providers and their clients were inclined to participate in the provision of protection in a rapid and effective way—even if that ability relied on the use of illegal means. As Dojčinović put it, "Private security companies and crime have overlapped since the breakup of Yugoslavia in the 1990s." And, in his words, "that violent tradition continues today. With no regulations, and no political push to change the laws and reign in security companies, today's owners operate much like their predecessors" (Dojčinović 2010).

In a context marked by the tacit acceptance of the role and power of PSCs, even state agencies relied on these companies to do their "dirty laundry." Revealingly, an investigation conducted in 2008 showed that officers of Serbia's security agencies had hired PSCs to carry out activities that involve the violation of the privacy of many Serbs (Petrović 2010: 22). In particular, state security agencies used PSCs in actions that involve surveillance and reconnaissance, in an effort to escape legal constraints—given that state agencies would have needed a court order to act, whereas PSCs were willing to operate in secret, without seeking to obtain such an order.

The importance of forms of capital associated with the past in the first years of post-communist transition is reflected in one of the most interesting, under-analyzed aspects of the process of security reform in former communist states: in contrast to processes of security privatization in other parts of the world (Abrahamsen and Williams 2011), in the first years after the fall of communism the rich, powerful multinational security companies—which were seeking access to East European markets—were unable to play significant roles in Bulgaria, Serbia, Bosnia, and Romania. In the words of a senior official representing one of the most powerful multinational PSCs, G4S, "it was impossible to operate successfully in markets where what was really valued was not superior technology and professional expertise, but a security firm's privileged access to powerful players within the state who could guarantee special perks to their clients, and, in some cases, a willingness to resort to techniques of intimidation and surveillance of the client's alleged enemies or competitors that were completely illegal and morally unacceptable in the eyes of our company."[44]

The Dynamics of Illicit Internationalization in the First Years of Transition

While in the first few years of post-communist transitions international PSCs were unable to gain prominent positions in the field of security, a different type of internationalization was taking place: an illicit internationalization, involving the participation of security providers from ex-communist states in international networks of organized crime. While it is impossible to have a full picture of the nature and extent of that internationalization—not least because we do not have full knowledge about all illicit activities—the information we do have suggests that instances of illicit internationalization of the field of security were quite frequent. Not surprisingly, the same kinds of capital that enabled some PSCs to acquire powerful positions in their countries in the context of weak legal infrastructure, lack of enforcement, and widespread corruption were also valuable in facilitating the insertion of those companies into international criminal networks. Particularly valuable appears to have been the cultural capital linked to the past, including expertise in "enforcing contracts"[45] and collecting debts even in the absence of a stable law-enforcement system, surveillance skills, and, more broadly, training in using a variety of means, including violence to protect their "cargo" in a variety of circumstances.[46] Also helpful in this context were the material capabilities (money and security-related technologies) inherited by many East European PSCs as a result of their special access to state assets, as well as specialized intelligence skills that enabled them to escape capture while operating across national boundaries. Interestingly, even in cases of polities emerging from ethnic conflict, many participants in illicit security practices were willing to cooperate with actors from opposing ethnic groups in order to enhance their position in the international criminal world.[47]

For instance, in Bulgaria contraband was one of the main types of illegal income in the post-communist transition years. Following the liberalization of the Bulgarian economy, up to 80 percent of GDP came from imports and exports.[48] In the 1990s, the growing reliance on imports from Asia and Turkey had a negative impact on the Bulgarian industry and agriculture, while at the same time helping to build up the shadow economy in the country. Both organized criminal groups and corrupt security officers aspired to control the transborder traffic of goods, not least because goods-smuggling channels run by local and foreign criminal groups were also used to traffic drugs, people, and arms. The 1992–6 embargo of Yugoslavia gave further impetus to the mutually beneficial relationship between the security sector and criminal and quasi-criminal trafficking/smuggling groups. Systematic, organized violations of the sanctions led to a massive influx of money, allowing criminal groups to capture significant shares of the regular economy. Security reports from that period reveal many embargo violations on the part of economic groups led by former police officers and nomenclature members—some of whom had established private security companies.

Apparently, criminal organizations had a clear division of labor: corrupt enterprise managers allocated fuel and other raw materials; former policemen and agents secured contracts in the customs and border security administration; and contract enforcers acted as haulers and guards of the embargoed freight (CSD 2004: 25). The latter became the key players in the business. At first, they were only employed by larger companies as escorts to their vehicles, but eventually the security companies themselves started transiting fuel and cigarettes along old and new channels into Serbia. In order to breach the embargo without trouble, it became important for the smugglers to bribe border state officials. This is how customs, security, and police officers, as well as other state officials, came to cooperate with the criminal world (CSD 2004: 26). Such alliances were easy to build because, as noted above, many PSC directors/managers were former policemen. In addition, in the mid-1990s many serving officers were working part-time as private guards to businessmen. Consequently, companies with illegal business were illicitly provided with information from the Ministry of Interior. It could be argued, therefore, that it was the Yugoslav embargo that catalyzed the formation of Bulgarian organized crime, facilitating the alliance between criminals, ex-policemen that had come to be affiliated with PSCs, and the economic elite in Bulgaria.

As regards former Yugoslav polities, an EU-funded report titled *Examining the Links between Organized Crime and Corruption* also blamed the nexus of private security and organized crime in part on UN sanctions imposed during the Yugoslav wars of the 1990s. According to that report, the fact that smuggling various essential goods was necessary for surviving the UN-imposed embargo, and that money from illegal trade was also necessary for financing the waging of war and other state functions, facilitated the involvement of the security services in forging links with organized criminals who were able to supply the badly needed goods and/or funds.[49]

In Serbia, the unreformed security sector enabled a massive infiltration of organized crime into the economic and political fields. By the mid-1990s, some criminal circles had already accumulated substantial wealth as a result of war profiteering, sanction busting, black marketeering, plundering of state assets, and foreign currency dealings. Several large, well-organized criminal clans emerged and came to permeate the government, the police force, customs, and the judiciary. As noted above, Serbia's elites also established a number of PSCs by taking advantage of their privileged position and contacts within the state. For instance, the country's notorious paramilitary leader, widely known as Arkan, founded a security company that trafficked drugs—in addition to running casinos, arranging political assassinations, and engaging in a host of other illegal activities (Dorsey 2010). Serbia's institutions generally operated via clan networks and circles of relatives and friends, instead of through a legal framework (CSD 2004: 56). The profits earned via illicit activities, including the smuggling of drugs, arms, oil, and excise goods—in collaboration with illicit networks from countries like Bulgaria and to a lesser extent Romania—were laundered and sent abroad through an elaborate network of foreign-based companies and bank accounts. These companies and accounts had been established during Yugoslavia's socialist period, and enabled Serbian companies to continue conducting business in international markets after economic sanctions were imposed on Serbia. Some of these companies and bank accounts were located in Greece and Cyprus, others in countries like Switzerland, Germany, and South Africa. In other words, Serbia was far less isolated than one might have expected under international sanctions, and in large part this was due to the activities of networks of actors which transcended the private/public boundary, and were able to cooperate closely not only with illicit networks in other states but also with legitimate foreign businesses, including international banks.

As regards Bosnia, keeping in mind that it emerged from the 1992–5 war with a destroyed economy, deep ethnic divisions, and inefficient law enforcement, it is hardly surprising that it came to be deeply affected by illicit actors and practices (CSD 2004: 76). It also became one of the centers of regional smuggling networks. Law-enforcement institutions, especially the police and customs, were often involved in conducting criminal acts. Indeed, it could be argued that in Bosnia and Herzegovina smugglers, arms traffickers, and quasi-criminal combatants did not merely profit from the war but "were decisive in its outbreak, longevity and outcome" (Brady 2012: 16). And, as noted above, many of those who had been involved in wartime crimes emerged from the war as part of Bosnia's elite, with close ties to politicians and the security services (especially through PSCs with strong political connections). A potent symbiosis emerged between the criminalized political economy and political elites, with those hybrid networks engaging in practices that went far beyond the borders of Bosnia. Routes that had been used for trafficking arms and drugs during the war were consolidated and expanded after the war, with former soldiers and combatants becoming middle men, and former enemies developing joint smuggling ventures. The ability to transcend ethnic divides, quasi-impossible in the political life of Bosnia, became an important reality in the criminal life of that country, enabling the growth of thriving smuggling networks (Brady 2012: 16).

The outcome of these developments was the expansion, in the 1990s, of a powerful "Balkan Route" of illicit trafficking in drugs, arms, and human beings that stretched from Central Asia to Western Europe. Within that route, many Bosnian actors of diverse ethnic backgrounds played important roles, acting in collaboration with criminal groups from Serbia, Bulgaria, Macedonia, Albania, and other countries from that region. A series of PSCs were apparently involved in a systematic fashion in these illegal practices, working in cooperation with illicit actors from other countries to smuggle drugs, weapons, and human beings in and out of their countries.[50] More broadly, as Umberto Pascali has cogently argued,

> a large part of the Balkans have been swallowed up, and tentacles are stretching out across the Black Sea, through the Caucasus, to merge with another such spot centered around Afghanistan. The "spot" does not respect national borders or ideological, ethnic, or religious differences, it just keeps spreading, bringing misery and destruction—on which it thrives. The "spot" is what was, until recently, labeled as the "black economy," or "illegal economy," or organized crime. In fact, it is a much more pervasive and totalitarian phenomenon. It represents the creation of a new perverse form of society: a modern form of feudal anarchy.   (Pascali 2001)

In this complex, transnational illicit world, PSCs have occupied powerful positions—not least as protectors of the illicit cargo, and violent enforcers of arrangements among various actors involved in this type of trade.

Of the polities examined in this project, Romania is the country that seems to have been least affected by the dynamics of organized crime. This, however, does not mean that the country has been immune from the influence of organized criminals—and here, as in other ex-communist states, PSCs appear to have played important roles in the illicit activities. For instance, it is alleged that citizens of the Republic of Moldova who operated protection rackets in their home country and in Russia also became involved in running several prominent Romanian PSCs, often partnering with former members of the Romanian security service (Prisacariu 2010). Reportedly, former members of the Moldovan secret police founded a private security company that catered to former Russian nationals living in Romania. It specialized in protection and extorted those who did not want its service, according to police records. The company had an impressive client list, including Russian companies like Lukoil, Targoviste Special Steels Works, UPET SA Targoviste, Nova Bank, Lada Niva Motors, and Troika Restaurant (Prisacariu 2010). In addition, it is alleged that some individuals affiliated with Romanian PSCs operating in the port of Constanta and in towns close to the border with Serbia profited from the blockade during the Yugoslav wars, becoming involved in transnational smuggling networks, in collaboration with organized criminal groups from Kosovo, Bosnia, and Serbia. Following the end of the blockade, those insecurity professionals reportedly continued to operate within the framework of a transnational illicit network, in particular by participating in the smuggling of cigarettes, alcohol, and some stolen goods.[51]

All the developments examined above reveal that in the first years of post-communist transition the field of security was profoundly affected by processes of (corrupt) privatization. A series of domestic and international factors combined to enable what amounted to a problematic commercialization of security—indeed, one could argue a partial criminalization of key institutions that were supposed to provide public goods. Yet, that was not the end of the story. In the countries emerging from the collapse of Yugoslavia, as well as in Romania and Bulgaria, the field of security was to change yet again in very significant ways in the late 1990s and 2000s, especially as a result of the growing integration of those polities into international political and economic structures. It is to those developments that we must now turn our attention.

Notes

1. South Eastern Europe Clearinghouse for the Control of Small Arms and Light Weapons (2005); see also CoESS 2011.
2. This was one of the leitmotifs that came up during the author's interviews with dozens of practitioners and security analysts in Romania, Bosnia, Serbia, and Bulgaria (the interviews were conducted between May 2011 and June 2014, in Sofia, Belgrade, Sarajevo, and Bucharest). See also Ganev 2007.
3. Ganev 2007.
4. As explained in the next chapters, however, there are aspects in the evolution of practices of security governance and provision in Eastern Europe that can only be understood if we extend Bourdieu's analysis of fields. For instance, in order to better understand dynamics of cooperation, contestation, and competition among various groups within the field of security, and to shed light on practices through which coherence is maintained within those groups, it is useful to draw on the theory of fields developed by Fligstein and McAdam (2011, 2012, 2014). Processes of cooperation, contestation, and competition in the field of security as well as practices

aimed at maintaining cohesion within groups became particularly significant in East European societies in the context of processes of Europeanization and globalization, which led to the rapid rise in the number and diversity of security providers in each of those societies. As we shall see later in the book, by building on Fligstein and McAdam's analysis of group practices within a given field, and shedding light on the performative dimensions of those practices, we can gain a more sophisticated understanding of practices of security governance and provision in the contemporary era.

5. My research generated findings that are similar to the findings of Maria Los's analysis of developments in Poland. See her analysis in Los 2003.

6. I borrow this phrase from Vadim Volkov (2002), whose analysis focuses on the dynamics of privatization in the Russian case.

7. Interviews with two EU officials involved in accession negotiations with Bulgaria and Romania, Brussels, May 15–16, 2010.

8. Author's interviews with three political analysts, one of whom was a former government official, Sofia, June 6–20, 2012.

9. This was similar to dynamics pointed out by Volkov (2002) in his analysis of the Russian case.

10. Author's interviews with former senior government officials, Sofia, June 2012.

11. The existence of this community of practice in the field of security was one of the key themes that came up in my interviews with more than two dozen interviewees, including Bulgarian and Romanian security analysts, NGO representatives, as well as representatives of G4S (a multinational PSC) who were complaining about the challenges they encountered when their company first sought access to the Bulgarian and Romanian markets. The interviews were conducted in Bucharest, Sofia, London, and Budapest in May–June 2011 and May–June 2012.

12. This section draws on Tzvetkova 2008, Gounev 2007, as well as reports by the OCCRP network of investigative journalists under the title of *Security Chaos* (OCCRP 2010).

13. On practices and problems of policing following the collapse of communist regimes see also Caparini and Marenin 2004; Fogel 1994; Kadar 2001; Pagon 1996; Shelley 1999; van Steden and Sarre 2010b; Ugljesa 1998.

14. International Crime Victim Surveys cited by Caparini and Marenin 2005.

15. While it is difficult to obtain strong written evidence about this, more than a dozen Bulgarian and Romanian investigative journalists and experts affiliated with think tanks and non-partisan institutes such as the Centre for the Study of Democracy (Sofia) and the Romanian Centre for European Policies (Bucharest) (interviewed by the author in Bulgaria and Romania between 2011 and 2014) argued that such PSC warnings to businesses occurred repeatedly in the 1990s.

16. Interviews with five security analysts (three of them former practitioners) affiliated with the Centre for the Study of Democracy, Sofia, June 2012. On similar dynamics in the Russian case see Volkov 2002.

17. I am borrowing a phrase coined by Volkov (2002) in his analysis of the making of Russian capitalism.

18. The next chapters revisit the issue of various forms of capital mobilized by PSCs in an effort to enhance their prestige and strengthen their position in the post-communist field of security.

19. Interviews with two Bulgarian and two Romanian investigative journalists, June 1–2, 2011 (Bucharest) and June 15–16, 2012 (Sofia).

20. Interview conducted on June 15, 2012, Sofia.

21. While it is impossible to establish with any degree of precision the number of instances in which PSCs operating in Eastern Europe were involved in the collection of sensitive information and its use in blackmailing schemes, more than a dozen independent analysts and investigative journalists from Bulgaria, Romania, Bosnia, and Serbia confirmed that such practices did occur (interviews conducted in Bucharest, Sofia, Belgrade, and Sarajevo, 2011–14).

22. Haggerty and Ericson (2000: 609) explain that a whole range of desires "now energize and serve to coalesce the surveillant assemblage, including the desires for control, governance, security, profits and entertainment."

23. Interviews with three Romanian and three Bulgarian owners of small businesses (in each country, two of the three were clients of PSCs, and one was not) and two investigative journalists in each country, Bucharest, June 1–5, 2011, Sofia, June 14–20, 2012.

24. Following Maarten Hajer, I define storylines as condensed statements summarizing complex narratives, used by people as shorthand in discussions (Hajer 2009: 61–3).

25. Interviews with owners of small businesses and investigative journalists (see note 23 above).

26. For a broader discussion of questions of trust and public reassurance linked to the presence of PSCs in different contexts see also Rowland and Coupe 2014. Also relevant is van Steden and Sarre 2010a.

27. Interviews conducted by the author between May 2011 and June 2014 in Sofia, Bucharest, Belgrade, and Sarajevo.

28. Interviews as in note 27.

29. This was confirmed by all my interviewees in Bulgaria and Romania.

30. Interviews with four investigative journalists from Romania and Bulgaria, Bucharest and Sofia, June 2012–13. This was confirmed by a security analyst from the Centre for the Study of Democracy in Sofia, and a former member of a leading Romanian PSC (with connections with the former Securitate).

31. For broader analyses of the dynamics and challenges of contemporary peacebuilding, see also Jarstad and Belloni 2012; Millar et al. 2013; Richmond 2006, 2010.

32. The 1995 Dayton peace accord set up two separate entities: a Bosniak-Croat Federation of Bosnia and Herzegovina, and the Bosnian Serb Republic, or Republika Srpska (RS), each with its own president, government, parliament, police, and other bodies. Overarching these entities is a central Bosnian government and rotating presidency. In addition there exists the district of Brcko, which is a self-governing administrative unit, established as a neutral area placed under joint Serb, Croat, and Bosniak authority. Above these structures, Dayton established

the Office of the High Representative (OHR), as the authority responsible for the implementation of Dayton, with the power to "compel the entity governments to comply with the terms of the peace agreement and the state constitution."

33. There is no hard data on this, but a Sarajevo-based security analyst and two former OHR officials interviewed between June 24–7, 2013 suggested that more than 60 percent of the PSCs engaged in such behavior.

34. Interviews with two Bosnian security experts and a member of the NATO Delegation to Bosnia, June 27, 2013 and March 11, 2014.

35. Interviews with two security experts affiliated with the Atlantic Initiative and the director of a Bosnian PSC, Sarajevo, March 11–14, 2014.

36. Interviews as in note 35.

37. Interviews with two Bosnian investigative journalists, Sarajevo, June 25–7, 2013.

38. Up until 1993, all the entities that were part of Yugoslavia had a Law on Social Self-Defence. That law, however, was repealed on the grounds that it was inadequate in a situation in which several different types of property had come to coexist within Yugoslavia (Petrović 2010).

39. Interviews with two Serbian security analysts affiliated with the Belgrade Centre for Security Policy and two investigative journalists June 17–19, 2013.

40. Interview, June 17, 2013.

41. Interviews with two investigative journalists, June 18–19, 2013.

42. This was reiterated in the author's interviews with two investigative journalists (see note 41 above).

43. This was confirmed by all my interviewees in Serbia and Bosnia.

44. Interview with senior G4S official, May 10, 2012. For a broader discussion of the power exercised by local PSCs see also Gounev 2007; Petrović 2010; and Tzvetkova 2008.

45. Here, again, there are interesting similarities to the Russian case. See Volkov 2002.

46. Interviews with eight investigative journalists from Romania, Bulgaria, Bosnia, and Serbia, June 2012–June 2014.

47. United States Institute of Peace (USIP) 2002. See also Brady 2012.

48. The information used in this section comes from CSD 2004, as well as the author's interviews with more than two dozen security experts from Bosnia, Serbia, Romania, and Bulgaria, May 2012–June 2014. See also USIP 2002.

49. An interesting discussion of the links between private security firms and organized crime in the Balkans can also be found in Dorsey 2010.

50. Interviews with two Bosnian investigative journalists, Sarajevo, June 25–7, 2013.

51. Interviews with two investigative journalists, Bucharest, June 5, 2011.

3

Toward a New Political Economy
of Security Provision

The Impact of Europeanization and Globalization

It is indisputable that the peculiar, corrupt liberalization processes that occurred in Eastern Europe in the early years of post-communism had a profound impact on the dynamics of security provision in the countries of the former Soviet bloc. In some ways, that impact is still felt today. Yet, it would be a mistake to underestimate the extent to which practices of security have evolved since the early 1990s, particularly in the context of the growing integration of those polities into Euro-Atlantic institutional structures and the global economic system. This chapter is devoted to an analysis of the dynamics and implications of those processes, with a focus on developments that started in the late 1990s and continued into the 2000s. As we shall see, processes of European integration as well as the growing participation of East European polities in global economic flows, which involved a substantial influx of transnational capital and multinational corporations, contributed to the liberalization and professionalization of the field of security in the former Eastern bloc. In a situation in which East European elites were seeking admission to Western institutions, especially the EU, they became more receptive to the views (and the pressure) of those institutions. Indeed, it was often under international pressure that new legislation was introduced in East European countries. In the field of security, new laws helped to open the door to foreign PSCs, sought to limit the abuses committed by the private security industry in the early 1990s, and sought to consolidate the partnership between public/private security actors.

Simultaneously, leading PSCs operating in Eastern Europe took advantage of their integration into the European security field—most notably through membership in the Confederation of European Security Services (CoESS)—to push for more rapid and more extensive reforms in their national arenas. Through an analysis of developments linked to European integration and growing participation in the global economy, this chapter sheds new light on the ways in which developments in the political and economic fields have affected the field of security—specifically by contributing to a revalorization of various forms of capital available to security providers. Thus, in a context marked by an effort to integrate into the EU and by the influx of multinational corporations with global standards of security provision, forms of capital such as Western expertise and professionalism as well as superior technology became far more valuable than they had been in the early 1990s, enabling PSCs that possessed those types of resources to strengthen their position in the field of security.

The most significant and obvious form of international influence exercised in the mid/late 1990s and 2000s concerns the integration into Euro-Atlantic structures via the East European polities' accession to, or at least efforts to move closer to, the EU. In particular, in the context of accession negotiations—and, in the case of the former Yugoslav republics, within the framework of growing EU involvement in their post-conflict reconstruction—the European Union has been very active in pressuring East European governments to better regulate PSCs within the framework of broader efforts to combat corruption and organized crime. Yet, even in examining that influence we are reminded of the observation made by Sassen and other theorists of glocalization: international factors may be powerful, but they are always filtered through the particular circumstances of the polities in which they occur (Sassen 2006; also Robertson 1992; Swyngedouw 2004; Abrahamsen and Leander 2015). In this case, European influences were shaped—and in some ways limited—by the transformations that were occurring in various former communist states.

EU involvement in reshaping practices of East European security provision has been a particularly important international source of influence in the area of PSC regulation, in a situation in which emerging global rules and norms for the behavior of the private security industry were still too weak to make a substantial difference during the period of time covered in this book.[1] True, in recent years—following numerous criticisms of the inadequacy of international legislation in this area—there have been some significant global efforts to establish international norms and law to govern the activities of PSCs (Abrahamsen and Leander 2015; Shearing and Stenning 2015; DeWinter-Schmitt 2015; Katz and Maffai 2015; Percy 2015).[2] In the future, those norms and rules may well have a profound impact on private security regulation around the world. However, at least in the first couple of decades of post-communism in Europe the situation was very different.

From a legal perspective, arguably the most significant global effort to govern private security concerns the UN *Draft Convention for the Regulation of*

Private Military and Security Companies. Thus, in March 2009 the Human Rights Council tasked the Working Group with consulting with intergovernmental organizations, NGOs, and academic institutions on the content and scope of a possible draft convention on Private Military and Security Companies (PMSCs), and to share elements of a possible draft convention with member states. The Working Group developed and circulated a draft to more than 250 stakeholders and engaged in a broad consultative process. On the basis of that extensive consultative process, the Working Group prepared the text of a Draft Convention for consideration by member states, and presented it to the Human Rights Council in 2010. Intended as a starting point for further discussion by member states, the Draft Convention proposes a series of "inherently state functions," which states may wish to consider as inappropriate for outsourcing to private actors (Katz and Maffai 2015). The list includes activities such as waging combat operations, but also law-making, espionage, intelligence, and police powers, especially powers of arrest or detention. The impact of such a Convention, if approved, would be significant. The move to restrict the outsourcing of the above-mentioned functions would dramatically affect the reach of the private security industry as it has come to operate. It would also have a substantial impact on practices of security provision in states (including in Eastern Europe) that have come to rely so heavily on private security companies as a source of manpower and expertise.

In practice, however, it is precisely the anticipated impact of an internationally binding instrument that would prohibit the outsourcing of particular activities to the private security industry that has proven a significant obstacle in the open-ended intergovernmental working group process. So far, states continue to hold very different views concerning the desirable scope and nature of regulations that should apply to the private security industry. It is interesting to note, in fact, that in 2015 the Working Group carried out a national legislation study on a regional basis, with the aim to identify trends, gaps, and good practice to be presented to the Human Rights Council and the General Assembly. The Working Group's key conclusion, however, was that, while some countries had adopted legislation regulating the private security industry, there were massive discrepancies with respect to the specific ways in which privatization is approached (Working Group 2015). Differences were particularly prominent in areas such as the licensing of companies and vetting of personnel, duties on the part of the private security industry to respect international human rights legislation, rules governing the acquisition and trafficking of arms, etc. At present, such discrepancies persist, making it very difficult to conclude a UN Convention.

In addition to work under UN auspices, a number of non-binding, multi-stakeholder initiatives have also sought to elaborate the human rights obligations of states vis-à-vis the private security industry, and best practices for companies (Shearing and Stenning 2015; DeWinter-Schmitt 2015; Katz and Maffai 2015; Percy 2015). Particularly significant has been the 2008 Montreux Document on pertinent international legal obligations and practices for states related to the operations of private security companies during armed conflict. The Montreux Document reaffirms the existing obligations of states under international law, in particular international humanitarian law (IHL) and human rights law, relating to the activities of private military and security companies (PMSCs) in situations of armed conflict. It also lists good practices designed to help states take national measures to implement these obligations.[3] The Montreux Document highlights the responsibilities of three principal types of states: Contracting states (countries that hire PMSCs); Territorial states (countries on whose territory PMSCs operate); and Home states (countries in which PMSCs are headquartered or based). While the Montreux Document itself is not a legally binding treaty, it does seek to provide guidance on the basis of existing international law. However, that document is less relevant to this study, which does not cover conflict zones (or companies involved in conflict zones).

Linked to the Montreux Document, there is also the *International Code of Conduct for Private Security Service Providers* (ICoC). The ICoC was developed to supplement the Montreux Document by articulating the obligations of private actors. The ICoC was drafted in a conference that concluded in September 2010 and was facilitated by the Swiss government.[4] The conference involved representatives from private security providers, industry associations, governments, such as the US and UK, and non-governmental organizations. The code reinforces and articulates the obligations of private security providers particularly with regard to international humanitarian law and human rights law. The ICoC also sets the foundation for developing an institutional framework to provide meaningful and independent oversight of and accountability to the ICoC. It has been designed to apply in complex security environments, meaning any areas experiencing or recovering from unrest or instability, whether due to natural disasters or armed conflicts, where the rule of law has been substantially undermined, and in which the capacity of the state authority to handle the situation is diminished, limited, or non-existent. While the arrival of the Code is a significant development for the private security industry, there is no evidence that it had any significant impact on the countries—and during the period of time—examined in this book. At the time of writing, the East European countries I discuss were not members of this Code, and with very few exceptions (e.g. Securitas), the private security companies that operated in that region did not subscribe to the ICoC.[5]

Yet, the limited global legal instruments that were available for the regulation of the private security industry during the period of time covered in this book should not lead one to conclude that international factors did not play important roles in the reconstitution of practices of security provision in Eastern Europe. On the contrary: regional influences were quite strong—with the EU playing a particularly important role in promoting security sector reforms as preconditions for accession to, or closer partnership with, the Union.

Returning to Europe, (Re)constituting the Field of Security

Following a few years of pathological politics after the collapse of communism, in the mid-1990s, both Romania and Bulgaria started to embark upon significant political transformations. Thus, ex-communist governments were replaced by more liberal, pro-West political actors, who began to reverse or at least minimize the impact of some of the measures that had been adopted by their predecessors. The new elites explicitly embraced liberal principles—including the idea of security commodification—but sought to correct at least some of the abuses that had been committed in the implementation of those principles in the early 1990s. In the field of security, one of the issues that was seen as requiring urgent attention was the growing power of PSCs—increasingly perceived as a potential threat to the authority of the state. Domestic concerns about the power and behavior of PSCs became particularly acute in a situation in which the new political elites in Bulgaria and Romania embarked upon campaigns to bring their countries into the EU and NATO. Consequently, in the late 1990s to early 2000s, Bulgarian and Romanian elites became particularly open to the influence exercised by Western actors, especially the EU. In that context, the European Union came to play a key role in the transformation of Central/East European polities. It did so particularly in the course of accession negotiations, when EU officials systematically monitored and—in numerous instances—actively guided legislative and institutional reforms in those countries.[6] To a large extent, EU efforts to monitor and promote reforms in candidate states focused on liberalization in multiple issues areas, including domestic security. Thus, European officials sought to promote free trade in security services across Europe, and, as part of accession negotiations, encouraged candidate states to allow free and fair competition in the security services—including by opening up the field of security to international competition.[7] For instance, in a series of rulings, the European Court of Justice had determined that EU member states could not limit employees of private security companies to their nationals, as such a restriction would violate the principle of free mobility of workers within the Union.[8] Consequently, established and new or aspiring EU members—including Bulgaria and Romania—had to adjust their national laws so as to eliminate discrimination against citizens of other EU states that wanted to work in the security industry in their jurisdictions.

European pressures for change became quite intense in the course of accession negotiations with the EU, leading the elites in Bucharest and Sofia to take steps to limit some of the worst abuses that had occurred in the field of security—including by placing greater constraints on PSCs.[9] Yet, the Bulgarian and Romanian governments did not try to address the problems and challenges posed by PSCs by completely outlawing them. Rather, by mobilizing the liberal discourse about the legitimacy of private actors in the sphere of security, and responding to the demands and pressure exercised by powerful actors within the state that had links to the PSC industry, Romanian and Bulgarian elites embarked on a process of change aimed at identifying and banning those PSCs that were guilty of some of the worst types of abuses. Simultaneously, they took steps to empower other PSCs to act—within certain limits—as partners of public agencies in the provision of domestic order. In adopting this approach, Romanian and Bulgarian policymakers were embracing a type of practice that was already taken for granted in established EU member states. What was different in the case of the East European polities, however, was that they were empowering PSCs to act as partial agents of public power despite the private security industry's recent history of violent behavior, and despite concerns expressed by civil society organizations and security experts, who continued to regard the private security industry as a potential threat to the authority of state institutions.[10]

As Philip Gounev has pointed out, under pressure to meet NATO and EU membership criteria, in 2004 Sofia passed the Law on Private Guarding Activities, which was meant to bring Bulgaria to the level of European "best practice"—for instance, by strengthening the definition of private security activities, requiring all private security employees to undergo specialized training, and stipulating that private security companies can only operate in Bulgaria if they have a license issued by the Bulgarian authorities (Gounev 2007). The 2004 legislation authorizes the expansion of PSC activities, which have come to include the provision of security in public places/facilities, such as the protection of power plants, ports, and provision of public order during sporting and cultural events. For instance, the document governing the activities of private security companies, the Law on Private Guarding Activity,[11] legitimizes the role of PSCs not only as protectors of private property but also as providers of "the public peace" and partners of the Bulgarian public authorities in the fight against crime. According to Art.2(1) of the Law, "The Private guarding activity is an activity related to guarding sites, events and persons, their rights and legal interests against illegal encroachment." As stated in Art.3, "that activity shall be carried out by observing the following principles: respect for the rights, freedoms and dignity of the citizens;

interaction with the Bodies of the Ministry of Interior in the fight against crime and the protection of the public peace."

It is not difficult to see that the focus of the new legislation was on establishing legal and institutional arrangements through which such firms could operate—within certain limits—as responsible agents of public power in the field of security. Consider, for example, how the Bulgarian Law on Private Guarding Activity empowers PSCs as active partners of the public authorities in everyday policing activities. The focus there is on constituting private security companies as agents that enhance the power of the state in risk-management practices. In essence, PSCs are expected to act as producers of knowledge about a complex security environment, and to use that knowledge in conducting preventive actions. According to Art.3 of the law, the private guarding activity shall be conducted by guaranteeing security and safety in the guarded sites and carrying out preventive activity on the grounds of analysis of the causes of tort in the guarded sites. To enable them to perform their activities, the law gives PSCs the right and also the duty to detain persons in the region of the guarded site when those persons have committed a crime or even when they are deemed (by PSCs themselves) to pose a danger to the life, health, or property of others (Art.32). In addition, private security companies are granted the right to use force when they cannot fulfill their duties otherwise (Art.34).

It is particularly interesting to note the ways in which this law extends to PSCs the function of preventive policing—that is, a function that, following the rise to prominence of norms and practices of risk-management, became a significant attribute of public authorities in the modern age. For instance, the Bulgarian Law for the Private Guarding Activity empowers PSCs to participate in the function of classifying people according to the degree of risk they allegedly pose, and on this basis apply different treatments to them. For example, Art.7 of the law states that the activity of protection carried out by PSCs "may include the introduction of admission regimes on the sites [protected by those companies]." Individuals and groups deemed by PSCs as "risky" can be excluded from the particular events and/or sites that they are guarding. Interestingly, those sites include not only private businesses but also important public spaces and sites of interest to the Bulgarian society at large. The private security industry's involvement in risk-management goes far beyond long-established activities of private security employees—such as, for instance, working as bouncers in bars or nightclubs. In the new context, PSCs were empowered to carry out risk-management practices at times and in spaces—for instance, in ports or during mass cultural or sporting events—where the security of valuable public assets or large numbers of individuals could be at stake. More broadly—consistent with the logic of preventive policing—PSCs were given the right to assess the security risks in the areas that they are protecting, and are also assigned the duty to detain individuals suspected of a crime or deemed as a risk to the health or property of others.

In enacting the functions prescribed by the Law for the Private Guarding Activity, a series of prominent Bulgarian PSCs continued to use assets whose origins were linked to the problematic process of privatization that occurred in the early 1990s. They also continued to articulate a discourse that casts them as more efficient than the state not only in ensuring the protection of private individuals and their property, but also in the provision of a key function traditionally associated with sovereign authority: public security. A recurring theme in the discourse articulated by those companies was that their experience, expertise, and technology—which was portrayed as superior to the cash-strapped state agencies—enabled them to respond in an efficient manner to a changing security environment. In the words of the director of a leading Bulgarian PSC, "we have everything we need to respond to the security needs of our clients, big or small, public or private. No job is too small for us, but, equally, we're perfectly ready to protect big companies, with more complex security needs."[12] In a similar vein, the manager of another PSC based in Sofia stated: "the successes we have had since the end of the Cold War, the fact that many of our clients have continued to rely on us over the years is clear evidence that we can be trusted to provide good solutions to any security problem or concern that our clients might have."[13] What is obscured in this discourse is the fact that in the case of many prominent Bulgarian PSCs "success over the years" was closely linked to their political connections, willingness to engage in illegal practices, and ability to siphon off poorly monitored state assets.

In Romania, too, in response to EU pressure to fight corruption and strengthen the rule of law, several steps were taken to provide a stronger framework for regulating PSCs, and to identify and shut down some of the companies that had been involved in criminal activities.[14] Simultaneously, the Romanian authorities, like their Bulgarian counterparts, have sought to build a stronger partnership between the state and the newly regulated PSCs, giving them new powers to participate in the provision of public security. It is revealing that, according to Art.2 of Law 333/2003 (the Law Regarding the Protection of Goods and Persons), it is now the responsibility of private companies, working in partnership with public organizations, to ensure the protection of goods/valuables on their premises, as well as of the goods they transport on Romanian soil. In other words, through Law 333 the duty of protection of property conventionally attributed to the police is partly devolved to private persons, companies, and individual public organizations, who have the right—and indeed are encouraged—to resort to the services of specialized private security companies. Furthermore, according to Law 333, PSCs can carry out the function of protecting the environment, and have the right to produce reports regarding the risks to private property, to particular individuals, or to society and the environment as a whole (Art.20).

And—again, similar to the situation in Bulgaria—through the Law on the Protection of Goods and Persons, private security companies acquire the power to set up admissions regimes on the sites that they are protecting (involving the right to classify people and subject them to different treatment based on the degree of risk they allegedly pose). As a corollary to this, PSCs are also given the legal duty to detain and surrender to the police all those individuals suspected of criminal activity in the sites that they are protecting (Art.48). In short, the Romanian legislation introduced in the 2000s defines new norms of security provision that cast private actors in the role of (partial) agents of public power, endowed with special rights as well as responsibilities to contribute to the provision of public security. Those rights and duties involve not simply conventional functions of physical protection of individuals and property but also risk-management tasks, through which PSCs participate in the production of knowledge about different categories of individuals, and are allowed to subject those individuals to different regimes based on the different degrees of risk they allegedly pose to the PSCs' clients and—at least in theory—to society at large. In other words, PSCs were empowered to exercise not just coercive power (for instance in preventing/responding to burglaries) but also productive power, participating in efforts to reconstruct individuals and businesses as responsible subjects.[15] On this logic, responsible subjects are those who understand the need to contribute to their own security in the area of cuts in public spending—and are thus willing to take all possible precautions, including by hiring private security—to ensure that they do not become victims of violence.

As a result of all those changes, starting in the 2000s the field of security became more diverse, as a number of international PSCs started operating in both Bulgaria and Romania, usually by acquiring a local company and turning it into the national branch of multinational PSCs (especially G4S and Securitas). At the same time, a number of domestic firms with no political connection to the ex-communist elites were also created. This was in sharp contrast to the first few years of post-communism, when, as noted above, the key private security actors were domestic firms with strong ties to the old regimes.

The new openness to international PSCs arrived at a particularly opportune time for global private security companies. Thus, the ascendance to power of more pro-liberal elites in Sofia and Bucharest, and the moves by those elites to pursue accession to the EU and NATO, generated international confidence in Bulgaria and Romania—and that, in turn, translated into an influx of foreign companies and especially banks. Those companies required Western standards of protection, going beyond what the local police and other law-enforcement entities could offer. The standards required by foreign companies involved not only technologies and skills/expertise (for instance, for the transport of cash and other valuables) but also Western principles of professionalism and ethical behavior. This was important in a situation in which companies opening branches in Eastern Europe could not afford to be seen by their stakeholders as having any connection to the abusive behavior and corruption associated with many local PSCs. Under these circumstances, foreign companies became a major source of highly lucrative contracts for security companies that could offer such standards. Particularly important has been the connection between the development of the banking sector via the arrival of international banks and the growing presence of global PSCs in Eastern/Central Europe.

Western banks started to enter the East European markets in the 1990s, and strengthened their positions in the 2000s, as their host countries were carrying out more liberal reforms in an effort to gain admission to the EU. Through those efforts—and based on the prospects of EU membership—East European polities were also starting to be perceived as more predictable, safer markets. Consequently, by the 2000s, large Western banks had become a dominant force in Central and Eastern Europe, to the point where foreign ownership reached 70 to 90 percent of banking assets.[16] Between 2000 and 2008–9, Western banks (e.g. Raiffeisen Bank International, Erste Bank, UniCredit, Société Générale, Intesa, KBC, and Santander) increased their loan books and asset base in Central and Eastern Europe by 10 to 30 percent per year in Euro terms (which was considerably higher than loan growth in their domestic markets), and opened thousands of branches in the former communist space. Currently, the average leading Western bank in Central/Eastern Europe has over 2,000 branches spread across former communist countries. In total, the top Western banks have some 250,000 employees in those countries (Klingen et al. 2013: 49). While less important than major Western banks, some regional banks also came to play powerful roles in several East European polities. For instance, banks with Greek capital became significant players—with hundreds of branches—in the banking sector in Bulgaria, Romania, and Serbia. In spite of the adverse home-market conditions they face, Greek lenders have retained their presence in Eastern Europe.[17]

One of the key implications of the influx of foreign banks into Eastern Europe was that leading global PSCs quickly became prominent players in the field of security. In the 2000s, global PSCs became the security companies on which a large number of banks starting to operate in the former communist bloc were relying. For instance, in both Romania and Bulgaria more than 70 percent of Western banks hired the powerful multinational companies Securitas or G4S, in a situation in which local security providers—both public and private—were seen as unable to provide Western standards of protection.[18] In Bulgaria, G4S alone came to control 40 percent of the cash solutions market, with a similar percentage of control being reported in the case of Romania.[19] It was in that context that G4S and Securitas came to employ thousands of individuals in both Bulgaria and Romania, and started to provide a multitude of functions ranging from individual/business protection to the transport and management of cash and valuables, as well as ensuring security and domestic order during public events.[20]

This situation is not unique. Indeed, it could be argued that the process of security privatization has been linked to, and has facilitated, the insertion of polities regarded as risky into the global economic system.[21] Global PSCs systematically invoke their global standards and ability to provide a wide range of services to international and local businesses, and in particular insist on their ability to make the variety of risks that companies/banks may face in new/developing democracies manageable and thus insurable (O'Reilly 2010: 185). Also, as Abrahamsen and Williams have explained in their study of security provision in Africa, private security companies play important roles in the process of expansion of global capital, and have become vital to the daily activities of global business (Abrahamsen and Williams 2011: 51–2). For many multinational firms, the availability of private security services is often perceived as a precondition for becoming involved in new or emerging markets, particularly when those markets are in unstable regions. Consequently, global PSCs like G4S and Securitas often expand their operations in tandem with their clients; as international banks, multinational retailers, and other entities with operations in different countries move into new countries, they often consult about risks and strategies for reliable, market-efficient protection and frequently take their private security companies with them. There is, then, a trend toward a situation in which multinational corporations use the same PSC for their operations in different countries. To a significant extent, this is due to the fact that large, multinational businesses are much more likely to trust PSCs than local authorities to understand the risks facing them, and to devise solutions to minimize—if not completely neutralize—those risks.

While countries like Bulgaria and Romania were far from being regarded as just as dangerous as some other polities—particularly those emerging from (or still affected by) violent conflict—they were nevertheless seen by foreign banks and other large international companies as significantly riskier than Western societies. That had to do with the persistent weakness (and often corruption) of state security institutions, the inefficiency of the justice system, as well as the links between some public actors and organized crime.[22] In the words of the director of a major Western bank currently operating in Bulgaria,

the image that we had when we opened a branch in Sofia was that of a country that was full of economic potential, but also plagued by inefficiency, corruption and, worst of all, high levels of criminal activity. For us, that was a major concern.

We didn't want to take any chances, and we didn't know how far we could trust the police, so we decided to hire G4S—a company that we know well and trust, having worked with them in the past. We knew that they understood and were able to address our needs. Furthermore, we knew it would have been unacceptable to our shareholders to work with local PSCs that were involved (or at least suspected of involvement) in any type of racketeering or other forms of criminal activity.[23]

In a similar vein, a senior member of the management team of one of the leading Western banks that started to operate in Romania in the 1990s pointed out that,

we had a responsibility to ensure Western standards of security, and neither the local police nor domestic PSCs could be trusted to do that. In fact, the police were very clear that we needed to hire extra security for the bank. For their part, most domestic PSCs could not be trusted, not only because some of them had a record of cooperation with some shady characters but also because most domestic PSCs simply didn't have the technology and know-how to take care of our needs. So the choice was clear: hire a Western private security company, and then stop worrying about this.[24]

What is particularly interesting about these statements is the way in which they reveal that practices enacted by global PSCs had a powerful performative dimension. Thus, PSCs cast themselves as the kinds of actors that could not just effectively provide protection to foreign banks, but do so in a manner that was appropriate for a security institution working for Western clients—by respecting the rule of law and principles of accountability and respect for human rights (in contrast to some of the domestic private security actors). That was important in a situation in which global PSCs like G4S and Securitas understood that, in order to maintain their international reputation, foreign banks could simply "not appear to be linked to any private security provider that was linked, or seen as linked, in any way to any form of racketeering or some other illegal or shady type of activity."[25]

To put this discussion in a broader perspective: developments linked to the influx of foreign companies and PSCs into Eastern Europe once again shed light on the ways in which transformations in the political and economic sectors impacted the field of security. What was involved in that context was a revalorization of different forms of capital in the security field. As discussed in Chapter 1, the value attached to different forms of capital in a given field can change over time as a result of changes in that field or in other domains of social life. In our case, changes in the political field (with the rise to power of pro-liberal, pro-Western elites and the resulting move closer to the EU) and, linked to this, changes in the economic field—with the arrival of foreign banks, as well as large corporate clients requiring Western standards of protection—led to a redefinition of what was valued in the security field: globally competitive technology, expertise, experience, and a reputation as serious security providers that did not participate in criminal activities. Private security companies that had those types of resources now found themselves far more valued—and valuable, by virtue of their ability to gain large lucrative contracts—than domestic security providers that had a reputation for violence rather than Western-style expertise and experience.

In their discourses about the (in)security of businesses and individuals in Eastern Europe, international PSCs often placed the emphasis on what they regarded as an endless complex of interconnected risks, offering to manage those risks for their clients. In essence, companies like G4S and Securitas drew on material resources and technologies that were superior to those of public authorities or local private security players, as well as non-material capital (especially prestige derived from the commodification of security and their recognized positions in global markets) to seek recognition for their claims that they had the kind of expert knowledge needed by businesses that wanted to be successful in a risky environment—that of former communist Europe. The notion involved in the global PSCs' discourses was that, while East European polities may be different from Western countries, the experience and expertise accumulated by leading private security actors in various places around the world put them in a strong position to contribute to the process of bringing universal principles of liberalization and security commodification to the ex-communist states.[26]

In the words of a senior member of the management team of the Bulgarian branch of G4S, "this is a company that has proven, in many places around the world and sometimes in difficult conditions, that it can retain its professionalism and effectively deal with a multitude of challenges in protecting its clients—all that without deviating from the principles and standards that our stakeholders expect. We can assure our clients that our rich experience enables us to deal with whatever issues may arise in any location, at any given time, while fully respecting those principles and high standards."[27] And, in commenting on the activities of G4S in Eastern Europe, a London-based representative of the company insisted: "our customers in the former Eastern bloc can be sure that they are working with a good company, which has high ethical standards and makes a positive impact on society, not just as a result of the service it offers, but also because of the way it behaves. They can be confident that we will always operate to the highest standards and will not compromise their reputation as a result of unethical conduct. We are fully committed to protecting our clients from whatever risks they may face today or tomorrow, of course, but in addition we are also helping East European societies acquire the kinds of professional, effective, and accountable security services that they could not even have dreamed of for such a long time."[28]

The PSCs also mobilized the key themes in the official discourses articulated by Romania and Bulgaria in the late 1990s and 2000s to cast themselves as crucial players in security provision. In particular, they reiterated the neo-liberal discourse inscribed in the security legislation adopted by many East Europeans in the 2000s, according to which it is the responsibility of individuals/companies to take measures to protect themselves from a variety of potential security challenges. The notion involved here is that, in a context marked by limited (often inefficient or unreliable state resources) and unlimited risks, individuals and businesses simply cannot expect the state to provide for all their security needs. Instead, they should rely on experts who combine globally recognized expertise and superior technology, but also—through their local contacts—an understanding of the local challenges and security needs.[29] PSCs thus focus both on prevention and on minimizing the potential consequences of danger (e.g. minimizing the danger to a bank/company's personnel in case of a burglary). They thus seek to reassure clients that they have done everything possible to protect. There is, however, no final resting point to this process: the multitude of risks in the contemporary world and the fact that they are constantly evolving in response to changing circumstances (e.g. changing *modus operandi* of local and transnational criminals) requires that firms commit to a permanent focus on precaution, identifying risks, deterring violent incidents, and if/when necessary ensuring a quick response to attack (Krahmann 2011).

In both Bulgaria and Romania, security analysts and members of foreign banks' management teams have pointed out that, in meetings with them, private security companies often invoked not just their global expertise and experience, but also the limited effectiveness of the local police and justice systems. They also drew their clients' attention to—what were portrayed as—the multiple risks posed by actors ranging from petty criminals seeking to take advantage of weaknesses in a variety of security arrangements (for instance, by stealing money from the banks' cash dispensers), to organized criminals that sought to target foreign companies (for example by planning "cash-in-transit robberies," which involved attacks on vehicles transporting money and other valuables). Under these circumstances, the PSCs' argument went, if foreign banks/corporations wanted to operate profitably in the East European markets, they needed to rely on security companies with strong, internationally acquired reputations of reliability and efficiency. On this logic, only those companies had the expertise, know-how, technology, and unquestionable commitment to excellence that was required to ensure the effective protection of businesses.[30]

A further effect of the influx and growing prominence of global corporations has been the emergence of local PSCs interested in (re)structuring themselves on Western models of private security providers, and on this basis securing domestic and international recognition as actors who could be trusted as professional, crime-free security providers. A key aim of those companies has been to secure lucrative contracts with corporations (particularly foreign companies) and private entrepreneurs who expected fully legal, high standards of security provision. While East European PSCs generally understood that at least in the first few years they would not be able to compete with global PSCs in terms of technology, expertise, or prestige, they believed they would be able to assert themselves in niche markets—for instance, by working for Western-oriented local businesses that were not prepared to pay the fees of global PSCs, or by working in cooperation with global PSCs that were looking to outsource some of their services (e.g. placing guards at the entrance of banks).[31]

In the words of the director of a Romanian PSC based in Bucharest:

> sure, we cannot claim to have the same quality and quantity of technology or personnel as a company like G4S or Securitas. Everyone understands this. Those are global companies with huge budgets, and they've also been in the business forever. Everyone knows about them, and the rest of us can only dream of the kinds of resources that they control. But, on the other hand, not all the companies or individuals who hire a private security company need that kind of technology or budget. Our aim is to establish ourselves as a serious, reliable company that has no connections to the "underworld," does not use illegal force or fraud, and that—in exchange for a reasonable fee—can provide effective protection to individual citizens and businesses that don't have particularly complex needs. If we achieve that, I think we'll do very well in the next few years.[32]

Seeking to "Normalize" the Western Balkans after the Yugoslav Conflicts

While Serbia and Bosnia have not yet been admitted to the EU and NATO, processes of bringing them closer to Western Europe and preparing them for eventual integration into those institutions have also had a profound impact on their security fields. Let us start by considering the case of Serbia. As discussed in Chapter 2, even after the end of the Yugoslav conflicts, the security sector was plagued with serious problems. Above all, the deeply flawed privatization process and absence of adequate legislation had led to the emergence of powerful networks of security providers in which PSCs had links to key individuals within the public realm and in some instances organized crime. Over the years, pro-reform Serbian actors—especially civil society actors grouped in and around liberal NGOs and think tanks—joined forces with international actors such as the American Chamber of Commerce in systematically criticizing persisting practices of corruption and the links between some Serb PSCs and organized crime.[33] They also argued in favor of adopting legislation based on liberal norms of transparency and accountability. These actors were joined by some global PSCs that began to operate in Serbia following the fall of the Milošević regime, when the start of the liberalization process translated into the arrival of international banks and retailers that needed Western-style security arrangements. Similar to the cases of Romania and Bulgaria, there was a clear link between the arrival of foreign banks/corporations and the proliferation of global PSCs—given the lack of trust of those foreign banks in both public authorities and local private security actors in Serbia. In the words of a member of the management team of a foreign bank, "even if we actually thought that local PSCs had the expertise and technologies needed to respond to the complex security requirements of a bank—and we did not—it would have been hard to justify such a move to our shareholders given the widespread perception in the West that local companies were as bad as the police in terms of efficiency and reliability."[34]

The arrival of global companies also prompted some Serbian actors who were keen to gain lucrative contracts with those players to build new companies (or transform old ones) around Western standards of professionalism.[35] Pro-reform PSCs established the Private Security Association within the Serbian Chamber of Commerce as a professional association seeking better regulation in this field. Together with Serbian civil rights activists, and with the support of the American Chamber of Commerce and the Confederation of European Security Services, they sought to persuade the Serb government and parliament to adopt the kind of legislation that would impose in their country norms of private security similar to the standards that are expected (though not always fully respected) in established liberal democracies.[36]

Yet, for a long time those efforts did not bear any fruit. Thus, pro-reform domestic actors were far weaker than the powerful networks that opposed the regulation of private security, and were thus unable to bring about any significant change. Also, unlike Bosnia, in the early and mid-2000s international actors did not have a sufficiently powerful presence in Belgrade. Serbia, of course, was not governed by international administrators, and, at least in the first few years of post-communist transition, the EU—the most active actor involved in promoting liberalization elsewhere in Eastern Europe—was not systematically involved in efforts to reform this ex-Yugoslav state.[37] Consequently, Serbia was the only country from its region that, at the end of the 2000s, still did not have a comprehensive legislative framework governing the private security industry.

More recently, however, the situation began to change. Particularly important was Belgrade's decision to submit its application for joining the EU (in 2009), and the subsequent start of accession negotiations. Even then, however, the EU's attention was focused on the apprehension of Serb war criminals, and the conclusion of an agreement between Belgrade and Pristina. It was only once those two conditions were fulfilled that the EU gave Serbia the green light for accession negotiations, which began in January 2014. As the government in Belgrade has identified accession to the EU as one of its key foreign policy aims, the need to reform the security sector, to bring it into conformity with norms prescribed by the EU, acquired new urgency. In that context, the domestic and international advocates of regulation in the private security industry were able to articulate a potent argument: only by reforming its security sector, including putting an end to the abuses committed by PSCs, would Serbia become the kind of polity that qualifies for inclusion in the EU club (Jovanović 2013). In addition, in recent years a series of violent incidents involving PSCs added further pressure on the government to regulate the private security sector.[38]

In response to those developments, after more than a decade of transition, at the end of 2013 a Law on Private Security together with a Law on Detective Activities adopted in Belgrade (CoESS 2014b). The adoption of these new laws represents a significant step forward in the process of implementing in the field of security liberal-democratic norms of transparency, accountability, and respect for human rights. In particular, by introducing a system of licensing and by defining the boundaries of acceptable behavior by PSCs (including limits on their ability to exercise violence), the new laws hold the potential to eliminate the abuses that have marked the process of security privatization until now. In other words, here, again, we can talk of a revalorization of different forms of capital in the field of security. Thus, changes in the political field, with the move closer to the EU, led to a situation in which those security providers that could offer skills, expertise, and technology compatible with Western standards became more valued than they had been during the Milošević era and immediately following the end of the Yugoslav wars.

In Bosnia, international actors had an even more direct involvement in (re)-shaping the field of security. While initially the international administrators did not place much emphasis on the practices of private security companies, by the early 2000s the growing power and abusive behavior of many security professionals operating under the umbrella of PSCs was generating growing concerns—both within the international administration and among Bosnian civil rights activists and pro-reform politicians—that the unfettered security privatization could constitute a security challenge.[39] Fearing that the activities of private security professionals could undermine the fragile stability of the country, international actors led by the Office of the High Representative (OHR) pressured Bosnian politicians to adopt legislation aimed at regulating PSC activities.[40] As a result of that pressure, new laws on PSC activities were passed in the Federation and in the Republika Srpska (RS) in 2002 and in the

Brčko District in 2004. Furthermore, the Federation law was amended in 2008 in an effort to eliminate some weaknesses. The new laws represent a significant step forward in the process of regulating the process of security privatization by establishing clearer boundaries to the kinds of activities that PSCs can and cannot perform. For instance, PSCs are allowed to offer technical and physical protection services to individuals and companies, but they do not have the right to arrest individuals (Kržalić 2009).

The decentralized nature of the political system in Bosnia is reflected in the system of regulation of PSCs: private security companies are licensed by the interior ministries of the different Bosnian entities, and are required to register separately in each of the regions in which they wish to operate: in each Federation canton, in the Brčko District, and in the five policing and court districts in the RS. These laws also establish certain conditions that persons who wish to establish PSCs need to fulfill—above all, they must not have criminal records. The laws further define the percentage of PSC employees that are allowed to carry weapons (20 percent in the Federation; 50 percent in RS). Both the PSC employees and their weapons are registered with the interior ministries (in the RS at the entity level and in the Federation at the cantonal level), and PSCs are allowed to use force only for self-defense purposes (Kržalić 2009; Azinović et al. 2011).

The adoption of these laws was a clear reflection of the power of the international community in Bosnia: given the antagonism between Bosnia's main ethnic groups, it would have been virtually impossible for Bosnians themselves to promote new legislation on PSCs in the absence of strong pressure by the international actors under the leadership of the OHR.[41] It is revealing that even the strongest Bosnian supporters of regulation of private security—mostly NGOs and think tanks such as the Atlantic Initiative, Transparency International, and the Centre for Security Studies—regarded a decisive intervention by international administrators as the best hope for reform in this area.[42] There are also reports that, behind closed doors, members of Bosniak political parties repeatedly appealed to the international administrators, asking them to take stronger steps to regulate private security providers before they became a threat to the integrity of the state.[43]

In addition to demonstrating the power of the international administrators in Bosnia, the private security legislation adopted in the 2000s also reveals the commitment of those administrators to the neo-liberal project of security commodification. In spite of their concerns related to the abuses committed by PSCs, the international actors did not seek to impose a complete ban on private security companies. Importantly, from their perspective, private security companies were a normal presence in the security landscape of a modern liberal democracy. In the words of a former OHR official: "our aim—and our challenge—was not to get rid of private security companies; it was to ensure that they did not act in a manner that was inconsistent with the principles of Dayton, and that they did not undermine our mission in Bosnia."[44]

This is certainly not to suggest that international actors have always acted in conformity with liberal norms and principles in seeking to regulate the private security industry in Bosnia. In fact, during and immediately following the Yugoslav wars, some foreign PSCs were responsible for serious human rights violations. For instance, as one of the first foreign security companies to operate in the region, MPRI trained Croatian forces and prepared them for a military operation, Storm, aimed at retaking the so-called RS Krajina from Serb forces. The operation took place in 1995 and resulted in serious crimes against the civilian population.[45] Furthermore, in post-Dayton Bosnia a PSC that was working for the US government, DynCorp, was directly involved in human trafficking—apparently with the complicity of some UN officials (Bolkovac and Lynn 2011). Despite all these problems, in the period immediately following Dayton the international administrators allowed PSCs to act with impunity. As noted above, it was only in the early 2000s that the OHR took advantage of its power to promote legislation in this area. Once the campaign to promote change in this area did start, however, the international administrators were able to promote legislative change quite quickly.

As in the cases of other East European polities, further progress in the process of liberalization of the field of security came as a result of the influx of international corporations and especially banks in Bosnia in the late 2000s, leading to the demand for private security services that were seen to be acceptable by those corporations—above all, services provided by actors that were not involved in mafia-like activities.[46] As in so many other East European states, the majority of foreign banks and other international companies operating in Bosnia relied on global PSCs, especially Securitas, in a situation in which local PSCs were seen as lacking the expertise, technology, and reliability needed by global corporations.[47] Furthermore, in the new environment some of the leading Bosnian PSCs sought to reorganize their practices and improve their image in an effort to obtain lucrative contracts with international firms. Consequently, in the late 2000s Bosnia experienced a process of partial professionalization of security, in which the addition of new actors led to revalorization of forms of material and non-material capital that had previously been undervalued in Bosnia. This included professional training for PSCs; modern technologies; and the adoption of security practices consistent with respect for human rights and the rule of law—as opposed to illegal practices, such as racketeering. In the words of a Bosnian PSC director: "it became clear to many of us that if we wanted to prosper in this business we would need to make our companies look like the kind of companies with which international banks and retailers would want to do business."[48]

In essence, Bosnia as well as Serbia—similar to developments in Bulgaria and Romania—witnessed a revalorization of different forms of capital in the field of security in the early 2000s. Thus, primarily as a result of transformations in the political field, leading to more systematic international involvement in the promotion of reform of security practices, as well as changes in the economic field (especially the growing presence of international financial institutions), this led to a situation in which those security providers that could offer skills, expertise, and technology compatible with Western standards became far more valued than they had been in the 1990s.

Transnational Mobilization in the Context of European Integration

While the reforms undertaken under pressure from the EU constitute the most obvious aspect of European integration, there are also other ways in which Europeanization has affected the field of security in former communist polities. In particular, the process of acceding—or at least getting closer—to the EU has also translated into a growing integration of PSCs operating in Eastern Europe into the European network of security professionals. Especially important in this context has been the involvement of PSCs from Eastern Europe in the practices enacted by, or under the auspices of, the Confederation of European Security Services, CoESS. Just as the new laws implemented in the context of European integration have empowered PSCs while at the same time placing constraints on their function as agents of public power, so, too, the inclusion in European professional networks placed PSCs from Eastern Europe in a stronger position in the field of security in their domestic arenas, but at the same time imposed certain duties on them. In particular, membership in the Confederation of European Security Services meant that PSCs from the ex-communist states had a transnational forum for gaining expertise in/ knowledge about international standards of security provision, and contributing to transnational efforts to enhance the legitimacy and power of private security in Europe. Simultaneously, their association with a recognized European professional institution of security providers gave East European representatives of the private security industry enhanced credibility and a new platform from which they could advocate for further reforms in their national arenas.

The Confederation of European Security Services, founded in 1989, is the European umbrella organization for twenty-six national private security employers' associations, which translates into some 60,000 private security companies employing a total of 2.2 million private security employees. At the pan-European level, CoESS acts as a powerful lobby group that has been systematically involved in pursuing region-wide recognition and regulation that is favorable to the private security sector. CoESS has published several documents (including white papers) on the role of private security in Europe, as part of its effort to help construct a European legislative framework that is harmonious, balanced, and "conducive to the expansion of the private security industry" (CoESS 2008: 13). As CoESS repeatedly points out, it is the only representative European employers' organization defending the interests of the private security services industry. It is also recognized by the European Commission as a European sectoral social partner in accordance with the European Treaties. CoESS represents nineteen EU member states and a total of twenty-four countries. In a situation in which the European private security services industry generates a yearly turnover of approximately €34.2 billion, CoESS has argued that Europe can only protect its security by adopting an integrated global approach. On this logic, the Confederation can and should play a key role in defining this global approach as an advisor, a central player, and a driving force behind policy implementation (CoESS 2008: 13).

Chapter 4 offers a fuller account of the ways in which CoESS has been involved in efforts to legitimate and expand the contributions provided by the private security industry in Europe. As a prelude to that analysis, it is worth examining here some of the ways in which private security associations from ex-communist states have mobilized CoESS in an effort to consolidate their positions and pursue more reforms in their national arenas. To explain this evolution, we need to understand CoESS as a manifestation of what Didier Bigo has called the transnationalization of the field of (in)security, in which the key protagonists are networks of European security professionals. The European field of security is a transversal field, which transcends divisions between national/international and internal/external, and in which many security professionals affiliated with agencies that previously held marginal positions (e.g. customs, immigration, national guards, etc.) now occupy prominent positions. In a sophisticated analysis of the features of the contemporary European field of security professionals, Bigo and his colleagues have argued that against the background of various disagreements and oppositions, the actors that participate in the field of security share a doxa, a common sense of what is at stake in European security. At the heart of this shared common sense lies an assumption that frontiers are not the main line of defense in today's Europe; rather, the focus is on targeted control over the population and the tracing of individuals.[49] In fact, the main objective of participants in the provision of European security is to anticipate and counter the threat before it crosses the internal or external borders of Europe. In addition, as they become involved in security issues, all these security professionals focus on global, transnational, or regional security—as opposed to local violence. In other words, the emphasis is on "policing at a distance"

(Bigo 2007), leading to the emergence of a security continuum in which the difference between internal/external security breaks down. Relatedly, contemporary security professionals focus on technological solutions to security challenges. Furthermore, through their discourses and practices they all seek to convey "a sense of centrality of the question of the relevant priorities regarding threats" (Bigo et al. 2010: 53).

This, however, is not to suggest that the European field of security is a homogeneous space. On the contrary: as the next chapters will show, against the background of these shared assumptions, there are many oppositions and forms of competition among participants in security practices. Indeed, Bigo and his colleagues point out that the field of security is structured around a general competition around the legitimate classifications of threats. In essence, this security field, which transcends national boundaries, creates forms of collaboration but also competition between agencies that previously had little contact with one another (armies, border control services, military police, civil security units, etc.) (Bigo 2006). This can be characterized as a field of (in)security professionals, or of the management of unease, which depends less on the possibility of exerting force, as classical sociologists would suggest, and more on the capacity of agents to produce statements on unease and present solutions to facilitate the management of that unease (Bigo 2006: 22). Professionals of unease therefore establish a field of security in which they recognize themselves as mutually competent while competing with one another for the monopoly over legitimate knowledge over what constitutes a "real risk" (Bigo 2006: 8). In this context, (in)security professionals adopt a strategy of overstepping national boundaries and forming corporatist professional alliances to reinforce the credibility of their assertions and win internal struggles in their respective national security fields (Bigo 2006: 8).

In analyzing oppositions, contestations, and various forms of competition within the European field of security, it is also useful to draw on the work of Fligstein and McAdam, which extends Bourdieu's sociology of fields in interesting ways. In particular, Fligstein and McAdam develop an analysis of the micro-foundations that inform field dynamics and, they argue, all of social life. In their view, social life does not rely on habit and interest alone, but requires socially skilled actors to create collective identities, produce meaning, and actively create, contest, and defend the social orders they inhabit (Fligstein and McAdam 2012, 2014). Fligstein and McAdam regard fields as meso-level social orders that are political by nature as they reflect the outcome of political processes. From their perspective, any given field is embedded in a broader environment consisting of countless proximate fields as well as states, which are themselves organized as intricate systems of strategic action fields (Fligstein and McAdam 2012). Under these circumstances, the source of many of the opportunities and challenges faced by a given field can be found in its relations within this broader environment. Crises and opportunities for the transformation of different fields often arise as a result of developments within proximate state or non-state fields. Applying this argument to our cases, it is interesting to note that, as shown in Chapter 2 and earlier in this chapter, many of the changes that occurred in the field of security in East European polities were inextricably linked to developments in other fields, in particular the economic one. For Fligstein and McAdam the same field dynamics operate at the level of individuals, groups, organizations, and states. All fields are centered on the emergence, stabilization/institutionalization, and transformation of socially constructed arenas in which multiple actors compete for material and status rewards (Fligstein and McAdam 2012).

In a situation in which the thinking of various players in the field is shaped by their experiences and their positions, they will have different interpretations of what is going on. This means that, according to Fligstein and McAdam, there is less consensus in any given social field than we tend to assume, competitions and conflict are normal, and, consequently, fields are frequently less settled than we assume. One of the key differences between their approach and most versions of institutional theory is that Fligstein and McAdam regard fields as only rarely organized around a truly consensual definition of reality (Fligstein and McAdam 2012). In contrast to the emphasis that many institutionalists place on routine social order, Fligstein and McAdam argue that there is constant jockeying taking place in fields as a result of their contentious nature. Different actors make moves and other players in the field have to interpret them, reflect on their choices, and act in response. Many are consistently seeking to make adjustments to the conditions of the field, given their position and the actions of others. This leaves significant latitude for competition and sometimes changes in the positions that participants occupy in a given field. Thus, even in settled times weaker actors can learn how to take advantage of different aspects of the field, and on this basis seek to improve their positions vis-à-vis others.

Fligstein and McAdam add a new layer of complexity to Bourdieu's analysis by examining how cooperation and competition that occur not only at the individual level but also between collective actors actually structure fields (Fligstein and McAdam 2011, 2012).[50] As they explain, Bourdieu's analysis is pitched mostly at the level of individual actors "who find themselves in fields where they then act" (Fligstein and McAdam 2011: 19). This focus on the individual level means that Bourdieu has relatively little to say about the problem of collective action. By contrast, Fligstein and McAdam place the focus of their analysis firmly at the group level. These groups face not just competition from other groups, but also the challenge of maintaining their own cohesion. Consequently, "skilled strategic actors operate collectively, not just in their own interests, to act vis-à-vis other groups, but also to hold their own groups together" (2011: 19). This view leads Fligstein and McAdam to argue that fields are composed of incumbents, challengers, and governance units (Fligstein and McAdam 2012). Incumbents are those actors who exercise disproportionate influence within a field, and whose interests and views tend to be reflected in the dominant organization of the field. Challengers, by contrast, occupy less privileged positions within the field and generally have little influence over its operations.

An important role in maintaining this group cohesion is played by "internal governance units" (for instance, trade associations or standards-setting organizations). Internal governance units are charged with overseeing compliance with field rules and, more broadly, facilitating the smooth functioning and reproduction of the system (Fligstein and McAdam 2012). They disseminate particular ideas and information about what is going on in their groups, and also inform challengers or potential challengers about their actions. In addition, internal governance units play important roles in representing their field to governments and to other fields. For instance, trade associations cultivate allies in various state fields that exercise nominal control over the strategic field in question. Consequently, they are in a position to call on these allies for help if or when a crisis develops within their field. It is important to point out that virtually all governance units reflect the influence of the powerful incumbents in the field. Regardless of their legitimating discourse, the units are generally there not to serve as neutral arbiters of competition and conflict between incumbents and challengers, but to reinforce the dominant perspective and protect the interests of the incumbents.

In the context of our analysis, one can interpret the emergence and practices of CoESS as an example of security professionals forming a corporatist professional alliance at the European level. In that capacity, one could argue that CoESS has come to act as an internal governance unit, acting to stabilize the field of security in particular ways by helping to construct a new identity as members of the European community of security providers, disseminating a particular type of information about what is going on and its vision of what should be going on—in particular, what norms should govern the private security industry and its relationship with public actors. It has also been engaged in practices aimed at teaching its members and associates how to effectively and legitimately perform the functions of security providers in contemporary Europe. As we shall see, CoESS has further played important roles in representing the private security industry in interactions with public officials, including representatives of EU institutions as well as national authorities in various European states. In those interactions, CoESS has often contested prevailing public understandings of the limits of PSC mandates as well as interpretations of the logic of European integration in the field of security. At the same time, CoESS can be seen as an institution that, by helping to define and disseminate norms of proper behavior (or "best practice") for members of the European community of PSCs, has acted to protect the interests of the established members of that community against challengers. In this context, a particularly significant and potentially problematic set of challengers has been the category of unregistered private security providers, whose illicit activities threaten to undermine the reputation of private security in general.

Key players in CoESS are both global PSCs represented in national associations and those local players that are keen to distance themselves from PSCs with links to organized crime in order to secure lucrative contracts with global clients. Those actors, acting collectively, have sought to reinforce the legitimacy of private security providers, enhance the credibility of their assertions regarding the nature of contemporary security challenges and solutions to those challenges, and win competitions with other players (including security-related state agencies) in their respective domestic arenas.[51] That role has been particularly important to the national associations of East European states. Many of those associations have joined—and have been active members of—CoESS in an effort to enhance the position of the private security industry in their respective national arenas, and within that industry to strengthen the position of their own, internationally oriented PSCs. Those actors have focused in particular on the promotion of national regulations that benefit the industry, transcending the stigma of association between PSCs and organized crime, and securing support for the idea of partnership between various (European and national) public security agencies and PSCs in the governance and provision of security. In other words, participation in the transversal European field has been seen by East European PSCs with an international orientation as a source of power in their efforts to further reform national legislation and security practices. That source of power has also been important in the quest to compete more efficiently against PSCs that refused to "play by international rules"—for instance, by failing to provide adequate training to, and protect the labor rights of, their employees, resorting to illegal practices and, in some instances, maintaining links to the illicit economy.[52]

There are several ways in which private security associations from Eastern Europe have sought to benefit from their involvement in CoESS. Above all, CoESS has acted as a forum for socializing East Europeans into the principles, norms, and rules of the game regarding the role of private security that are regarded as acceptable in Europe. While there is no single European legislation on private security, CoESS has been keen to convey to the "new Europeans" the message that there are certain taken-for-granted norms and rules that unite members of the EU.[53] These include, in particular, a shared recognition of the need for legislation that governs the private security industry so as to avoid abuses of power and prevent links between PSCs and criminal organizations; the principle that private security ought to act as a partner of public authorities, with specific rights and duties and placed under the control of the state; the principle that the authorities of an EU member state ought not to discriminate against PSCs that originate in another member of the Union; and the principle that workers in the private security industry ought to be recognized as members of a legitimate sector of the economy and thus entitled to labor protections.

As national associations from Eastern Europe joined CoESS, they were facing difficult domestic circumstances—in large part precisely because of the inadequate regulation of PSCs in the years immediately following the collapse of communism, and the fact that, domestically and internationally, the private security industry was perceived as closely connected to organized crime. As noted above, in the context of efforts to achieve greater integration into Europe and the global economic system, a series of PSCs—both global companies operating branches in those countries and some national players seeking to obtain lucrative contracts with Western businesses—embarked upon initiatives aimed at changing the image of the industry and enhancing their symbolic capital. Their objective was to (re)build—and secure domestic and international recognition for—the private security sector as a Western-style sector. That involved drawing a clear boundary between the legitimate, carefully regulated, and trustworthy PSCs that deserved to be key players in the provision of public and private security, and the "rogue elements" of the industry: those PSCs who maintained links to organized crime and therefore had to be delegitimized and removed from the field of security.[54] Indeed, many PSCs from Eastern Europe that were seeking recognition as legitimate, professional actors regarded the very inclusion of their national federations in CoESS as a key step in the right direction.[55]

Representatives of the private security industry repeatedly sought to invoke their new membership in a European professional association with significant prestige to enhance their symbolic capital in their own domestic settings. They used CoESS as a stage from which they could more effectively perform the role of responsible security providers. That internationally accepted stage was particularly helpful in enabling them to gain recognition as legitimate actors in a performance conducted, on the basis of a shared set of assumptions, at the European level. As a corollary to this, CoESS also provided the East Europeans with information about the roles of private security in Europe and, more broadly, with widely recognized scripts of private security actors as reliable partners of public agencies. In the words of the manager of a Bulgarian PSC: "the fact that we were now able to speak not just as an entity providing commercial security services in Bulgaria but as members of a powerful, respected European institution made it easier for us to talk to our own policymakers, who could not dismiss us as just a bunch of guys who were at best unprofessional and at worst criminals."[56] And, as the former director of a Romanian PSC noted, "because we were able to invoke our affiliation with CoESS it became easier for us to argue that not all PSCs were corrupt. This made it possible for us to recruit some international clients, and also to push for greater dialogue with the police over the regulation of private security."[57]

Linked to this, CoESS has defined "best practices" for the conduct of private security companies and their collaboration with public authorities, and has taken steps to disseminate those practices via white papers and other publications on the role of private security and its possible forms of partnership with public actors, and by organizing workshops and presentations in Eastern Europe.[58] Those "best practices" can be seen as internationally sanctioned scripts to guide the performance of security provision. Those include information about the nature and extent of types of collaboration in the governance and provision of security that could emerge between public actors and the private industry. They also include guidelines on the ways in which the state, in collaboration with professional associations of the private security industry, should act to identify and shut down PSCs engaged in criminal activities. In their quest to strengthen their domestic positions, representatives of the private security industry of East European states actively sought to take advantage of those scripts and learn the European-defined roles. Thus, they repeatedly consulted with CoESS as they were advocating for particular legislative provisions in the regulation of PSCs in their countries. Consultations apparently included seeking the advice of CoESS on the substance of those provisions (particularly concerning the involvement of PSCs as partners of the police not only in responding to incidents but also in preventing them), as well as tactical advice on how to lobby and collaborate with national authorities. For instance, especially in the early days of membership in CoESS, there were several instances in which representatives of PSCs from Bulgaria, Romania, and Serbia reportedly expected CoESS to play a role similar to the European Commission in the context of EU accession negotiations, telling the governments of those states what they were doing wrong (in this case, by failing to provide adequate regulations concerning PSCs) and providing detailed instructions on how those problems could be fixed.[59]

CoESS apparently had to teach actors representing the private security industry from those countries that such a *modus operandi* was inappropriate given the nature and mandate of the Confederation. Nevertheless, CoESS was able to provide them with advice on how to consult with their public authorities (based on models of interaction developed in Western Europe). Representatives of the Confederation reportedly further provided advice on the kind of legislative/institutional arrangements that PSCs should advocate for in order to enhance the position of the private security industry. In addition, in Serbia—where, as noted above, there was no comprehensive legislation governing PSCs for a particularly long time—CoESS was also involved in systematic efforts, in collaboration with Serbian pro-reform activists, some PSCs, and other Western actors like the American Chamber of Commerce, to persuade Serbian authorities that the absence of appropriate legislation in this sector was a major problem, and could impede the country's efforts to become more closely integrated into Europe.

In recent years, CoESS was also mobilized by the private security industry in Eastern Europe in efforts to secure more rights and better protections for the employees of legitimate PSCs. This has been particularly significant in a situation in which in most East European polities' ordinary employees—in contrast to the senior management—in the private security sector have been among the most vulnerable in the workforce. Thus, representatives of the private security industry from various European states have collaborated under the auspices of CoESS to identify the key problems faced by PSC employees in their respective national arenas, and to collectively advocate for change. In other words, representatives of PSCs from Eastern Europe—acting within the framework of CoESS—were able to draw on European norms of protection of workers to push their governments to enact change in the regime governing the treatment of employees in the private security industry.

The starting point to their arguments has been the assumption that private security is a major industry in modern societies. Thus, "Private security is a specific and socially delicate industry. If we take into consideration the risks of modern life, private security is mandatory. It exists at different developmental and legal levels in all countries, new EU member states, as well as in both countries that are still in the process of joining the EU" (Badea 2014: 11). In that context, the argument went, PSCs needed to be able to perform security functions in a manner consistent with the prevailing rules of the game in established liberal democracies and especially EU polities—including respect for basic labor protections/rights of employees.

The argument that was repeatedly invoked by representatives of PSCs in discussions with policymakers has been that, since this industry would not vanish or become less important in the future, it was incumbent upon decision-makers in each European state to take the necessary steps to ensure that the basic rights of those who work in this sector are protected.[60] In examining the situation in the East European states, CoESS concluded that even in the late 2000s:

> many East European polities were facing "major development problems," often involving problems concerning the status of private security and the rights of workers in the sector. A lack of social dialogue, or problems with the full conclusion and implementation of the reached agreement, are further problems experienced by several former communist states.   (CoESS 2014b: 11)

Several kinds of problems plaguing the security industry in each East European country were highlighted by PSCs as urgently needing solutions. For instance, in Romania:

> Security personnel are poorly unionized and the average monthly net salary of a security guard is estimated at 250 EUR. In Romania the number of security personnel is estimated to be around 80,000 employees. [The usual] price of security services by hour is estimated at 1, 75 EUR, placing most workers in this sector below the poverty threshold. (Badea 2014: 15)

As in many other countries from that region, in Romania a persisting practice is that in public tenders the companies that are selected are those which offer the lowest price for performing the private security services. In general, contracts are awarded on the basis of the cheapest bid. Public authorities do not interfere in this matter in order to control unfair competition and undeclared work. Lowest price competition also leads to weaken the infrastructure of the performance system, including staff training, supervision, and quality management (not to mention lack of benefits and protections for the workers in the industry). Cutting costs also lowers service level by employing cheaper labor and having as a result poor quality services (Badea 2014: 15).

In a similar vein, in Bulgaria the average monthly net salary of a security guard is about 250 EUR, placing PSC personnel in a very vulnerable economic position, often without social protections/benefits and no employment guarantees. In the field of private security employees have not concluded a collective agreement. No negotiations are taking place in this area (Badea 2014: 15). Here, as in Romania, the situation is made worse by the fact that in public tenders the companies that prevail are those which offer the lowest price for performing the private security services. More and more contractors save from security and buy responsibility, but not quality services. A lot of public institutions stimulate the "gray" economy by public tenders (Badea 2014: 17). Not surprisingly, in Bulgaria—as in Romania—this situation translates into poor work conditions and a precarious position for workers in the private security industry.

The situation in Serbia has been even more difficult than in Bulgaria and Romania: as late as 2013 the average monthly net salary of a security guard was 180 EUR. For a long time, all employers in the private security sector were waiting for a law on private security to be adopted in order to start negotiations for collective agreement for the security sector. Meanwhile, there was no social dialogue and practically no communication between employers and employees. The lowest offer was found to persist as the dominant principle in public tenders. The normal price of security services by the hour is 1.70 EUR to 2.50 EUR. Low wages, low price of working hour, and delayed payment for services combined to produce a very difficult situation for Serbian workers in the private security industry (CoESS 2014b: 20). Similar problems were also found in Bosnia, where workers in the private security industry are also affected by low wages, very few benefits, and generally a precarious position made even worse by competition from the "gray economy."

In response to those conditions, national associations of the private security industry embarked on systematic campaigns—both transnationally and in their respective national arenas—in an effort to improve the situation of employees in their industry. For instance, at the European level they worked within the framework of CoESS working groups to produce reports, issue joint statements and recommendations regarding the governance of PSCs, and organize events aimed at raising the awareness of decision-makers and the public on the challenges faced by workers in this industry—and the dangers to public safety associated with those challenges. In their respective national arenas, associations from various European countries represented in CoESS used the authority of the findings published by the Confederation to identify problems with the regulation of the private security industry, and recommend possible solutions to those problems. What was important to representatives of the private security industry was that, by acting under the auspices of CoESS, they were able to present their arguments and claims as not simply the idiosyncratic preferences of an insignificant set of local PSCs, but as issues that were recognized at the European level as problems requiring urgent solutions. Consequently, what would have been marginal local voices were able to gain a powerful platform in their domestic arenas by drawing on European networks and symbolic capital. Thus, CoESS reports and white papers have been disseminated to private security providers, their clients, as well as public authorities in an effort to challenge old attitudes and principles, educate the public as well as decision-makers involved in the regulation of the private security industry, and achieve better protections and higher wages for PSC employees. Yet, so far the results of this campaign to promote change via transnational mobilization have been mixed. As we shall see later in the book, some protections were gained for employees in the private security industry, but overall their situation remains precarious.

This chapter has sought to shed light on the European and global dynamics that have contributed to the evolution of the field of security following the collapse of communism in Europe. That evolution, and in particular the integration of private security actors operating in Eastern Europe into the European network of security professionals, has translated into a situation in which security entrepreneurs from the former communist states are now participating in the wider European practices of security governance and provision. In that capacity, as Chapter 4 demonstrates, they are part of complex processes through which private security actors cooperate and compete with public agencies at the European level, as they seek to enhance their profile and power as performers of protection in the twenty-first century.

Notes

1. On this, see also Dzhekova and Rusev 2015.
2. For a broader discussion see also: Born et al. 2006; Kontos 2004; Seiberth 2014.
3. A discussion of the key aims and provisions of the Montreux Document is available at: http://www.mdforum.ch/en/montreux-document.
4. More details about the ICoC can be found on the Code's website: https://www.icoca.ch/.
5. More recently, efforts to regulate the private security industry have also involved a series of business initiatives. However, those initiatives arrived too late to make a meaningful difference to post-communist transformations of security provision in Eastern Europe. For an analysis of some of the most interesting transnational business governance initiatives, see in particular Rebecca DeWinter-Schmitt's chapter in the Abrahamsen and Leander Handbook (Abrahamsen and Leander 2015).
6. On the role of European institutions in guiding and shaping Central/East European polities in the context of integration into the EU, see, for instance, Vachudová 2005; Epstein 2008; Schimmelfennig and Sedelmeier 2005.
7. Author's interviews with former senior government officials from Bulgaria and Romania, conducted in Sofia and Bucharest, May–July 2012.
8. ECJ Rulings: Commission v. Spain C-114/97 (1998); Commission v. Italy C-465/05 (2007).
9. Interviews with two Bulgarian retired government officials as well as a retired Romanian senior official and an investigative journalist, May–July 2012, Bucharest and Sofia.
10. Interviews as in note 9.
11. The Law on Private Guarding Activity was amended several times in 2005 and 2006.
12. Interview conducted by the author, Sofia, June 19, 2012.
13. Interview with a senior staff member of a Bulgarian PSC, Sofia, June 20, 2012.
14. A series of Romanian interviewees, including two retired government officials, and officials from the British and French Embassies in Bucharest stressed that the EU had applied constant pressure on Bucharest to take steps to remedy the problem of corruption and to protect the rule of law if Romania wanted to gain accession to the EU (interviews conducted in Bucharest, June 6–16, 2011).
15. On productive power, see in particular Barnett and Duvall 2005a, 2005b.
16. For a more detailed analysis, see in particular Klingen et al. 2013: 47–9.
17. Contrary to the expectations of many observers, Greek banks have suffered only gently declining market shares in Eastern Europe—at least until now. They have shrunk their balance sheets by only about 10 percent since 2008 (Klingen et al. 2013: 58).
18. Interviews with two Romanian and two Bulgarian investigative reporters, as well as three security experts affiliated with the Centre for the Study of Democracy, Bucharest, June 1–7, 2011, and Sofia, June 15–20, 2012.
19. For more details see G4S 2011: 37.

20. By the time Bulgaria and Romania completed their integration into the EU and NATO—and were thus seen as reasonably safe countries for foreign business, G4S was one of the top five security companies in both countries. Author interview with three Bulgarian security experts affiliated with the Centre for the Study of Democracy, Sofia, June 13–20, 2012.

21. For a very interesting account of the relationship between the private security industry and the insertion of countries perceived as "high-risk" environments into the global capitalist system, see O'Reilly 2010: 183–206.

22. Interviews with three Bulgarian security experts affiliated with the Centre for the Study of Democracy (Sofia) and two Romanian security experts affiliated with the Romanian Centre for European Policies (Bucharest); interviews conducted between June 13–20, 2012 (Sofia) and on July 3, 2012 (Bucharest), as well as the local directors of a leading Western bank operating in both Bulgaria and Romania, May 17–18, 2011, Bucharest, and June 13–15, 2012, Sofia.

23. Interview with the director of a major Western bank currently operating in Bulgaria, Sofia, June 15, 2012.

24. Interviewed by the author on May 17, 2011, Bucharest.

25. Interviews with two senior members of the management teams of G4S (one in Bulgaria and one in Romania) and two members of the management team of Securitas in Romania, as well as the local directors of a leading Western bank operating in both Bulgaria and Romania. The interviews with the PSC management teams were conducted in Sofia, June 25–8, 2012, and in Bucharest, March 20–3, 2014. The interviews with the local directors of a leading Western bank operating in both Bulgaria and Romania were conducted May 17–18, 2011 in Bucharest, and June 13–15, 2012 in Sofia.

26. Interviews as in note 25.

27. Interview conducted on June 14, 2012, Sofia.

28. Interview conducted on June 3, 2013, London.

29. On this, see also the analysis provided by Krahmann (2011).

30. See note 25 above.

31. Interviews with three Bulgarian security experts affiliated with the Centre for the Study of Democracy (Sofia) and two Romanian security experts affiliated with the Romanian Centre for European Policies (Bucharest); interviews conducted between June 13–20, 2012 (Sofia) and July 3, 2012 (Bucharest).

32. Interviewed by the author on June 15, 2011.

33. Interviews with a senior member of the management team of the Serbian branch of G4S, June 19, 2013, and two investigative journalists, June 20, 2013.

34. Interviewed by the author on June 18, 2013, Belgrade.

35. Interviews by author, June 17–20, 2013.

36. Interviews as in note 35.

37. According to security experts, investigative journalists, and NGO members interviewed by the author, the EU representatives were so focused on promoting an accord between Serbia and Kosovo—regarded as vital for promoting European security—that they were willing to close their eyes to many problems of transition,

including the alleged involvement of political actors in criminal activity, often through their links with PSCs (interviews by author, June 17–20, 2013).

38. Interviews with two Serbian investigative journalists and a former senior official from the Serbian Ministry of Interior, Belgrade, June 18–21, 2013.

39. Within Bosnia, the political actors that were particularly concerned about the potential impact of security privatization were members of the Bosniak community (interviews with two analysts affiliated with the Sarajevo Centre for Security Studies, June 25–7, 2013).

40. Interviews with former OHR official, June 25, 2013, and with two analysts affiliated with the Sarajevo Centre for Security Studies, June 25–7, 2013.

41. Interviews as in note 40.

42. Interviews as in note 40. See also Perdan 2008.

43. Interviews with two former OHR officials, Sarajevo, June 25–7, 2013, and two members of the EU Delegation to Bosnia, March 12–14, 2014.

44. Interview, June 26, 2013. This view was reiterated by two members of the EU Delegation (see previous note).

45. See also Singer 2004.

46. Interviews with senior member of the management team of the Bosnian branch of Securitas, June 28, 2013, and with two Bosnian experts affiliated with the Atlantic Initiative Sarajevo, March 11, 2014.

47. Interviews with two former OHR officials (see note 40 above), and with two analysts affiliated with the Sarajevo Centre for Security Studies, June 25–7, 2013.

48. Interview by the author, June 27, 2013.

49. See in particular Bigo et al. 2010.

50. See also Fligstein 1990, 1996, 2001.

51. We shall return to those competitions in Chapter 4.

52. Interviews with members of Romanian, Bulgarian, and Serbian PSCs represented in CoESS, Brussels, March 4–7, 2014.

53. Interview with senior CoESS representative, Brussels, March 6, 2014.

54. Interviews with senior CoESS representative (see note 53 above), as well as members of Romanian, Bulgarian, and Serbian PSCs represented in CoESS (Brussels, March 4–7, 2014).

55. Interviews as in note 54. Bulgaria and Romania are active members of CoESS, being represented, respectively, by the National Association of Industrial Security Companies (NAFTSO) and the Romanian Security Industry Association, RSIA. Serbia has the status of Associated Member (represented by the National Commission of Private Security Companies, NCPSC).

56. Interview with the manager of a Bulgarian PSC, Sofia, June 14, 2012.

57. Interview conducted on June 20, 2011.

58. For more information about the types of publications and events promoted by CoESS see its website: http://www.coess.org/.

59. Interview with senior CoESS representative (see note 53 above).

60. Interviews with members of Romanian, Bulgarian, and Serbian PSCs represented in CoESS, Brussels, March 4–7, 2014.

4

Contestation, Cooperation, and Competition in (Re)Defining European Security

If processes of European integration and insertion into global economic flows had a profound impact on practices of security in former communist polities, we should not conclude that they produced a static set of arrangements. Rather, the changes enacted in the context of Europeanization and globalization set the stage for complex forms of cooperation but also contestation among various security providers. Within the framework of those practices of cooperation and contestation, the commercialization of security is constantly negotiated and redefined, as private security actors both accept and contest the rules of the game governing security governance and provision.

It is important to note that these practices of collaboration and contestation do not take place only in the national arenas of East European polities. Rather, they are enacted within the broader context of—and are shaped by—complex forms of collaboration and competition among public and private actors over the redefinition of norms governing security at the European level. This occurs in a situation in which East European polities now participate in the European field of security. Consequently, they are both affected by and help shape the dynamics of that field. It is that broad level of European cooperation and contestation that is the subject of this chapter.

To understand dynamics of competition and contestation in the field of security, it is useful to examine the ways in which actors mobilize various forms of capital—and seek to (re)valorize different kinds of resources so as to enhance the value of those types of capital that they possess relative to that of other resources. The outcome, as discussed below, is a new political economy of security provision in which actors are reconfigured and struggle to (re)shape the field of security in particular ways, alliances are forged between different players (including former enemies or rivals), and certain forms of capital gain value while others are devalued. Within the resulting field of security, old divides between domestic and international, public and private, and security and economics are becoming increasingly blurred.[1] Starting from a Bourdieu-inspired image of social fields as sites of struggle, as discussed in previous chapters, we can conceptualize PSCs' strategies deployed in struggles over positions as reflecting the setting of the field of security and being designed to demonstrate partial compliance with the basic rules of the game, while at the same time challenging the field setting and seeking to partly redefine the roles of the private security industry. What is being fought over in this context is the definition of the roles of PSCs as producers of public security. The aim pursued by private security actors is to broaden the mandate of PSCs as key producers of public security, with the ability to perform a more prominent position in the governance and provision of security than is currently allowed. To this end, PSCs enact performances of security in which they deploy strategies aimed at accumulating capital to support their positions in the security "game," and to effectively compete and struggle over definitions over who has what rights and responsibilities in the governance and provision of security.

If we are to understand how strategies can perform functions of both compliance and contestation within a social field, we need to start from the assumption that strategies are situational (they vary depending on the specific "game" involved), positional (struggles take place to maintain or improve particular positions), and dispositional (they are generated from the feel for the game and the actors having been immersed in the game) (Bourdieu and Nice 2000: 112; Mérand and Forget 2013: 98). What is particularly important for us in this context is the situational nature of strategies: in other words, what constitutes a good strategy in one game may not be suitable in a different game. As a corollary to this, actors that do not have a solid sense of the game run the risk of formulating inappropriate strategies. For instance, we noted in our analysis of the early years of post-communist transition (Chapter 2) that, despite the fact that they had long been immersed in security games around the world and they had substantial material and non-material assets, international PSCs were largely unable to secure strong positions in East European polities because they did not have the kinds of resources that were valued in the specific contexts of those polities. While international PSCs had material capabilities that went far beyond those of national or local private security providers, as well as globally recognized expertise and experience, they did not have access to the local networks of influence, and were not trained in—or allowed to use—the type of coercive practices of protection that, in Eastern Europe, was widely seen as valuable in the context of the mafia-like capitalism. Consequently, they did not enjoy the kind of prestige that they enjoyed in other parts of the world. Linked to this, it could be argued that international PSCs did not have a sufficient "feel for the game" to be able to formulate effective strategies. Thus, they did not know how to perform security in a manner that would have sounded convincing to (public and private) clients who were used to coercive, communist-style methods. That was problematic because, as noted in previous chapters, in order to effectively perform particular roles—in our case, to secure the recognition of their audiences that they were genuine, trustworthy providers of security—PSCs must act, and be seen as acting, in a manner that conforms to the prevailing habits, law, and etiquette of the society in which they are operating.

However, as discussed in Chapter 3, the situation started to change significantly following processes of European integration and insertion into global flows. Those transformations empowered but also placed a series of constraints upon the private security industry. Importantly, they also set the stage for more extensive collaboration—while at the same time opening the door to systematic competition—among public and private actors involved in security governance and provision. A close analysis of practices conducted by PSCs reveals that they have both collaborated extensively, in many areas, with public security agencies and, at the same time, been engaged in what could be called *doxic* battles with them. To recapitulate: *doxa* is the prevailing understanding within a field; it is the "truth," or what is taken for granted within that field (Bourdieu 1977: 166). In its basic form it comes without articulation and denotes a situation in which, as Bourdieu put it, "when there is a quasi-perfect correspondence between the objective order and the subjective principles of organisation (as in ancient societies), the natural and social world seems self-evident" (Bourdieu 1977: 164; Bourdieu 1990: 68). Going beyond a shared understanding of meanings, doxa is the joint subscription to "encoding and decoding operations" referring to the same system of constant relations (Bourdieu 1990: 26). The implication of this is that when newcomers join a specific field they have to learn the rules and play by them in order to gain a position from which they can attempt to influence doxa. This needs to happen even in situations in which the newly arrived actors disagree with the dominant understandings within the field that they have just joined.

According to Bourdieu, we need to differentiate between doxa, orthodoxy, and heterodoxy (Bourdieu 1977: 168–9). As noted above, in its basic form doxa is unarticulated. However, if or when challengers contest the doxa (representing a situation of "heterodoxy"), they compel the dominant actors to articulate it. Doxa is thus transformed into orthodoxy in order to be defended. Challenging the doxa or orthodoxy of a field is particularly interesting in the field of security, where the arrival of new actors with new practices can represent a challenge to the dominant logic of the field. The term "heterodoxy" refers to situations where dissent exists over what doxa is. Consequently, a struggle between challengers and dominant actors subscribing to the orthodoxy may ensue, as dominant actors seek to maintain their monopoly over defining which forms of capital are valued in a given field.

Following Bourdieu's logic, when the world of "opinion" opens, heterodoxy comes into play, as the dominated actors (or, in Bourdieu's terminology, classes) "have an interest in pushing back the limits of doxa and exposing the arbitrariness of the taken for granted" (Bourdieu 1977: 169). Conversely, the dominant actors "have an interest in defending the integrity of the doxa, or, short of this, establishing in its place the necessarily imperfect substitute, orthodoxy" (1977: 169).

The term "doxic battles" has been used by scholars who embrace Bourdieu's ideas to describe situations where agents in a field struggle over doxa, mobilizing their accumulated capital in an attempt to articulate the legitimate version of the social world (Swartz 1997: 89). Doxic battles occur against the background of a doxic baseline, which is largely uncontested by the actors who participate in the field of security. In our case, one could point to a shared sense between public agencies and private actors that a partial commodification of security is both acceptable and desirable, that the principle of market efficiency is also relevant in the sphere of security, and that in a complex world of multiple risks and reduced budgets private actors need to play significant roles—in partnership with public institutions—in security provision. All these ideas are largely uncontested by public and private security actors alike. What is also uncontested is the idea that the state still has primary responsibility for security provision, but exercises that responsibility in a field that includes both public and private actors, and in which certain functions are performed by PSCs. What *is* contested is the specific application of the vision of public–private partnership. Private security actors seek to secure broader, official recognition as privileged partners of public agencies in the production of knowledge about security threats and risks, and solutions to those risks. They also seek to be recognized as actors who are competent to perform more functions—that is, to be included in areas of security governance and provision from which they are still excluded.

In essence, we can speak of a doxic battle as being identifiable in the debate over how to define the boundaries of the appropriate role of PSCs: many PSCs and their professional associations favor a definition that is far broader and more ambitious than that supported by European institutions and many EU member states. In other words, while, as noted above, public agencies, acting in the spirit of neo-liberal norms, have advocated the commodification of security and a powerful role for PSCs, they have not gone sufficiently far—at least not in the eyes of most private security players. Therefore, private security actors have enacted a script that undermines certain aspects of the existing doxa, and, simultaneously, have striven to accumulate various forms of capital to deploy in the overall (doxic) struggles over how to define the reality of European security in the twenty-first century. The outcome of these struggles is not yet clear as the field of security remains a very dynamic and contested one. But, in the longer term, these struggles will have significant implications for the spaces that private actors can occupy in the governance and provision of security. A close analysis of security practices enacted in recent years suggests that such doxic battles occur at both the European and the national level. Let us start with the European level, by examining several instances that reflect strategies mobilized by the private security industry in an attempt to play a more prominent role in (re)shaping the European field of security.

We noted above that strategies are dispositional, emerging from the feel for the game and the actors having been immersed in the game (Bourdieu and Nice 2000: 112). To be strategic, "position-taking has to be in line with their position and the dominant symbolic representations (or doxa) of the field" (Mérand and Forget 2013: 98). In our case, PSCs have drawn strategically on dominant representations, particularly prevailing neo-liberal discourses of market efficiency and the role of private actors in performing roles traditionally attributed to the state. They have done so in an effort to accumulate forms of capital for their positions and reject the elements of traditional definitions that do not benefit them. In particular, PSCs have systematically struggled for enhanced positions in consultation on legislation about security, and in risk-assessment exercises, going beyond what is possible under the current legislation. In their efforts to enhance the power of the private security industry, representatives of PSCs have often argued against the positions adopted by EU institutions (especially the European Commission) as well as national authorities from many European states—including those studied in this book. Those public officials have often advanced arguments criticized by PSCs (for instance, as noted above, on the logic and sequence of EU-wide harmonization of rules governing private security), and have been reluctant to involve the private security industry in the governance of security to the extent desired by the latter. To put this in the language of performances, we can say that PSCs have assembled and staged a script that casts members of the private security industry as more prominent—more deeply involved in security governance and provision—than prevailing shared understandings and existing rules of the game allow. In order to gain recognition as actors that can play such a prominent role, they have sought to stage their ability and willingness to perform security according to the dominant neo-liberal ideas regarding the discipline of the market.

In contesting the current rules of the game of security commercialization and definitions of appropriate boundaries of private actors' involvement in the formulation and implementation of security solutions, PSCs have sought to obtain the institutionalization of their role as privileged partners of public authorities in the provision of security. In particular, PSCs have been advocating for the inscription of a mention of their role as "privileged partners" in European legislation. To them, this type of inscription would be important as it would mark the public authorities' recognition that the involvement of the private security industry in security provision is not just an ad hoc, temporary arrangement, possibly subject to change as soon as (for instance) public budgets dedicated to security can increase. Rather, the systematic involvement of PSCs would be recognized as a lasting feature of the new security environment, which responds to the needs of the era of multiple risks and high uncertainty. Linked to this, PSCs have sought recognition of their role as effective and responsible producers of knowledge on European security, able to perform correct diagnostics and solutions in key areas of European security—including by correctly interpreting the meaning of European harmonization in the field of security, and defining the rules of the game of public procurement of security services. Their argument is that recognition of actors that can be involved in the production of knowledge about European/national security and in the provision of protection in sensitive areas should be granted according to their experience/expertise/capability, not according to whether the actors are public or private. From their perspective, private security actors can fill important gaps caused by shrinking public budgets and a proliferation of risks; indeed, in some areas, the expertise and superior technologies possessed by certain PSCs means that they could perform certain security functions in a manner that is more efficient than the state. Hence, by cooperating with the state they can effectively strengthen the ability of public authorities to enact state sovereignty.

The discourses that representatives of the private security industry have mobilized and sought to enact revolve around the neo-liberal idea of security commodification and the value of the discipline of the market in multiple areas and domains of life, including security. On this logic, based on their expertise in various areas of security provision, their commitment to the principles of market efficiency, and their superior material capabilities (especially sophisticated technologies), PSCs deserve to be recognized as having the ability to be equally if not more effective security providers than public agencies.

The Struggle to (Re)constitute the European Field of Security

In recent years, one of the most interesting developments in the European field of security has been the growing effort of the private security industry—again, especially within the framework of CoESS—to put forward a script that contests moves by European institutions (especially the European Commission and the ECJ) to maintain and reproduce a clear hierarchy between public and private security providers. From the point of view of the private security industry, it is problematic that, even though PSCs are increasingly collaborating with public agencies in areas ranging from the protection of critical infrastructure to maintaining public order during cultural/sporting events, the European Court of Justice (ECJ) in particular has insisted that such functions do not translate into greater public authority for the private industry. In its rulings, the ECJ has insisted that: "merely making a contribution to the maintenance of public security, which any individual may be called upon to do, does not constitute exercise of official authority."[2]

CoESS representatives have also expressed frustration and disappointment over the failure to inscribe in EU legislation a formal recognition of the status of PSCs as official "partners" in the provision of security in Europe.[3] As they put it, there is a wide and counterproductive gap between the reality of growing reliance of public authorities—both at the EU level and in individual member states—on private security for a wide range of functions traditionally attributed to the police, and the persistent refusal to acknowledge that reality in new European legislation. From this perspective, "it is hard to understand why, when the PSCs' contracts with public authorities have grown exponentially all over Europe, when private security is increasingly accepted by the public and increasingly visible in the protection of European and governmental buildings, assuring security at airports and protecting critical infrastructure in many EU states, we still do not even have one paragraph of European legislation to confirm the status of PSCs."[4] According to the private security industry, the inclusion of such a provision in EU legislation would represent a step in the direction of ensuring that laws reflect European reality in the twenty-first century; it would also be important as it could grant greater legitimacy to the private security sector, thereby enabling its members to perform systematic roles in the provision of public security. For instance, PSCs could be more extensively involved in supporting the police by performing all non-core functions. In turn, it is argued that involving PSCs more systematically in policing activities—under clear legislation—would be a vital step in responding to the growing security needs and diminishing budgets in Europe.

It is interesting to note that CoESS objections to the current status of private security in Europe echo discussions around an initiative promoted in the early 2000s by the Spanish Presidency of the EU. Soon after the 9/11 attacks, the Spanish Presidency proposed the adoption of a Council Decision according to which a "network of contact points of authorities with responsibility for private security" should be established (Permanent Representation of Spain to the EU 2002). The idea was that such a network would facilitate coordination and cooperation between the various national bodies, exchange experience in the handling of information provided by private security firms, and establish best practices in security provision. The initiative contemplated the creation of a network of contact points as an initial step toward the establishment of common requirements in member states regarding the authorization and supervision of the supply of private security services, and the unification of aspects that would allow the parties involved in the private security sector to extend their business interests to any member state (Gestri 2012: 64). More broadly, the Spanish proposal raised the idea that private security companies form part of the network of national security agencies of EU member states. After successive drafts of the proposal in January and February, the EU Council Legal Service delivered an opinion clearly opposing any Council Decision on the grounds that it "encroached upon the sphere of Community competence and was not feasible under Article 47 of the Treaty on the EU (TEU)." This opinion was quickly countered by the legal service of the Spanish State Secretariat for Legal Affairs, as the Spanish Presidency was determined to press ahead with the proposal. Its key argument was that private security was inextricably linked to public security provided by the state, and therefore a matter for the EU Justice and Home Affairs Council.

A comprehensive analysis of struggles between European institutions over the limits of the sphere of Community competence is beyond the scope of this chapter. What is particularly interesting for our purposes is the type of argument used by the Spanish Presidency to justify this initiative—language that has subsequently been used very frequently by CoESS and other representatives of the private security industry as they have sought to secure recognition for PSCs as key partners of public authorities in the provision of security in Europe. This can be interpreted as a move by CoESS to cast itself as the kind of actor that can think—and perform security functions—like an EU state rather than simply like a corporation. According to this narrative, an institution like CoESS can use the same logic that was used by Spain to provide a knowledgeable diagnostic of the European security situation. More broadly, the CoESS focus on the similarities between its argument and the position adopted by a key European public actor can also be seen as an effort to secure European recognition for the material resources (superior technology) and cultural capital (expertise) of the private security industry, and on this basis to enhance its symbolic capital, facilitating a more systematic, official involvement in the provision of public security.

The Spanish Presidency summarized their argument as follows: "The [European] Court of Justice has described private security as an economic activity subject to the freedom of movement provisions of the Treaty. It has ruled that the derogations from the freedom of movement of persons under Article 39(4) of the EC Treaty (TEC)—concerning employment in the public service—and from the freedom of establishment under Article 45 of the TEC (exercise of official authority) do not apply to the activity of private security undertakings and their employees, and that such activity does not in itself constitute a threat to public policy (Articles 39(3) and 46(1) of the TEC)"

(Permanent Representation of Spain to the EU 2002). Furthermore, in a move that effectively embraced neo-liberal principles of security commodification, the Spanish Presidency argued that private security companies had an integral role in providing public security and that the basic economics of supply and demand meant that "they are now part of the essential nucleus of exclusive competence attributed to the State in security matters."

The Presidency document further argues that the state's monopoly on security should take precedence over Community law. The notion involved here is that "if security in the abstract is the exclusive competence of the state and if security is understood to mean the result of the activities of public security services plus the result of private security activities, the logical conclusion is that private sector activities are also the competence of the state, i.e. of the public security authorities." On the need for private security, the Spanish Presidency made two further observations: there is a "disequilibrium between the supply of security services by States governed by the rule of law, which are subject to budgetary constraints, and the demand for protection from businesses and individuals"; and "predominant crime prevention philosophy places more stress on 'defensible spaces' and thus on 'situation prevention.' These are concepts which have enabled businesses, sellers and installers of protection services to present their private economic interests (doing business) as being in the general interest of society and, on the other hand, have enabled the public authorities to make a virtue of necessity, as shown by the fact that targets considered particularly vulnerable to crime (e.g. banks, jewellers, etc.) are frequently required to protect themselves 'privately'" (Permanent Representation of Spain to the EU 2002).

The Spanish proposal was widely regarded as legally incompatible with the EU Treaties and a number of rulings by the ECJ, and thus did not get very far. In the end, the Council enacted a Recommendation that is limited to the provision of measures of police cooperation among national authorities, especially with respect to the handling of information generated by the activities of PSCs. Importantly, the Recommendation avoids any reference to exchanges of information on the national rules regulating security firms, or to the need for coordination among member states in that field (Gestri 2012: 64). But some of the core ideas of the Spanish initiative were subsequently mobilized by CoESS to oppose a type of EU-level harmonization that it perceived as detrimental to the interests of PSCs, and to lobby for greater involvement of the private security industry in European security governance. In other words, CoESS tried to delegitimize the script of harmonization proposed by the European Commission and the ECJ, and proposed an alternative script, in which the key storyline depicted PSCs as perfectly able to play a bigger role in security governance and provision.

In CoESS's repeated efforts to advocate a more substantial and systematic role for the private security industry in European security governance and provision, a prominent strategy has been to invoke the new logic of the field (risk-management) and the importance of superior technology, professional expertise, and knowledge, and to depict private security companies as actors that have the kind of material and non-material capital that are required and valued in this field. In other words, there has been an effort to use the European authorities' own characterization of the field to contest their opposition to greater PSC participation in this field. It is noteworthy that CoESS has explicitly sought to link the evolution of private security to the widely accepted idea concerning the rise of the risk society, thus seeking to cast itself as an actor that understood and was willing to perform security functions in a manner consistent with that logic of risk-management. Thus, in its *White Paper on the Socio-Economic Added Value of Private Security in Europe*, CoESS explicitly linked its evaluation of European security to the language used in EU documents by stating:

> Today, the welfare state, which was created in Europe after the Second World War, is evolving into a risk society. In the context of the welfare state, the status of the keeper of the established order has evolved into a social redistributor and trouble-shooter. In the risk society, the individual and/or organised citizen, and with him or her, the individual and/or organised business community, as well as the public authorities, focus all their political attention on crime, the subjective and/or objective feelings of insecurity and nuisance.   (CoESS 2013a: 9)[5]

The evolution of the security environment is associated with a "new moral order," which "must be based on a desire for security, safety and risk reduction." According to CoESS, with the advent of the global economy, our society has come to be characterized by more and more economic free trade, and will evolve into an increasingly advanced information society that is sustained by globalization. Briefly put, "the global village is becoming a reality." In this context, the debate involving public or private responsibility for security and safety is "under the microscope." Private companies can already offer services that "seemingly belonged to the exclusive jurisdiction of the public authorities." It would appear that "by analogy with the 'market failure', a 'state failure' has occurred. The national and sovereign state is no longer the centre around which the political community is organised" (CoESS 2013a: 9).

CoESS went so far as to invoke classical liberal arguments about the invisible hand of the market to support its claim that in a society of multiple risks PSCs can perform important roles not only in securing private businesses and individuals but also contributing to the provision of security as a public good. The idea stressed in its discourse is that "civilians and companies' investments in self-interest also increase public interest in private security services" (CoESS 2013a: 12–13). This evolution is depicted as consistent with the current debate on core tasks for the police related to public security management (justice, police, and defense), and thus cast as particularly relevant. Key, from this perspective, is the fact that the private security concern "no longer competes with public security management, but adopts a genuine complementary character." In practical terms, this means that end-user investments in private security services increase the overall level of security and allow public security actors to move away from non-core policing tasks and focus on more fine-tuned priorities. That is, "public security actors can, independent of the very definite current budgetary constraints, once more choose far more, better quality and more targeted services in the areas that can be served by private security actors" (CoESS 2013a: 13). A logical division of labor can thus be established, in a situation in which the private security industry can focus more on the proactive and preventive aspects of insecurity phenomena, and "public security actors can concentrate on the curative and repressive links in the security chain" (CoESS 2013a: 13).

According to CoESS, this complementary role is justified by the fact that private security offers multiple advantages. These include legal advantages, such as contractual freedom of choice, responsibility, liability, and the elimination of the type of rivalry which is sometimes present in public service provision. From an economic perspective, the key benefit is that labor distribution "leads to specialisation, which in turn implies improved efficiency and effectiveness." Furthermore, some important social advantages can be gained from this situation, which is expected to generate high employment levels of lower educated people and risk groups in the labor market, professionalization, education, training, and the harmonization of social and labor laws (CoESS 2013a: 13).

A similar line of argument regarding the value of PSCs to the provision of security as a public good was adopted by CoESS with respect to critical infrastructure as well as military infrastructure (CoESS 2010, 2013a).[6] The starting point for the CoESS argument is the widely accepted observation that critical infrastructure in Europe is "owned, operated, regulated and protected by a complex mix of public and private organizations." "Under these circumstances, CoESS, as the representative organization for European private security services, strongly believes that there is a far greater role to be played by its members and their affiliated private security companies in securing and protecting critical infrastructure in a way which brings benefits to all—the responsible authorities, the infrastructure owners and operators, the end-users of critical infrastructure, the private security companies and the general public at large." Specifically, "the added value of the private security concern for the security of critical infrastructure must be sought in specialisation. Private security services companies can develop know-how specific to these organisations and/or institutions by focusing on specialised market segments. These include energy, chemicals, pharmaceuticals, automation, airports and aviation, banks, insurance, maritime affairs and healthcare" (CoESS 2013a: 17).

Central to the CoESS position is a critique of the current state of affairs. Thus, while most EU member states have recognized, in principle, the importance of protecting critical infrastructure, and have adopted a plethora of programs and policies to achieve this aim, "it is CoESS' feeling that these programmes and policies remain too much on a political level and do not provide sufficient guidelines or directions/instructions for the actual day-to-day security and protection of critical infrastructure" (CoESS 2010: 7). Furthermore, some European countries do not even have an official definition of critical infrastructure, and therefore "no rules on how it should be protected and secured" (CoESS 2010: 7). This is particularly problematic in "the current global security environment," in which security—understood as activities designed to reduce the likelihood of a multitude of risks, including "criminal and terrorist action," and resilience, meaning the ability to "withstand and recover from deliberate or naturally-occurring disruption—must be built into the design and operation of critical infrastructure" (CoESS 2010: 10).

Under these circumstances, CoESS argued, it is important to "see the security and protection of critical infrastructure maximized through an explicit recognition by policymakers of the complexity of the issue, involving as it does public, private and in some cases hybrid actors. CoESS wishes to see an explicit allocation of roles and responsibilities for protection" (CoESS 2010: 7). Interestingly, CoESS mobilized the EU's own discourse about the importance of public/private partnerships to advance its claim about the need for greater public/private cooperation in the protection of critical infrastructure. Thus, CoESS reminded the European authorities that in November 2009 the European Commission had launched its Communication on Developing Public/Private Partnerships, which identified such partnerships (PPPs) as a "policy priority" for the Commission, and was therefore "fully in line with CoESS' vision on public–private partnership in the field of security" (CoESS 2010: 11).

In essence, the CoESS strategy has been to argue that the very logic of PPPs explicitly embraced by the Commission, and, more broadly, the European authorities' adoption of a (neo-liberal) approach, stressing principles of market efficiency and outsourcing of public services, require greater involvement of the private security industry in the protection of European critical infrastructure. The notion involved here is that:

> Securing and protecting critical infrastructure is one of the most suited areas for public–private partnerships, given their often public (national or local) character, which is translated in public ownership or public management or public objective. It is undoubtedly a development in Europe in general regarding private security that more and more sectors and assets are taken away from public security to the

benefit of the private security sector. CoESS does not want to make a judgement on this development, but witnesses in all European countries an increasing presence of private security companies and private security guards in the public domain.

(CoESS 2010: 10)

From CoESS's perspective, the reasons behind this evolution—and also the reason why the private security industry needs to play a greater role in the protection of critical infrastructure—revolve around the fact that many PSCs possess the kind of material and non-material capital, ranging from superior technology to specialized skills and rich experience, that are particularly valuable in a situation characterized by a declining ability of public agencies to fulfill society's complex security needs. In CoESS's words, the reasons for the enhanced presence of PSCs in the public security domain include: "the increasing feeling of insecurity amongst all parts of society, the limited resources of police and other public security bodies, the ever-increasing quality and professionalism of private security services and, last but not least, the innovative and flexible added value private security can provide based on its longstanding expertise" (CoESS 2010: 10).

The argument put forward by CoESS with respect to critical infrastructure was also extended to military infrastructure and international security institutions. Once again, CoESS explicitly invoked widely accepted neo-liberal policies and practices of security commodification to legitimize its own argument regarding the expansion of private security services to new areas. On this logic, once the political taboo has been dismantled, there is no reasonable reason for public authorities to refuse to allow a greater role for the private security industry. On the contrary, by expanding the mandate of PSCs, public authorities would contribute to the public good by enhancing the security of European citizens in an era marked by a multitude of security risks and challenges, which cannot be addressed by governmental and intergovernmental actors without support from the private sector. As stated in its 2013 *White Paper on The Socio-Economic Added Value of Private Security Services in Europe,*

Guarding and securing military infrastructures and even performing military tasks is no longer a political taboo. With regard to guarding and securing military infrastructures we note that private security guards are already performing certain tasks that provide added value for defence because professional military personnel can focus exclusively on core tasks . . . In addition to these tasks, private security services could also be embedded in the operations of, for example, Europol and Eurojust, in addressing international environmental crime, organised crime and cybercrime. By expanding specialist "know-how", they could contribute to the compilation of so-called "threat assessments", which are necessary for these international institutions to act. (CoESS 2013a: 17)

Gatekeeping and Social Capital in the Private Security Industry

It is also interesting to note that, in an effort to protect the credibility of the private security sector, CoESS has been adamant that only PSCs with the proper accreditation and sufficient expertise should be allowed to participate in public–private partnerships in the protection of critical infrastructure. By contrast, PSCs that, due to lack of expertise or proper training, cannot provide high-quality service should be excluded from all PPP programs, particularly those concerning critical infrastructure. In other words, as the organization that portrays itself as the voice of European private security services, CoESS has been keen to not only secure a privileged position for PSCs in the protection of critical infrastructure, but also to act—and be seen as acting—as a "gatekeeper," performing the function of denying recognition and excluding from the domain of private security providers those companies that fail to live up to the standards of professionalism as defined by the Confederation. The function of gatekeeping can be seen as a potent manifestation of CoESS's role as internal governance unit in the European field of security. As noted in Chapter 3, by helping to define and disseminate norms of proper behavior (or "best practice") for European PSCs, CoESS has been protecting the interests of the established members of the private security industry against challengers. A particularly problematic set of challengers has been the category of private security providers whose illicit activities threaten to undermine the reputation of private security in general, thereby endangering the industry's quest to enhance its profile and power in the provision and governance of security.

The enactment of the role of gatekeeper has, once again, involved all three aspects of performance (Schechner 2002): carrying out the function of protecting public/private clients from illegal or unscrupulous private security actors; doing so in a manner that conforms to prevailing European norms and laws concerning the activities of PSCs and their roles as partners of public agencies; and showing or staging what they are doing, especially via participation in regular meetings with EU officials. In enacting this role, CoESS has resorted to a technique that is often adopted by actors in their quest to convince the audience of the authenticity of their performance (Alexander 2011). Specifically, CoESS representatives have enacted a script that involves a clear good/bad dichotomy: casting the Confederation as the voice of virtuous security providers, able and willing to protect the public against a multitude of dangers and risks. This is in clear contrast to the category of PSCs depicted by CoESS as unprofessional and corrupt. Those PSCs are seen as lacking relevant expertise and experience, and in some cases maintaining links to criminal circles. Consequently, one of CoESS's self-defined missions is to weaken and delegitimize the unprofessional PSCs which threaten to undermine the credibility of the entire private security industry.

CoESS's enactment of the role of gatekeeper has also involved a systematic mobilization of social capital. Here, again, Bourdieu's analysis is particularly insightful. As he argued, social groups delegate the right to speak on behalf of the group to an agent or a small group of agents "with the aid of this collectively owned capital" (Bourdieu 1986: 251). This agent or group of agents has the authority to expel or "excommunicate embarrassing individuals" in order to protect the reputation of the group as a whole (Bourdieu 1986: 251). In our situation, delegating this right to exercise symbolic violence on behalf—and for the protection—of the group at the European level is seen in the setting up of CoESS as an umbrella organization representing national associations or federations of PSCs. By consistently displaying professionalism, insisting on its commitment to protect the industry from PSCs engaged in illegal practices, and demonstrating an ability and willingness to work with European and national public authorities, CoESS has converted its social capital into symbolic capital, reflected in its recognition as a "social partner" by EU authorities.

As part of its campaign to display and protect its professional image and credibility, CoESS has been at the heart of self-regulation efforts at the European level. At the level of industry representative bodies, restrictions apply to private security companies wishing to become affiliated with national federations that are members of CoESS. In a similar vein, it is not the case that every national federation automatically becomes a member of CoESS.[7] In the eyes of CoESS, it is particularly important to be seen by European authorities as an organization that is serious about excluding from its ranks associations/ entities that do not meet its criteria of professionalism.

At a European level, self-regulation has taken place in the form of the European Code of Conduct signed by both CoESS and UNI-Europa (representing the trade unions) (Born et al. 2006). This Code covers a wide array of topics, ranging from the selection, recruitment, and training of workers to the relations with the police and other private security companies. This is not to suggest the European Code is perfect; in fact, it can be seen as relatively weak in the sense that its provisions are very vague and, for example, do not set minimum standards on what should constitute the minimum level of training. This weakness can be seen to stem from the fact that regulations differ to such an extent from one European country to another that it is not possible to stipulate a minimum guideline. However, CoESS and UNI-Europa perceive this Code as a first step toward the harmonization of the sector in the region. In this context, the Code of Conduct can be seen as one of the avenues through which CoESS has been performing its role as internal governance unit in the European field of security, disseminating norms and standards of appropriate behavior for PSCs in Europe. In addition to the Code, CoESS and UNI-Europa have also agreed upon a *European Vocational Training Manual for Basic Guarding*. Although it remains a training manual, it is an important piece of self-regulation for the private security industry, as it introduces the standards which should be considered as a minimum basis for the training of security guards.[8]

CoESS has been particularly keen to project the image of professionalism for the private security players involved in the protection of critical infrastructure. In its words, "it is important that, when policies are considering cooperation with private security companies for the security and protection of critical infrastructure, the necessary attention should be given to quality." The problem, from the Confederation's perspective, is that although many national legislations on private security ensure at least a minimum level of quality through strict legal criteria for setting up private security companies or for working as a private security guard, there has been a failure to give special attention to—and establish special conditions that reflect—the specificities of critical infrastructure. Under these circumstances, CoESS recommends that national legislations regarding private security include a special license or authorization when critical infrastructure security and protection is concerned. This could be achieved "through additional licensing and operational criteria for private security companies wishing to secure critical infrastructure or through compulsory specific training programmes for private security guards in this area" (CoESS 2010: 12).

One of the key arguments advanced by CoESS in the context of this campaign has been that the Confederation should be recognized as an authoritative, trustworthy source of knowledge about best practices in the domain of protecting critical infrastructure. In a situation in which a series of PSCs have been involved in critical infrastructure protection at the national level, "CoESS is well placed to influence the European Commission's thinking on critical infrastructure site protection" by drawing on the best practices developed in countries like the UK, Germany, and Spain. Thus, some of the key activities that should be standardized and regulated include inspections/approval; corporate governance; establishment/maintenance of standards; insurance; staff employment/training; and critical infrastructure contract infrastructure (CoESS 2014b: 1).

Contesting the Meaning of Harmonization in European Security

In its efforts to enhance the position of PSCs in the European security sector, CoESS has also been involved in a long campaign aimed at contesting the logic of harmonization of security services prescribed by the European Commission. Through that campaign, it has waged a long battle with the European Commission over the proper definition of the logic of harmonization in European security. Specifically, CoESS has opposed the application of the

2006 *EU Directive on Internal Market and Services* (Services Directive) to the private security industry, arguing that such an application would be counter-productive and could endanger public safety in EU countries. The EU's attempt to apply the Services Directive, which aims to remove internal barriers—including national regulations obstructing the free movement of services across the EU—reflects a commitment to the promotion of free trade across Europe. However, when the Services Directive was first implemented, private security services—more specifically the manned security services (guarding)—were left out of its scope, in recognition of the fact that existing national regulations were widely different from country to country. These differences included the screening of employees, training requirements, control systems, and sanctions—among other aspects (CoESS/ESTA 2005).[9] CoESS was from the start systematically opposed to the application of this Directive to private security because of a perceived lack of regulatory harmonization at the level of EU member states. The Confederation's aim was to prevent some providers of low-quality services from entering on the currently tighter nationally regulated markets.[10] In opposing the application of the Services Directive to the private security sector, CoESS cast itself as—and sought the EU officials' recognition as—an authoritative source of expertise, skills, and knowledge about the needs of the European security sector, and the best way to address those needs. Interestingly, it has also portrayed itself as having the moral authority to act in this area, by virtue of its commitment to the application of core EU principles of respect for the rule of law and human rights in the field of security.

The Confederation's campaign against the harmonization proposed by the Commission became especially intense in the late 2000s, in a situation in which the security sector's exclusion from the Services Directive was to be reviewed by the EU Commission at the end of 2010. The challenge, from the point of view of CoESS, was that there was strong support among many European officials for rapid harmonization of rules regulating private security services in member states—on the grounds that this step would enhance the global competitiveness of the Union. Thus, within the European Commission there was substantial support for the view that a Europe that maintained national barriers in this field could not be efficient or internationally competitive. Particularly in a situation in which private security was becoming globally competitive, the argument went, the EU had to extend to this sector the logic of European integration. This meant that if a company was registered in one EU member state it should be able to operate freely across the entire territory of the union, without any further need to register in the other countries in which it was providing services.[11]

This approach can be seen as part of a more general concern on the part of the European Commission about the fragmented state of the security industry in Europe, coupled with a view that a systematic, sustained effort was needed to remedy that situation. For instance, in a 2010 Commission document *EU 2020: An Integrated Industrial Policy for the Globalisation Era*, it was stated that the security industry was a most promising sector "in meeting future societal challenges." That potential, however, was compromised by the fact that: "The EU security industry faces a highly fragmented internal market and a weak industrial base. National regulatory frameworks differ widely and the market for security products is highly diversified, ranging from cameras to complex scanner systems. To provide a security system, manufacturers, system integrators, and service providers have to work closely together with clients. It is essential to develop a fast-track system for approval of priority technologies; to make substantial further progress on harmonisation, standardisation; to consider coordinated public procurement" (European Commission 2010).

In its lobbying campaign, CoESS sought to persuade EU officials that any effort to apply the Services Directive to private security in the near future would seriously undermine the quality of security provided across Europe by PSCs. The problem, as CoESS pointed out, was that the application of the principle of freedom of movement without first achieving high standards of regulation in each member state would result in a situation in which PSCs that had low levels of professionalism, inadequate equipment, and unreliable personnel with insufficient training might still be able to register in EU countries with weak regulation, and from there inundate the entire EU market. Thus, unprofessional PSCs would take advantage of their low cost of operation to push down prices and thus potentially drive out of business those companies that were providing far more professional services—but also had to charge higher fees in order to cover the costs of those services.[12] The concern, in short, was not only that the security of European citizens and businesses would be endangered through the influx of unprofessional PSCs, but also that such a move might compromise the entire private security industry and thus make it more difficult even for professional PSCs to be recognized as legitimate, reliable partners in European security governance and provision.

CoESS perceived as an important victory the EU decision to continue to exclude the private security sector from the application of the Services Directive after 2010. Far from resting on its laurels, however, following the adoption of the Directive the Confederation has continued its campaign against what it perceives as premature harmonization. As in the past, the problem—from the point of view of the Confederation—is that there are powerful voices advocating harmonization in the name of efficiency. For instance, the European Commission approach to security has been to focus on the idea that disparate legislative frameworks hurt EU firms' competitiveness, suggesting that in order to transcend this problem it is important to increase standardizing and certifying to harmonize legislation and achieve higher levels of competitiveness. In a 2012 *Action Plan for an Innovative and Competitive Security*

Industry the Commission argued that: "Thanks to their level of technological development many EU (security) companies are still among the world leaders in most of the segments of the security sector. Recent evolutions and market forecasts do, however, indicate that the market shares of European companies on the global market are bound to decrease constantly over the next years" (European Commission 2012).

The notion involved here is that the EU is at a significant disadvantage compared to the US. Thus: "The market leading US companies are still the technological front runners, they additionally also benefit from a harmonised legal framework and a robust internal market. This gives them not only a reassuring basis but also the benefit of a clearly recognised and distinguishable US brand, which has proven to be a highly valuable advantage compared to EU companies in terms of international competition" (European Commission 2012). Furthermore, "This lack of a similar 'EU brand' is especially critical if one considers that the central future markets for security technologies will not be in Europe but in emerging countries in Asia, South America and the Middle East" (European Commission 2012). Under these circumstances, "the aim of the Commission is thus to establish a better functioning Internal European Market for security technologies. Favourable Internal Market conditions, enhancing competition and lowering production costs through the exploitation of scale economies, are also essential to strengthen the position of the EU security industry in those emerging countries that represent the future of the security sector." To this end: "The Commission will make use of all the tools at its disposal to create a true Internal Market for security technologies, thus providing a strong home base for the EU security industry with a view to gain market shares in emerging markets" (European Commission 2012).

From the point of view of CoESS, the problem with this approach is that—as in the past—the Commission's focus on the creation of a "true internal market" in the security sector would translate into a premature, inappropriate dismantling of national barriers that protect countries with better regulation of PSCs. This concern has been repeatedly raised in the context of consultations with EU officials. Thus, the CoESS position on the *European Commission Consultation for Developing an Industrial Policy for the Security Industry* revolves around the claim that: "[G]iven the large variety in national legislation regulating private security services, the introduction now of EU-wide harmonisation or rules regulating private security services would be too premature and would lead to an even greater market fragmentation. Therefore, the primary objective should be to raise first, at the national level and where needed, the level of legislation. Once all national legislation is more on the same level...EU wide harmonisation and standardisation...can be envisaged" (de Clerck 2011: 7).[13]

As in the past, CoESS has not sought to challenge the idea of EU-wide harmonization of rules as a way to create a more unified, stronger European market. Instead, its argument has been that, in the absence of sufficient knowledge about the way in which PSCs operate in various EU countries, the harmonization strategy proposed by the Commission was flawed and dangerous. From this perspective, CoESS—as "the only representative European employers' organization representing the interests of the private security services industry"—is in a much stronger position to provide an analysis of the status of private security regulations and challenges in different EU member states, and on this basis to identify a viable strategy for achieving harmonization in the longer term. The aim, in essence, has been to secure the Commission's recognition of the symbolic capital of CoESS, and on this basis to strengthen its position as an authoritative producer of knowledge about the best way to implement liberal principles in the private security domain.

Changing the Rules of the Game in Public Procurement in Europe

In a similar vein, CoESS has been systematically involved in a campaign to shape the EU's approach to public procurement. The campaign was launched in the context of recent moves by the Commission to modify procurement legislation dating back to 2004. Thus, in December 2011 the Commission proposed the revision of Directives 2004/17/EC (procurement in the water, energy, transport, and postal services sectors) and 2004/18/EC (public works, supply and service contracts), as well as the adoption of a directive on concession contracts (Committee on the Internal Market 2011). CoESS was deeply concerned by the provisions included in the first draft of the new European directives, which, in the name of liberalization and greater competitiveness, envisaged an almost exclusive focus on price as the criterion for awarding contracts. Under these circumstances, CoESS joined forces with UNI-Europa to contest the vision proposed by the Commission. Specifically, the aim of that campaign was to persuade European officials that the liberalization strategy proposed in the Commission's initial draft was flawed and would undermine core European values, such as protection of social rights, as well as endanger European public safety. In that context, CoESS again sought to cast itself in the role of an expert with authoritative knowledge about the status, needs, and challenges of security provision in Europe, and on this basis to challenge the Commission's vision of liberalization.

In other words, what was involved in debates about European public procurement can be seen as yet another instance of doxic battle, in which the various players operating in the field of security provision (on the one hand the Commission, and on the other hand private security providers as represented by CoESS as well as the syndicates) agreed on the importance of upholding liberal principles in this area, but disagreed over the meaning of liberalization. CoESS's main argument was that, on the basis of the cultural capital possessed by its members (national private security associations or federations), the Confederation was able to provide a correct prognosis/estimation of the likely implications of the Commission's approach: a sharp fall in the quality of security provision; the rise to prominence of unprofessional, unreliable security providers; and the decline of professional, expert players in the domain of security provision; The European security needs in the twenty-first century are such, CoESS has repeatedly argued, that the definition of "best value" in security provision needs to be different from the definition proposed by the Commission. Specifically, it needs to encompass factors such as appropriate training, competence, experience, and respect for the basic values upheld by the EU (especially compliance with European "rules of the game" concerning the basic rights and protections of workers).

Ironically, in debates about procurement an organization representing private corporations (CoESS) criticized a powerful public actor, the Commission, for being too neo-liberal. According to CoESS, by focusing almost exclusively on lowering prices, the Commission has failed to provide adequate protections for European citizens that would be affected by the process of removing barriers to the market in the area of security services. In contrast to the Commission's neo-liberal approach, CoESS cast itself as the actor that had a more comprehensive, profound understanding of the correct way to implement the principle of liberalization—and thus perform security in a manner that was consistent with European values and norms.

Thus, in response to the European Commission's *Proposal for a Directive on Public Procurement COM/2011/0896* of December 20, 2011, CoESS joined forces with UNI-Europa and the European social partners of two other services sectors—the cleaning industry (UNI-Europa/EFCI) and the contract catering (EFFAT/FERCO) industries—and submitted a joint position with regard to this legislative proposal (CoESS et al. 2012) The position put forward in that paper was that the proposal needed a series of amendments to include social considerations in public procurement and in particular the elimination of the lowest price option, the respect of social legislation, and collective agreements including the respect of the employment terms and conditions applied in the place where the service or the work is performed. In particular, the authors of the joint paper stated that they:

firmly deplore the inclusion of the lowest price option as one of the award criteria. Not only price but also quality requirements as consideration of the skills and capabilities of the provider, the company and the contract management, the working conditions of workers along the supply chain and the respect of inter-national labour standards, national laws and collective agreements including trade union rights, amongst others, must necessarily be taken into account while awarding the services represented by our industries. Bidding for services solely in view of the lowest price will lead to a downward spiral of the quality of the services provided to the detriment of all stakeholders involved.   (CoESS et al. 2012: 1)

They went on to argue that: "High competitive pressure leads providers to present very tight bids, often to the detriment of the quality of the services provided. This often has a direct impact on lowering staff training and the level of supervision and management . . . What is more, although it will bring cost savings on the short term, in the long run, the race to the lowest price, highly encouraged in times of budget constraints, will result in reductions of taxes and social contributions paid (especially if companies violate social and tax laws), a cost for the health of workers and a lower quality. All in all, by taking indirect costs altogether, choosing the 'best value' approach will be economically most advantageous for contracting authorities" (CoESS et al. 2012: 1–2).

Furthermore, CoESS and its partners expressed concern about some of the security governance provisions inscribed in the Commission's proposal. The core argument put forward in the joint paper was that, while the draft included some positive steps, it did not go far enough in setting up arrange-ments that would ensure transparency and accountability in the area of procurement. In their words: "The social partners therefore welcome the provision setting up a national oversight body in each Member State in charge of the monitoring, implementation and control of public procurement and that the oversight bodies shall publish an annual report including an overview of sustainability policies and measures with explicit reference to environmen-tal protection, social inclusion and innovation" (CoESS et al. 2012: 3). How-ever, the authors of the joint paper also argued that these provisions should not only be mandatory but could also be more proactive in promoting sus-tainable development. For instance, what was needed was to organize "regular exchanges with social partners, civil society organisations and other stake-holders on the progress made towards sustainability to encourage a positive dialogue on evidence-based examples of sustainable policies and practices" (CoESS et al. 2012: 3). Again, then, CoESS sought to delegitimize the Com-mission's proposal by arguing that it was inconsistent with key norms and values around which the EU defined itself.

Not surprisingly, the authors of the 2012 joint paper regarded as a significant—if limited—victory the European Commission's decision, in the aftermath of the consultation campaign to revise its initial proposal, to move away from some of its most controversial provisions. The result was a com-promise position, which establishes some broad "rules of the game" at the

European level, but leaves most decision-making power in this area in the hands of national authorities. The directives were voted by the European Parliament on January 15, 2014 and adopted by the Council on February 11, 2014. Member States were subsequently instructed to transpose the new rules into their national law. In response to the new directives, UNI-Europa/EFCI, and EFFAT/FERCO issued a new joint position paper in which they argued that: "While the social partners would have preferred more specific thresholds for abnormally low tenders and the abolition of the lowest price criterion, there are several positive improvements in the new Directive. Compliance with environmental, social and labour obligations, including collective agreements, is now enshrined in the principles of the Directive. Furthermore, it is possible to exclude tenderers in case of non-compliance. Whilst there is still no mandatory mechanism for joint and several liability, doors are open for Member States to ensure that subcontracting chains become transparent" (EFCI and UNI-Europa 2014).[14]

In a situation in which the new Directive left substantial decision-making power in the hands of national authorities, the authors of the joint statement called upon member states "to improve some of the elements left to their discretion in the new text. For instance, they can prohibit or restrict the 'use of price only' criterion, and leave contracting authorities the choice between either assessing other aspects in addition to cost effectiveness, or base their purchasing decisions solely on that criterion. UNI-Europa and EFCI call upon Member States to take responsibility for the environmental and social impacts of public purchasing when implementing the new Directive in their respective countries. Favouring the lowest price criterion results in reduction of taxes and social contributions paid as well as the poor health of workers and lower quality in the services provided" (EFCI and UNI-Europa 2014: 2).

To achieve a proper implementation of the new Directive at the national level, the social partners explicitly urged their respective member organizations "to closely follow the transposition of the recently agreed texts. The EFCI and UNI-Europa expressed strong support for the national advocacy efforts, aimed at embedding sustainable and socially friendly procurement legal frameworks at national levels so as to enable a more just use of public money" (EFCI and UNI-Europa 2014: 2). In other words, following the adoption of the Directive, efforts to improve public procurement—and, more broadly, to broaden the mandates and powers of PSCs—shifted from the European to the national level. In that context, CoESS members became systematically involved in lobbying their governments to avoid relying on the lowest price as the primary criterion for awarding contracts. They also became involved in efforts to push governments into adopting a broader definition of "quality" security services, and embracing new best practices in the area of security provision. Those national-level efforts are examined in Chapter 5.

Notes

1. For insightful analyses of the new political economy of security, see also Williams 2012 and White 2012.
2. See Case C-114/97 *Commission* v *Spain*, paragraph 37; Case C-465/05 *Commission* v *Italy* [2007] ECR I-11091 §38, in European Commission 2011: 61.
3. Interviews with two senior CoESS representatives, Brussels, March 4–6, 2014.
4. Interviews as in note 3.
5. This language is similar not only to the proposal put forward by the Spanish Presidency but also with key documents on European security issued in the post-9/11 era. See, for instance, European Council 2003.
6. Critical infrastructure is commonly understood to encompass physical assets, networks, and organizations whose disruption or disabling would cause severe, lasting damage to social and economic life. This generally includes energy, water and food supplies, waste management, key transport networks (major airports and rail interchanges), financial institutions and cash supply, health services, and state emergency response organizations.
7. For companies to be members of CoESS implies that specific minimum levels of quality are met. By setting and applying such strict standards toward members, CoESS has been recognized by the European Commission as the official representative for the whole industry.
8. On this, see also Born et al. 2006.
9. See also Born et al. 2006.
10. Interviews with two senior CoESS representatives, Brussels, March 4–6, 2014.
11. Interviews with an EU official (DG Enterprise and Industry), Brussels, February 20, 2013; and with a senior CoESS representative, March 4, 2014, Brussels.
12. Interviews with two senior CoESS representatives, Brussels, March 4–6, 2014.
13. This was a full consultation aimed at collecting the views of different stakeholders regarding the EU industrial policy for the security industry. It was designed to help the Commission identify the best policies for overcoming the fragmentation of the European security market. In the case of CoESS, the response was provided by its Secretary-General, Hilde de Clerck.
14. While CoESS was not involved in drafting this statement, its representatives expressed support for its content (interviews with the author, March 4–6, 2014).

5

Between the Old and the New

Contemporary Dynamics of (In)Security in Eastern Europe

Efforts to internationalize and professionalize security provision, we now know, have had a powerful impact on East European polities. Yet, we should not conclude that they have been an unmitigated success. In many ways and in multiple arenas, what we are witnessing in each of the polities studied in this book is the coexistence of—and competition between—efforts to promote new, international norms and standards of security provision, and practices that either oppose or ignore those international standards, seeking to perpetuate old forms of capital and ways of acting in the field of security. The coexistence of those different logics of security provision is at the heart of the analysis developed in this chapter. The key aim here is to shed novel light on the interplay between domestic/international, public/private, old and new ways of thinking and acting in the evolving field of security, and in so doing to gain a better understanding of the ways in which "glocalization" actually occurs in specific national arenas.

There is a consensus among practitioners and experts in East European security provision that by the 2000s many PSCs in each of the countries examined in this book were seeking recognition as reliable, professional companies that had no connection to the abusive practices of the past, and could be trusted to provide Western standards of security to global companies as well as to national players with European or global aspirations.[1] Linked to that, PSCs started to seek more power and more systematic partnerships with public actors in their states. In that context, there has been a move by the largest PSCs, both global and national, to not only formulate a discourse stressing their professionalism, efficiency, and commitment to liberal-democratic values, but also to enact performances that represent those companies as actors that combine in the best possible ways the logics of action conventionally associated with two distinct realms: the public and the private. Thus, one can point to an effort on the part of those companies to cast themselves as players that resemble the state in terms of their commitment to the provision of the public good, but are even more efficient and reliable than public institutions by virtue of their superior technology, skills, and, in the case of global PSCs, internationally recognized expertise.

At the same time, similar to dynamics at the European level, in national arenas, too, PSCs have been engaged in systematic doxic battles with public authorities. Thus, while accepting the "doxic baseline" according to which the state retains a dominant position in security governance even as it is engaged in partnerships with private actors, PSCs have contested the interpretations of the limits of those partnerships as prescribed by public authorities in Eastern Europe. They have done so by invoking their superior material and non-material capital, and by drawing on the prevailing logic of market efficiency and security commodification to argue that the public good would be better served through their involvement in security governance and provision in ways that go beyond the limits currently set by public authorities.

At the national level, dominant PSCs—both individually and within the framework of their professional associations—have sought to push their governments to systematically include private security in consultations regarding security-related legislation and institutional reforms. They have also advocated for legislative change designed to define a clear division of labor between PSCs and public authorities, thereby transcending a situation of confusion and conflict of interest in which the police and other public agencies have the power to compete against or undermine the private security industry. In other words, PSCs have been engaged in campaigns to challenge what they perceive as the vestiges of the past: persisting attitudes and de facto rules of the game that prevent the private security industry from fully playing the role that it could play in the twenty-first century. In a similar vein, in recent years, one of the key efforts by PSCs across Eastern Europe has been to contest what they perceive as unfair criteria that govern public procurement. From their perspective, what is needed is a redefinition of principles governing public procurement, so as to move away from a predominant reliance on the lowest price and political connections, and to ensure that projects are granted on the basis of more appropriate criteria, including the quality of the security providers, their expertise, experience, and professionalism.

Against the background of reforms enacted in the context of European integration and growing insertion into global flows, campaigns for change can be interpreted as an effort on the part of the private security industry to put forward a new script, involving a view of (certain) PSCs as reliable, Western-style partners of the state. As actors that have no connection to the abusive practices of the early days of private security, the argument goes, professional PSCs are fully able and willing to contribute to the protection of the public, and, as such, deserve greater involvement in the performance of security functions. To support their script, PSCs have been involved in efforts to change old attitudes, and to cultivate a new habitus, structured around a collective perception of private security as a professional sector that is tied to the well-being of society, and deserves to be treated as such—rather than being seen as a shady sector linked to illegal violence. This campaign to change old perceptions and attitudes has often taken the form of persuasion campaigns targeting policymakers as well as broader efforts aimed at all players involved in security provision. A case in point has been the dissemination of "best practice" manuals and education seminars in which PSCs seek to change public thinking about the private security industry, and on this basis challenge existing models of public procurement.

Yet, we should not assume that legislative and institutional developments that occurred from the 2000s onwards—though important—were enough to eliminate all the vestiges of the early days of post-communist transitions. Instead, the implementation of the new legislation and the practices of PSCs, including global actors that are now prominent in the security field, have been shaped by complicated local dynamics, including the persistence of some old forms of capital which remain important at least in some areas of security provision. This complicated situation can be interpreted as signifying the emergence of competing logics of security provision—with pockets of resistance in the face of Europeanization, globalization, and the related professionalization of private integration in the European field of security.

The result is a dynamic, fluid, and complicated political economy of security provision, in which different types of actors cooperate but also compete, new alliances are forged while others are reconstituted or terminated, and competing logics of security provision coexist. Analyzing some of the main dynamics of those patterns of cooperation and competition is key if we are to understand the evolution of practices of security provision in contemporary Eastern Europe.[2]

Toward New Public–Private Partnerships in Security Provision

Similar to dynamics at the European level, in national areas, too, PSCs have been involved in systematic efforts to enhance their position in the field of security. In particular, they have been keen to push further the boundaries of public/private partnership defined by their national authorities, particularly by seeking recognition of their competence to participate in new areas of security governance and provision. As we noted in previous chapters, in the context of Europeanization and globalization, the private security industry in all the countries examined in this project was significantly affected by a number of legislative and institutional reforms aimed at constructing them as (partial) agents of public power. Consequently, they largely transcended the image of lawless, quasi-criminal entities that had been characteristic of the 1990s, and became legitimate partners of the state in the performance of various security functions—including those traditionally attributed to sovereign power. Yet, from the point of view of the private security industry, much more remains to be done by public authorities in Eastern Europe in recognizing the roles that PSCs can and should play in security governance and provision in the twenty-first century. Across Eastern Europe, in recent years leading representatives of the private security industry have been involved in systematic campaigns targeting public authorities with the aim of redrawing existing boundaries of public–private partnerships in the field of security. Thus, they have sought to not only perform (in the sense of carrying out) multiple security functions, but also to visibly display—and secure recognition for—skills and capabilities that, according to PSC discourses, justify their involvement in security governance and provision beyond the limits that still exist in their states.

Given the particular history of private security in each of those polities, campaigns to enhance the PSCs' positions in the contemporary field of security have involved efforts to distance themselves from the image of lawless, violent private security actors that were so powerful in the early years of post-communist transitions. Thus, as we have seen, in recent years East European PSCs have set up professional associations, integrated those organizations within the European Confederation of Security Services, and used them as platforms for enhancing the prestige of private security, disseminating an image of their industry as increasingly "clean" and "professional," and visibly taking steps to marginalize private security providers that engaged in illegal practices. In other words, similar to the role played by CoESS at the European level, these professional associations have acted as internal governance units in their national arenas. In that capacity, they have represented the private security industry in interactions with the public authorities, seeking to obtain more power and protections for PSCs. Simultaneously, the private security's professional associations have sought to protect companies affiliated with them—and, more broadly, the prestige of the industry—from challengers such as unregistered, illicit security companies. This, in a situation in which the behavior of illicit companies could potentially undermine the reputation of the entire sector, making it much harder for established PSCs to enhance their cooperation with public authorities in the provision and governance of security.

In the four countries studied in this book, in the context of processes of Europeanization and globalization, the prevailing strategy of many PSCs—be they global or national—has been to depict their skills and expertise as important forms of cultural capital in a context in which both public and private organizations require security providers that respect European standards of professionalism. Those skills, in combination with organizational resources and modern technologies (or material capital) that often surpass technologies available to state agencies, are presented as a guarantee that *select* PSCs can perform multiple security functions—ranging from physical security to surveillance and risk-analysis—required by globalized clients.

In seeking to enhance their position in the field of security, most PSCs have systematically cast themselves as agents of important economic players (local and global businesses), whose position is grounded in the principles of protection of private property—itself a vital ingredient to the functioning of that key institution in a liberal society, the market. In other words, PSCs have mobilized and invoked not only their own material and non-material capital, but also that of their powerful clients, which often tied their presence in those countries with their access to Western standards of security provision. This is particularly the case with respect to foreign banks, which, as noted above, have come to play dominant roles in the financial sector in all four East European countries. In Bulgaria as well as in Romania, Bosnia, and Serbia, the managers and owners of the leading PSCs have repeatedly stressed the link between their activities and the presence of Western banks and companies in their countries.[3]

The common theme stressed by representatives of the private security industry has been that only PSCs—especially those with internationally recognized experience and expertise—could be trusted to offer the know-how, technology, and, more broadly, professionalism needed for foreign financial institutions to operate in Eastern Europe. In interactions with government officials, the managers and owners of leading PSCs have repeatedly pointed out that their activities facilitated the continued presence in East European countries of the much-needed foreign banks, which represented a key ingredient in the economic well-being and the success of processes of liberalization of those countries. In the words of members of the management teams of Securitas in Serbia and Bosnia, political actors in those countries need to understand—and presumably do understand—that "there is no way that a serious foreign bank would operate in this part of the world if it had to rely on the police or local private companies for their security." Above and beyond questions of security per se, images of compliance with Western standards and norms were vital—and PSCs that could credibly be linked to such images became particularly valuable. Thus, foreign financial institutions "simply cannot afford to be seen by their shareholders as working in any shape or form with people or companies suspected of involvement in criminal activities, as many local PSCs are."[4] For PSCs, therefore, stressing—and displaying—their relationships to actors that contribute to economic growth became a key strategy in seeking to secure recognition for their capital—and thus also gain the authorities' support for the view that they deserved greater involvement in security governance and provision.

Indeed, one of the consistent, most striking images of foreign banks and most multinationals in Eastern Europe has been the visible presence of international PSCs—especially G4S and Securitas—on their premises. According to members of the management teams of banks like Raiffeisen Bank and Paribas, the presence of international PSCs was designed to not simply deter would-be criminals, but also to send a message of Western-style professionalism to their clients, and to the public at large. According to a foreign bank manager operating in Bucharest, "we want to be very clear that when you bank with us you can expect not just impeccable security for your money, but also the courtesy, expertise, professionalism of a Western financial institution."[5] In Serbia, meanwhile, a member of the management team of the Raiffeisen Bank pointed out that "when you bank here, you feel like a citizen of the Western world in every way: from security at the gate to Western-style etiquette in dealing with clients."[6] In a similar vein, in Bosnia the director of a Western bank that had hired Securitas was clear that his priority was to ensure that his clients knew their valuables were protected using the latest technology and proven expertise—not only at the bank but also during the transport of those valuables. In addition, however, the presence of Securitas on bank premises was meant to contribute to the image of a Western-style oasis—as a "world of normalcy" in the middle of "the messiness of political and economic life of Bosnia." In his words, "if you want to forget about Bosnia's problems, come and bank with us."[7] In essence, what was being performed in that context was not just the *de facto* protection but also the larger image of closeness to the West. As part of this, global PSCs were keen to not only effectively carry out functions of protection to their clients, but also to clearly display their ability to perform those functions in a manner consistent with Western standards of professionalism and norms of respect for human rights and the rule of law. In short, in addition to performing security, PSCs became involved in foreign banks' performance of Westernness in Eastern Europe.

To put this in a broader context, it is interesting to note that, in advocating more power and greater involvement in security governance in interactions with government officials from their countries, PSCs have also sought to draw legitimacy from broader transformations in the field of security.[8] Thus, they have used the social context marked by growing responsibilization of citizens and communities to cast themselves as actors that can offer a rational, efficient, and perfectly appropriate response to the increasing demands for security. In interactions with actual and potential clients—both private individuals/enterprises and public institutions—PSCs from all four countries have stressed that "you can't expect the police to do everything for you." Particularly in a situation in which "it is well known that the police lack modern technologies," "are often corrupt," and "don't really show much interest in the protection of private property," the only "safe option" for businesses is to "hire the real professionals," who "know what they are doing," have a "strong motivation," and—at least in the case of leading PSCs—"possess the modern technologies" needed to protect both national and international businesses.[9] It is also worth noting that, in the context of growing concerns about cyber attacks, some of the largest PSCs operating in Eastern Europe—both global and local—are even starting to develop cyber security capabilities. Not surprisingly, they are presenting this development as further evidence of their ability to respond effectively—based on their significant capital—to the multitude of security risks and challenges characteristic of the twenty-first century.[10]

For instance, in the case of Romania one of the most powerful voices in support of the private security industry has been the Federation of Security Services (Federatia Serviciilor de Securitate, hereafter FSS), a professional organization created in 2009 with the aim of promoting the interests of private security in interactions with public authorities, unions, and non-governmental organizations.[11] In a broader conceptual perspective, FSS can be seen as an internal governance unit in the field of security—similar to CoESS, but acting primarily in a national arena. FSS has represented the private security industry in interactions with the Romanian government, and has sought to protect established PSCs (the "incumbents," to use Fligstein and McAdam's language) from challengers such as non-registered, unlawful private security providers, whose behavior could undermine the reputation of the entire industry (Fligstein and McAdam 2012).

Since its creation, FSS has put forward a script according to which public authorities should involve the Federation, as the voice of legitimate private security providers, in a systematic fashion in the governance of security in Romania. The notion involved here is that the PSCs represented by the Federation have the kinds of material and non-material capital (skills, experience, expertise, and commitment to professionalism) that would be particularly valuable to public authorities as they seek to respond to a multitude of security needs in the context of budgetary constraints.[12] The private security industry, FSS stresses, has demonstrated that they can effectively perform key functions of protection in collaboration with public authorities—for instance, by helping them maintain public order and apprehending burglars that were subsequently surrendered to the police.

Once again, the performance of security in this case involves not simply carrying out functions of protection of the public, but also doing—and being seen as doing—so in a manner consistent with liberal-democratic norms of accountability and respect for the rule of law and human rights that are regarded as the foundation of EU member states. In the words of the FSS President, Gabriel Badea, "Today, the private security industry makes a decisive contribution to the protection of public and private property as well as the maintenance of public safety and domestic order. For instance, in 2014 alone PSCs responded to 16,734 attempted burglaries; of those, in 13,097 cases they were able to apprehend the burglars" (Badea 2015). To PSCs, this is important because it replaces the image of lawless private security actors associated with the early years of post-communism with images of efficient, modern, reliable providers of protection.[13]

The discourse articulated by FSS does not challenge the primacy of the state in the field of security. What it does, however, is suggest that, in the contemporary context marked by a complex security environment and limited resources, public authorities need to rely systematically on private security if they are to fulfill their function of providing this key public good. According to the discourse articulated by FSS, PSCs are particularly well suited for responding to security needs of a risk-management society: through their presence, they deter crime, thereby saving public resources that would otherwise have to be spent on the apprehension and punishment of criminals. This is particularly important in societies in which criminals (or potential criminals) are aware of the weaknesses and budgetary constraints of public authorities, and might therefore be tempted to commit crimes. In addition, in contrast to members of the police forces, who are often steeped in old ways of thinking and trapped in a slow, inefficient bureaucratic system, private security professionals are "trained to think ahead and minimize risk." The focus for the representatives of the private security industry has been on disseminating the image of PSCs that are professionally run and affiliated with professional associations as good liberal actors that respect human rights and the rule of law, protect communities from a variety of risks and threats, and do so in a market-efficient manner. Linked to this, PSCs are depicted as often possessing better technologies and being "more flexible than the state," which means that they can anticipate and if necessary respond to a multitude of security risks and challenges—ranging from crimes against private property to risks to public order—more efficiently than the state.[14]

The FSS ideas concerning the professionalism of the private security industry and their ability to contribute to the protection of society are echoed in statements put forward by leading PSCs. The dominant images put forward by companies like G4S, Securitas, and leading Romanian PSCs like BGS depict companies with strong national and international credentials, possessing the professional training, expertise, and experience to address multiple security needs. The companies, we are told, are adaptable to a variety of circumstances and possess the modern technologies that put them ahead of their competitors—including public agencies—when it comes to the ability to provide efficient security solutions. Their professionalism, as depicted in the PSCs' discourses, includes not just technical skills but also a commitment to work in full compliance with the principles and values of a modern liberal democracy: they are scrupulous in respecting existing legislation governing PSCs, would never—and do not need to—use inappropriate force, and only act on the basis of consultation with the clients.[15] G4S, for instance, stresses that: "As a leading security company, we are permanently focused on providing very high standards of security," and ensuring that "we constantly diversify the services that we offer, so as to provide the perfect solutions to our clients." On the basis of "the substantial expertise that we have accumulated in logistics, technology, and the management of services, as well as our experience in the management of the largest number of employees in the security sector, we create solutions for reducing various risks."[16] Consequently, "G4S plays an important role in society, helping state institutions to meet the expectations of citizens and providing them with concrete advantages, within strict budgetary limits."[17]

In a similar vein, BGS, the most important Romanian PSC, has articulated a discourse that stresses its ability—on the basis of its substantial material and non-material capabilities—to play a particularly important role in protecting not just private clients but society as a whole. Highlighting the role played by their company in supporting the police (in 2014 alone BGS apprehended and surrendered to the police more than 1,400 alleged burglars), BGS representatives repeatedly stressed that from their point of view the company is "a leader when it comes to the provision of security services, set apart from our competitors by our professionalism, modern equipment and ability to react quickly and effectively in response to incidents."[18]

Similar efforts by the private security industry to enhance its position in the field of security can be found in Bulgaria. Thus, since the early 2000s, NAFTSO, the Bulgarian association of the private security industry, has systematically invoked the material capital (especially modern technologies of security provision) and cultural capital (specialized knowledge, professional skills, experience) of the private security industry in an effort to enhance its symbolic capital. Thus, NAFTSO has sought to secure public recognition of the PSCs it represents as privileged partners of the state in the provision of protection to public and private actors. PSCs, according to the NAFTSO discourse, are actors that can fill the gaps left by limited state resources.[19] According to NAFTSO representatives, security and risk-management are key aspects of contemporary society, and "only an effective public–private partnership can address all sources of risk to private individuals/businesses as well as society as a whole" (NAFTSO 2011). On the basis of its superior technologies, skills, and experience—including, in the case of global PSCs—internationally gained and recognized expertise, PSCs can help public authorities ensure public order, deter crime, monitor criminals, and respond to incidents, and, in so doing, they help to create a safer environment for individuals and businesses residing in Bulgaria. Importantly, the PSCs are also depicted as useful in gaining intelligence about criminal organizations—particularly in towns and villages outside the capital, Sofia, where the police often find it difficult to obtain useful information about criminal networks due to limited knowledge and inadequate material capabilities.[20]

This vision of the merits of private security is also echoed in the individual discourses of leading PSCs operating in Bulgaria. For instance, a key theme stressed in G4S's discourse has been that of an experienced company with a strong global reputation, superior technology, and skills. This is combined with the idea of local knowledge thanks to the Bulgarian members of the management team of the company's branch operating in Sofia. On the basis of that combination, G4S representatives insist, their company can effectively perform functions of protection in a manner that is consistent with Western norms of respect for the human rights of both its employees and the public at large, the rule of law, and norms of accountability. According to a senior member of G4S's management team, "our clients know that with us they are getting not only top-of-line technology and the best experts, but also the confidence that the company will never stoop to some of the tactics of other PSCs."[21]

In Serbia, too, the professionalization of the private security industry has translated into efforts to enhance sector-wide organization and cooperation (Petrović and Milošević 2015). Thus, as noted in Chapter 3, in 2005 Serbia's PSCs established the Private Security Association within the Serbian Chamber of Commerce, and also set up the National Commission of Private Security Companies (NCPSC), which is an Associated Member of CoESS. Professionally organized members of the private security industry have advocated for wideranging regulation of the sector, and have been keen to be recognized as legitimate organizations, different from the private security entities with links to criminal organizations—and thus worthy of inclusion in the Serbian structures of security governance and provision, in partnership with public authorities. In particular, NCPSC has sought CoESS's support in learning the role of a Western-style security provider. This has involved, in particular, seeking guidance on how to develop and implement techniques for collaborating with national authorities, and on the kinds of provisions that should be included in legislation governing the private security industry. Simultaneously, NCPSC has invoked its affiliation with CoESS to cast itself as an actor that has the support of international private security forums—and has access to globally defined best practices in the security sector.[22] On this logic, by virtue of its international support and credentials, and as a reflection of the expertise and skills it embodies, the private security industry represented by NCPSC can effectively perform functions of protection in a manner that respects liberal-democratic norms of accountability and the rule of law. In other words, according to this script the private security providers can play a powerful role in providing security within Serbia and, more broadly, helping to bring the country closer to European standards—and thus helping to prepare it for greater integration within Europe by aiding in the reform of a key sector: security. In the words of an NCPSC representative, "it is impossible for the police, with all the problems that it is facing, to do everything that Serbia's citizens and businesses expect of it." Also, "as Serbia wants to move closer to Europe, it must find ways to ensure a safe environment for all who work and live here. This is where private security comes in: we can make a difference by providing reliable, efficient solutions to address many risks and challenges—just like PSCs do in all the Western countries."[23]

Acting through its professional associations—but also via individual efforts, particularly on the part of G4S and Securitas, the Serbian private security industry has advocated greater involvement of legitimate PSCs in the governance and provision of security. As noted in Chapter 3, Serbia was a latecomer in the area of legislative reforms concerning private security. In that context, representatives of the security industry were at the forefront of efforts to lobby the government for comprehensive legislation in their sector, aimed at formalizing the role of PSCs, clarifying their relationships to public authorities, and delegitimizing private security providers that engage in criminal activities. Following the adoption of the 2013 law, the private security industry has continued to push for greater regulation of their sector through the adoption of secondary legislation which would clarify aspects that were left unaddressed by the 2013 law. Throughout its campaign for enhanced recognition of the role of PSCs, representatives of the Private Security Association, as well as directors and managers of leading companies, particularly G4S and Securitas, have systematically depicted the private security industry as a reliable partner, able to fill the gaps in public security provision generated by Serbia's poor economic situation. Furthermore, by stressing their international experience and expertise, companies like G4S and Securitas have consistently cast themselves as companies that represent Western, liberal-democratic values and norms—and can therefore help to improve the situation and image of Serbia by contributing to the dissemination of those norms in the field of security. According to a member of Securitas's managerial team, for instance, "Our core values are integrity, vigilance and helpfulness. We are ready to lend assistance to all our employees, customers, and surrounding community. All employees within Securitas are honorable, honest, and sincere and that's why we have fully trust in them. Securitas Services never makes compromises about integrity" (sic).[24]

In a similar vein, G4S has portrayed itself as "a leading national security provider. Utilizing the know-how of the parent company in combination with the business philosophy, G4S Secure Solutions Serbia established itself on the Serbian security service market as a trustworthy partner that supplies excellent quality security services. Our customers are banks and companies, industry as well as retail, public institutions or private households."[25] It is because of the company's reputation for efficiency, accountability, and commitment to the rule of law and the well-being of the community that key institutions as well as private individuals "entrust their personal or their assets' security to us."[26] This view is echoed in statements issued by leading voices of foreign investors in Serbia, which have portrayed the presence of global PSCs and CoESS as a very positive development, based on the assumption that those actors can—and will—push national authorities to harmonize laws and practices with the European environment by using their "long-standing expertise and credibility." This, in turn, would help to ensure that Serbia moves closer to the EU, and ensures a safe and stable business environment in which international companies can prosper.[27] Furthermore, a series of Serbian PSCs have sought to attract foreign clients (and Serbian companies that work with foreigners) by casting themselves as performing roles that are similar—at least in terms of their professionalism—to global private security providers. In the words of a director of a Serbian PSC, "our company may not have the budget and technology of a global PSC, but we are pretty equal to them in terms of our skills and commitment to our clients. Our staff is professional, well trained and able to protect our clients and their valuables in an efficient manner."[28]

In Bosnia, efforts to organize the private security sector have continued to be hampered by the complicated political and administrative structures which, as discussed in Chapter 3, have also affected the field of security. There has long been a push by PSCs to establish a professional association to defend the interests of the industry and also respond to a need for a public good—acting as a pillar of the national security system and thus minimizing some of the problems faced by public authorities at a time of financial constraints. The problem, however, has been that the interests of PSC owners are still too divergent; some want such an association to establish better standards and defend the interests of their members, but not everyone agrees. Indeed, Bosnian security experts and journalists have argued that some PSCs, especially those with a dubious past, are doing all they can to thwart moves toward greater organization/centralization of this sector because they perceive that as a threat to their practices.[29] This situation constitutes a potent reminder of the diversity and multiple tensions that persist in the field of security, and of the fact that, in this complex field, private security actors play various roles, on both the licit and the illicit sides.

Even in the absence of a systematic campaign by a professional association representing the private security industry, however, there have been efforts by individual PSCs—particularly Securitas, as a leading player in the field—to advocate greater involvement of private security not only in the protection of individual businesses and individuals but also in the protection of the public good. Securitas's management team has repeatedly stressed that their company can play a key role in bringing Bosnia's security sector closer to that of its West European counterparts by promoting efficient solutions to a multitude of challenges/threats and risks, and ensuring that those solutions are consistent with the rule of law and principles of accountability that are vital to a democratic society. In the words of a senior member of the management team, "as a leader in the field, Securitas can help to define the rules of the game in security provision, taking Bosnia away from all the abuses that took place during and immediately after the war."

In other words, here again a PSC portrayed itself as not only involved in the provision of security, but performing a broader role in the (re)constitution of Bosnia on modern, liberal-democratic bases. Linked to this, Securitas can help to "clean up" the private security industry, by providing standards/best practice that other companies have to follow if they want to be competitive in a market dominated by international clients (IOs, international banks, international retail, all of which require international security standards of professionalism). Already, Securitas has helped to professionalize the field by teaching other players "ethical standards and rules," as well as specific procedures and technologies that can be applied in response to specific threats or risks. For this reason, Securitas is already working with public agencies, but much more could be done in the future.[30]

The ideas put forward in PSCs' statements are reinforced in the visual representations disseminated especially via the websites of private security providers. The websites of leading PSCs and their associations—in Romania, Bulgaria, Serbia, and Bosnia—use various "stage props" to represent PSCs as actors that combine state-like properties of order, clear organizational structure, and commitment to the public good with market-based efficiency and competitiveness. Thus, the images being put forward through the statements and visual displays of PSCs represent private security providers as players that are similar—and an invaluable aid—to the state in terms of their functions. An analysis of the websites of the main international PSCs (G4S and Securitas) as well as leading national companies in Bulgaria, Bosnia, Romania, and Serbia reveals a series of common images: smiling PSCs wearing well-designed uniforms are pictured next to new cars and expensive technologies of surveillance and control (e.g. CCTV cameras, or security equipment used at airports) as well as high-tech communication equipment.[31] Next to images that one might conventionally associate with private security provision (e.g. private firms and public institutions being guarded by PSCs) we also find images of private security employees looking after groups of children or directing crowds at large events, as well as providing relief from natural disasters like floods or fires. Images designed to convey an ethic of care—involving the commitment of private security actors to the well-being of the communities in which they operate—are thus dominant in PSC staging of their roles in society.

The more coercive pictures—such as a display of weapons—while still present in the images disseminated by PSCs from all four countries, are far less numerous or prominent than depictions of benign involvement in the well-being of communities. Those images seem designed to reassure clients that, if need be, PSCs are still able and willing to resort to coercive techniques. Nevertheless, it is clear, in all these representations, that the use of weapons is not the private security's preferred course of action. In essence, the message conveyed by those images is that today's PSCs are far from resembling, in any way, the shady, criminal entities that private security had been associated with in the early 1990s. Instead, they are modern, reliable organizations that can perform most of the functions that the police and other public agencies deliver—and often do so in a more efficient manner. Carefully excluded from the visual representations disseminated by the private security industry are pictures that might raise questions about the professionalism of PSCs. For instance, there are no depictions of PSC employees engaging in what might be seen as abusive behavior (e.g. using physical violence to restrain suspected burglars or individuals seen as potential risks to their clients). In a similar vein, images disseminated by the private security industry carefully exclude pictures of PSC employees relying on old, possibly inadequate technologies to perform their functions. Yet, this situation continues to affect some members of the private security industry—particularly lower-ranking employees of local PSCs, whose equipment is far more rudimentary than images displayed on the PSCs' websites would suggest.[32]

As part of its strategy to cast itself as a type of actor that can perform state-like functions, the private security industry has stressed the idea that it can integrate its security functions with other functions of good governance, providing a joined-up approach to local governance. In contrast with the first years of post-communism, when private providers were involved in limited (and, as we have seen, often problematic) security practices, in more recent years there has been a shift to a representation of PSCs as actors that can perform a variety of functions of governance going far beyond a narrow vision of security. What is involved here is a complex process of growing participation of those companies in everyday practices of management and surveillance of the population, often in situations in which state agencies are unwilling or unable (due to limited resources) to intervene. The message is clear: in an era of liberalization and budgetary constraints, collaboration between public authorities and private security providers enables the state to perform important functions of governance in an effective, market-like manner. Take, for instance, representations of the roles of those firms in providing protection during major cultural and sporting events. Thus, exhibitions, musical and film festivals, rock concerts, and soccer games are increasingly protected by global security players such as G4S, Securitas, and a few leading domestic companies from Bulgaria, Romania, Bosnia, and Serbia.

In describing their involvement in the protection of public events, PSCs portray themselves as not simply expert security providers but also effective participants in a broader process of population management. For instance, G4S and Securitas discourses cast the companies as actors that, through their management skills and commitment to the well-being of the public, effectively deal with problems such as accessibility to cultural/sporting events for disabled individuals, and the well-being of children and other vulnerable individuals before, during, and after the event.[33] More broadly, through their online images, PSCs are depicted as actors that look after children (by protecting their schools and looking after them during large-scale public events), provide emergency medical assistance (through a fleet of private ambulances that are more modern, better equipped than public ambulances), and offer support to the population during emergencies (e.g. helping to evacuate people in areas affected by flooding).

That ostensible commitment to an ethic of care is not reduced to the provision of security during isolated events. As noted above, particularly since the mid-2000s, security companies in Bulgaria, Serbia, Bosnia, and Romania have become involved in complex practices of management and surveillance of the population on sites where they provide protection, be they government property or private venues. In those sites—ranging from government offices to shopping malls, banks, and ports—what seems to be involved is the emergence of "bubbles of governance" in which people are constantly monitored and classified into different categories of "risk," to be subject to very different kinds of treatment.[34] While state police agencies, facing limited resources and personnel, are unable to provide constant monitoring of (potentially) vulnerable sites, private security companies have stepped in to offer constant monitoring as well as a host of services designed to facilitate the management of crowds in busy offices or stores. Their involvement is generally characterized by a continuous presence, an infrequent recourse to physical coercion, and often a degree of involvement in the operation of the businesses they protect in ways that are uncharacteristic of contemporary police practices (for instance, by helping shopkeepers to look after clients during busy times).

The involvement of PSCs in practices that follow a logic of care has reportedly played an important role in enhancing the prestige of those companies in the eyes of their employees—at least at the level of managerial teams. While a comprehensive study of employees from all security companies operating in the four countries examined here is well beyond the scope of this work, interviews with some thirty members of PSC managerial teams (mostly managers and deputy managers) across Romania, Bulgaria, Serbia, and Bosnia suggest that some version of developments that take place in the UK and Sweden is also occurring in Eastern Europe (Löfstrand et al. 2016). According to a recent study conducted by criminologists in the UK and Sweden, although the private security industry can now be seen as an increasingly dominant aspect of modern societies, it continues to be an industry that is also systematically affected by insecurities about status (Löfstrand et al. 2016: 298). This occurs in a situation in which, while the industry is "expanding in its scope and enjoying a measure of acceptance, it continues to be dogged by reputational problems" (Löfstrand et al. 2016: 298). Under these circumstances, Löfstrand et al. argue, PSC employees develop a range of strategies to construct a positive reframing of their work as important. More broadly, they share an occupational culture built upon shared norms that enhance occupational self-esteem by infusing their work with meaningfulness. In the East European polities studied in this book, the routine performances of protecting not only private clients but also public spaces and communities seem to play an important role in enabling at least the top echelons of private security employees to find meaning and take pride in their work. This is particularly interesting in a situation in which, as we have seen, the private security industry had a problematic start in those countries, and in which PSCs continue to be adversely affected by limited and imperfect regulations, and in some instances an uncertain future.

In a broader perspective, those reports of the quest for meaning reveal that performances are important not only because of the effects they have on audiences, but also by virtue of the ways in which they affect those that enact them. We noted in previous chapters that participation in CoESS has provided senior representatives of the private security industry—e.g. PSC directors and managers—with a community of European security professionals with whom they could identify, and from whom they could learn the roles of modern security providers. To borrow Fligstein and McAdam's terminology, CoESS has acted as an internal governance unit, seeking to stabilize the field of security by helping to construct a new identity as members of the European community of security providers, united around a particular set of norms and ways of thinking about the world. For their part—in a move that reveals the importance and power of identity-building practices—in several instances representatives of PSCs operating in the former Eastern bloc invoked their membership in the community of European professionals to strengthen their positions in their national arenas. In parallel to this, daily performances of security provision have enhanced the sense of membership in a community that performs a useful, important role in society. What seems to be involved here is a new form of "imagined communities" constituted through security performances.[35] Thus, the sense of purpose derived from their membership in a community of professionals performing useful, ethical work was a common theme in the descriptions of their work provided by members of PSC managerial teams in Bosnia, Serbia, Bulgaria, and Romania. Frequent depictions of that work were: "I know I'm doing something good"; "it matters to me that my company [Securitas] would never do some of the [criminal] stuff that other so-called security companies do. We are not like that." In a similar vein, "people know that we're there to help. Often, they come to us rather than call the police when they see something suspicious." The theme of being similar to—but better than—the police was also present in statements like: "often, the police are not fast enough to stop a crime. If it wasn't for us, there would be many more burglaries and acts of vandalism. We help to prevent a lot of ugly stuff, and that matters to me." And, "we've come to be respected. When people see our [G4S] uniform, they know they're dealing with professionals."[36] This is certainly not to suggest that PSC employees regard their work or community of security providers as perfect. In fact, they often complain about job prospects and persistent problems concerning the regulation of the private security industry. Despite all those problems, a key theme that emerges in their depictions of the work they do is that it matters to them to know that they are helping people and communities. There is a common sense that, in the absence of that sense of purpose, working for a PSC would be just thankless.

PSCs' Campaigns to Contest "the Rules of the Game" in the Twenty-First Century

We noted in Chapter 4 that, at the European level, PSCs cooperate with public authorities, but also contest some of the rules of the game established by those authorities. Similar combinations of cooperation and contestation can be found in the national arenas of each of the East European countries examined in this book. In other words, doxic contestations occur not only in EU circles but also in practices enacted in individual states. From the perspective of the private security industry, the problem with the existing status of PSCs is that of a persisting discrepancy between what they can achieve and limits upon their activities still imposed by national authorities. Indeed, similar to practices at the European level, in national arenas—both through their professional associations and in individual statements and practices—representatives of leading private security companies have contested and have sought to delegitimize and transform what they perceive as unfair constraints upon their activities, and have put forward scripts that involve greater participations of PSCs in practices of security governance and provision. In support of their campaigns, they have mobilized their material and especially non-material capital (expertise, experience, specialized skills) to cast themselves, and secure recognition by public authorities, as authoritative sources of knowledge on the problems characteristic of the field of security in the twenty-first century and effective solutions to those problems. Furthermore, they have invoked their links to international forums, particularly CoESS, as a way of accessing some of the cultural and symbolic capital enjoyed by that institution. Thus, they have cast themselves as actors that can be trusted because they are in sync with—indeed, are part of—a larger professional organization, which is internationally respected and recognized as a source/repository of knowledge/best practice in security provision. Campaigns to effect further change in the field of security have focused on both improving the implementation of existing legislation and the promotion of further legislative and institutional changes.

In Romania, for instance, FSS has systematically lobbied for greater inclusion of representatives of PSCs in the governance of the field of security (Badea 2013, 2014, 2015). One of its key priorities has been to secure greater recognition by the public authorities that the private security industry constitutes a source of authoritative knowledge about the ways in which security institutions and practices need to be (re)constituted in order to address the challenges of the twenty-first century. The FSS discourse revolves around the argument that significant progress was made through the legislation enacted in the 2000s, leading to a situation in which the private security industry is now involved in partnerships with the police and other public agencies. This includes consultations, within the framework of a working group with the Ministry of Interior—on the modification of legislation governing the private security industry. Nevertheless, much more remains to be done for those partnerships to achieve their potential. The problem, from the Federation's perspective, is that there is little *de facto* consultation within working groups with public authorities, primarily because the police and other state agencies retain old attitudes of mistrust and condescendence vis-à-vis private security providers.[37] As a consequence, public authorities have failed to consult with representatives of the private security industry on legislative modifications that would not only have facilitated the activities of legitimate PSCs, but also have benefited the state by allowing private security to partner with the police in providing efficient security solutions to a multitude of risks/security challenges.

Under these circumstance, FSS has argued for a substantial change of one of the key pieces of legislation that governs private security; a case in point being the campaign to modify law HG 301/2012. According to the FSS President, Gabriel Badea, the problem with this law is that it contains a series of provisions that would unfairly increase the administrative and bureaucratic burden on the private security sector (Badea 2015). In turn, this would have adverse socio-economic effects, preventing PSCs from fulfilling one of their key mandates: to prevent and stop crimes. In an effort to address what it had identified as key problems, FSS proposed a series of modifications to that piece of legislation and, having failed to achieve the desired outcome in interactions with the Ministry of Interior, also stepped in at the stage when the law became the subject of public debates, seeking to persuade a larger number of actors of the merits of those revisions (Badea 2015). In addition, building on their collaboration with the Romanian Police, FSS has formulated a draft protocol of collaboration with the Gendarmerie.

In advocating a fuller implementation via systematic consultation of the project of collaboration with the police, and the adoption of the protocol of cooperation with the Gendarmerie (Jandarmeria Romana), FSS has presented this initiative—and, more broadly, institutional arrangements designed to foster a systematic collaboration between public security agencies and PSCs—as a type of arrangement that was normal, indeed necessary in a modern liberal democracy. From this perspective, to oppose or fail to fully implement such an arrangement would be to fail to conform to the prevailing norms of the community with which Romania (like other East European polities) identified: the European Union. To achieve this effect, FSS has sought to enhance its capital by representing its position as similar to that adopted in established EU countries. The notion invoked here is that the changes advocated by FSS represent not simply the position of a Romanian organization of private security providers, but also the position accepted as rational and efficient by actors with a great deal of experience, expertise, and prestige in the provision of security in a modern liberal democracy. In particular, FSS has invoked the examples of the UK and Italy, depicting them as countries where such types of collaboration are an everyday phenomenon, to the benefit of all involved—including the public, which stands to receive better quality services at competitive prices (Badea 2013, 2015).

In a similar vein, the Bulgarian NAFTSO has led a long, sustained campaign to enhance the position of private security in Bulgaria, contesting and seeking to delegitimize the limits and obstacles created by the government. A concise expression of the ideas articulated in interactions with public authorities can be found—among others—in the 2011 *Appeal on the Occasion of the 10th Anniversary of NAFTSO*. In that appeal, NAFTSO starts by expressing the satisfaction of its members with the fact that, ten years following its establishment, NAFTSO has gained public recognition, "and is acknowledged as a leading representative employers organization in the private security industry at both national and European level" and as an organization "that strives for an active participation in the implementation of the European private security services model in the Republic of Bulgaria, and an efficient protection of sound private security service providers' legal interests" (NAFTSO 2011). Yet, NAFTSO points out that public recognition has not translated into a fully functional partnership between public and private security providers—and that is an unacceptable situation, particularly in a situation in which Bulgarian society is facing a complex set of "security and risk management issues," which are "gaining an even faster pace in our society and the private sector—and an even more important factor in securing the peace and quiet of Bulgarian and foreign physical and legal persons, and of their assets on the territory of the country." Under these circumstances, "public–private partnership, collaboration and constructive dialogue are a significant prerequisite for the development of effective private industrial security services to the best interest of society and for the prevention of criminal encroachments and attempts at terrorism" (NAFTSO 2011).

Instead of enabling the private security industry to fully perform that role, however, the Bulgarian government is accused by NAFTSO of creating unjustified obstacles, particularly in the aftermath of the financial crisis. Thus, in the *Appeal* NAFTSO expresses "its dissatisfaction and concern regarding private security services market status, associated with underestimating the private industry, late payments from public institutions, poor service quality and low professional level at work, enlargement of the 'grey service' and unregulated operations, vicious public procurement tenders and unfair competition, and lack of a more favourable business environment for the sound security service providers to deal with the state, contractors and company employees" (NAFTSO 2011). Similar to the Romanian case, NAFTSO has tried to enhance its symbolic capital by stressing the similarity between its position and the views held by prestigious actors, with widely recognized expertise and experience in the area of security provision. In particular, NAFTSO has repeatedly stressed that its position is supported by CoESS, and similar to practices adopted in established EU states.[38] From NAFTSO's perspective, all the practices that keep Bulgaria far behind other EU member states in the area of security-related public/private partnerships need to end. If the government is serious about providing security in a manner that is efficient, rational, and consistent with its liberal commitments to protect the market economy, legitimate private security providers need to be freed from unnecessary bureaucratic constraints, and empowered to cooperate with the state as they do in countries like the UK.

Meanwhile, in Serbia, representatives of the private security industry have consistently criticized the government for holding a contradictory position in the field of private security. Thus, because the government is a massive user of private security, it encourages the lowest bid in public procurement—often accepting unrealistically low rates (Petrović and Milošević 2015: 94). As stated in a report issued by the Private Security Association in the Serbian Chamber of Commerce, "the cost of labour in the provision of security services on the Serbian market is the lowest in comparison with 34 European countries, which for employers in the field represents a risk of bankruptcy, lack of employee motivation, low quality services and increased vulnerability for protected facilities" (Petrović and Milošević 2015: 94). Public sector personnel responsible for awarding contracts usually lack the expertise that would enable them to assess the quality of the services required, and contracts are often granted regardless of the expertise and capabilities of the winning company (Petrović and Milošević 2015: 92). Not surprisingly, this often results in poor-quality security provision—even in vital areas, such as the protection of critical infrastructure. According to representatives of the private security industry, such an outcome is inconsistent with the basic function of the government to provide high-quality security and also to ensure that its citizens pay taxes. For instance, representatives of the National Commission of Private Security Companies (NCPSCs) have insisted that, in order to address this abnormal situation, it is incumbent upon the government to introduce the necessary by-laws to clarify the recent Law on Private Security, ensuring equal treatment for all players in the field of security, protecting legitimate security providers from entities/individuals with links to the gray economy, and harmonizing its legal framework with European models of legislation so as to avoid conflicts of interest or a monopolization of the security sector by illegitimate players. Furthermore, from NCPSC's perspective, the government must encourage closer cooperation between security sector stakeholders (public and private), while also consulting systematically with professional PSCs, which can present and use their experience and best practices from other European states in which they operate.[39] As in other East European countries, the security industry's strategy has been to seek to enhance its capital in contesting government policies/practices by stressing that its arguments represent not just the views of Serbian private security providers, but are also accepted by international security experts including CoESS, which has repeatedly expressed concern about the legal situation of PSCs in Serbia.[40]

As regards Bosnia, as noted above, in the absence of a strong professional association to unite PSCs from across Bosnia and Herzegovina, individual PSCs, particularly Securitas (as the key international security firm present in the country), have played key roles in efforts to contest those limits and push for further change. Securitas representatives have reportedly forged informal alliances with—and have been supported by—international actors (especially officials from the EU and NATO, who are keen to see a further professionalization of private security), pro-reform Bosnian security experts, as well as individual politicians (especially in the Federation), who share the view that this sector is in need of further reform.[41] In particular, their concern is to enable legitimate private security providers to act systematically, within a clearly established legal framework, as partners of public authorities in order to compensate for the latter's limited resources and render Bosnia safe for its citizens and businesses.

In this context, Securitas representatives have invoked the company's cultural and symbolic capital—its skills, expertise, and international recognition—as an effective security provider in countries around the world. The aim in that context was to secure the public authorities' recognition that in Bosnia, too, it could be trusted to act as an authoritative source of knowledge about problems concerning private security, and potential solutions to those problems. From this perspective, one of the key problems in Bosnia is the persisting autonomy of cantons, which has resulted in a continued power struggle and lack of administrative coordination. Thus, each canton has its own administrative structure and is keen to keep it that way, so any effort at centralization—even within the Federation, not to mention Republika Srpska—is very difficult. PSCs, like other companies, need to register in every canton if they wish to operate throughout the Federation, which is an administrative nightmare. Also, different cantons have different laws with respect to the way in which firearms can be used and owned, and this means that a PSC transporting values from one canton to the other risks committing an offence simply because it has not adapted its behavior (regarding the use and possession of firearms, for instance) as soon as it has crossed the canton boundary. Only through greater efforts at coordination and harmonization across Bosnia can this problem be transcended and PSCs—like other companies—be in a better position to act more effectively. This, it is argued, would clearly benefit private citizens/businesses that would be better able to transport valuables across the country, and, indeed, would be an advantage to society as a whole (through the creation of a climate of greater safety).

According to Securitas's discourse, even leaving aside legal and administrative problems/inadequacies, there is the persisting problem of corruption affecting the way in which public authorities cooperate (or fail to do so) with PSCs. Consequently, the public sector is not as open to PSCs as it should be. In part, this is due to the fact that old mentalities persist, and large state companies (like Telecom, utility companies, etc.) do not want to fire their own, internal security departments in order to outsource security to companies like Securitas. This results not only in fewer opportunities for PSCs, but also in poor-quality security for those public companies (and the public that depends on them), as the "in-house" security arrangements are often built upon personal connections, not the expertise or capabilities of the security providers. Securitas has tried to delegitimize this state of affairs by portraying it as inconsistent with Bosnia's official narrative of its political trajectory—specifically, its self-declared goal of modernizing and moving toward closer partnership with (and eventually integration in) the EU. From this perspective, old mentalities need to be transcended and a genuine form of competition in the area of security provision for public companies needs to be set up in order to facilitate more efficient and reliable security provision by companies that have the right material and non-material capital.

Efforts to enhance the position of PSCs in the evolving field of security have also involved a sustained campaign to change the prevailing logic of public procurement in Eastern Europe. We noted, in Chapter 4, that following the adoption of the 2014 Directive, key decisions were left in the hands of national authorities. It will be recalled that the European Directive 24/2014 regarding public procurement stipulates that the criteria that should guide the acquisition of goods and services destined for the public must include not simply the lowest cost, but also considerations of the relationship between price and quality. Nevertheless, the Directive leaves national authorities significant room to maneuver in terms of deciding how to assess that relationship. This has translated into a series of campaigns at the national levels across Eastern Europe, in an effort to ensure an immediate, effective implementation of that Directive. In all East European polities examined in this project, the private security industry has lobbied for an immediate move away from the current practice of relying on the lowest price as the key driver of public procurements. Reforming that practice has been presented as a vital aspect in the process of protecting legitimate private security providers, excluding from the field of security individuals and companies with links to the gray economy and/or organized crime, and fostering a sustainable, profitable partnership between public/private actors. In each of the East European states, the aim of the campaign has been to reconstruct common-sense understandings of what counts as valuable private security provision by delegitimizing prevailing definitions that focus almost exclusively on the lowest price.

What is involved in that context can be understood as an effort to construct a new "habitus" in the field of security. Thus, the professional associations of the security industry from Bulgaria, Romania, and Serbia as well as representatives of Securitas in Bosnia have all confirmed that what they seek is to help bring about a situation where everyone—public authorities, PSCs, and their clients—take it for granted that the lowest price cannot and should not be the only criterion for selecting a security provider.[42] As Gabriel Badea, FSS President, explained: "It is important for us [FSS] that the European Directive 24/2014 be adopted as soon as possible, because it is a well-known fact that in the private security industry services are purchased—via auctions—at the lowest prices, and this leads to a whole set of detrimental effects" (Badea 2015, author's translation). As leading voices of the private security industry across Eastern Europe have repeatedly stressed, an exclusive focus on low cost as the most important criterion is counterproductive and, indeed, dangerous. Thus, its application fosters inadequate security practices which could render society unsafe (for instance, through the inadequate protection of critical infrastructure), empowers the gray economy, and potentially allows private security providers with links to criminal networks to proliferate. In other words, this definition encourages dynamics that take those countries away from the liberal-democratic path to which they were officially committed. What is involved here, in essence, is an effort by the private security associations to delegitimize their governments' definition of an appropriate or reasonable mode of providing a key public good. The PSCs' associations insist that this definition represents a flawed interpretation of what liberalism means and requires in the twenty-first century. Even in the age of security commercialization, the argument goes, public good provision requires that other criteria be taken into account in order to establish reliable, effective, and appropriate security provision arrangements. Ironically, then, PSCs have performed their roles as agents of public power by contesting governmental definitions of security commercialization, and insisting—in the name of the public good— that there are limits to the process of commodification of security. As a corollary to this, they have argued, it would be a mistake to base decisions concerning the protection of citizens and their property simply on the lowest cost. What is particularly interesting about this situation is that it problematizes the views of those who see PSCs as just contrary to public power. This view, reflecting, one could argue, a desire to protect neat boundaries between different social arenas, fails to see how select private security companies have become deeply involved in enacting public power.

Private security representatives have, once again, sought to mobilize the cultural and symbolic capital of CoESS to enhance their own positions in national arenas. Thus, they have consistently invoked CoESS-sponsored initiatives, and have drawn on the Confederation's discourse in an effort to enhance the legitimacy of their argument and to delegitimize their opponents' positions. Their core argument has been that experts all over Europe assign value to attributes like solid training, demonstrated competence, and professional attitudes, expertise, and experience—and so, too, should the governments of East European polities. Failure to do so would be synonymous with failing to perform their key function to provide fundamental public goods to society. For instance, the head of Romania's FSS has explained that his association is engaged in a public campaign to influence national authorities to implement as quickly as possible legislation in conformity with the European Directive 24/2014, in a situation in which most public agencies continue to privilege, and grant contracts to, PSCs that offer the lowest price (Badea 2015). In a labor-intensive sector like private security, it is argued, this situation has a series of adverse consequences, including very low salaries, the lack of proper training for PSC employees, inadequate equipment, lack of motivation, the de-professionalization of the field, and, consequently, a sharp decline in the quality of private security services.

In a similar vein, through multiple briefing sessions, workshops, and meetings, NAFTSO has been engaged in a campaign to persuade the Bulgarian authorities—and private clients of PSCs—that the criteria guiding public procurement have to change. What they demanded was a change in the Law on Public Procurement and, more broadly, a change in the culture surrounding procurement practices. It is imperative, from the perspective of the private security industry, to adopt the criteria put forward in the CoESS textbook, in order to move away from the practice of exclusive reliance on the lowest price. Like their Romanian counterparts, the Bulgarian private security association has sought to delegitimize the government's interpretation of public procurement criteria, arguing that decisions made on the basis of the lowest price, without any serious attention to the credentials of the security providers selling their services for that price, would put not just private clients but also public safety at risk—not least by encouraging the resurgence of links between PSCs, the gray economy, and possibly also organized crime. The leitmotif behind the various meetings/workshops and other events organized by NAFTSO (or its individual members) has been that it is unacceptable to fail to amend the Public Procurement Law and to end current reliance on the lowest price. Thus, it is abhorrent to "continue practices of holding vicious tenders and lowest price races" at the expense of quality—that is, to "save on security at times of high risks and criminal encroachments" (NAFTSO 2011: 2).[43]

For its part, as noted above, the Serbian Private Security Association—and, under its umbrella, pro-reform PSCs—have been involved in a campaign to push Serbia away from its current practice of encouraging the lowest bid in public procurement. Like their colleagues in Romania and Bulgaria, professionally organized PSCs have sought to delegitimize the reliance on the lowest price as the key criterion. In this case, one of the key arguments employed by the private security representatives has been that this definition and practice of public procurement is inconsistent with the country's efforts to transcend corruption, abusive behavior, and unfair competition in the field of security, and strengthen respect for the rule of law—as a vital ingredient in a modern European democracy. To enhance the authority of their claims, Serbian PSCs have invoked the textbook published under CoESS auspices, stressing the similarity between criteria outlined there and their own claims in order to cast those claims as representing not just Serbian views, but broader West European criteria of what constitute appropriate principles and practices of public procurement.[44]

From the point of view of professional security associations in Eastern Europe, public procurements driven by the lowest price push the private security industry toward practices of unfair competition, dumping, and tax evasion—all in an effort to survive in a hostile environment. Granting contracts based on the lowest price also leads to rates that are unsustainable—both from an economic point of view and from the point of view of compliance with the legislation, by providing too many incentives to PSCs to break the rules. By contrast, the implementation of Directive 24/2014 can enable the rise to prominence/triumph of procurement criteria that focus on the quality of private security services, thereby encouraging professionalism and innovation in this field, and thus also enhancing public safety.

The private security industry in Bulgaria, Romania, Serbia, as well as Bosnia has long argued that, in a situation in which the shift toward a focus on quality as key criterion in the selection of PSCs depends not only on the existence of appropriate legislation but also on the ability of those who select private security providers to discern the quality of services that particular PSCs can provide, it is imperative to educate decision-makers and government bureaucrats on how to assess quality. To this end, professional associations of the private security industry and multinational PSCs have disseminated the textbook on the acquisition of high-quality security services prepared under the auspices of CoESS.[45] This textbook explains all the aspects and issues that a client (be it private or public) should take into account when choosing a particular PSC in order to ensure that the company will be able to provide adequate services, in compliance with the existing legislation. Furthermore, the textbook contains some practical tools, including a set of tables that enable clients to calculate the "scores" of the bids coming from various PSCs, and on this basis to make an informed decision about which security provider to select for a specific job.

Within the framework of the campaign to promote high-quality private security services—and in collaboration with CoESS—private security associations in Romania, Bulgaria, and Serbia and representatives of global private security companies in all four countries have systematically sought to disseminate images of professionalism of leading PSCs. For instance, they have organized a series of meetings, seminars, and workshops with public and private clients of PSCs in their countries, aimed at explaining the importance of promoting high-quality private security, and offering practical advice on how to select private security providers. At the end of the period of time covered in this book (2015), these campaigns were still continuing, with PSC representatives arguing that change is slow, and that the economic constraints generated by the 2007/8 financial crisis were still being felt in many parts of the East European economies, providing extra incentives to focus on the lowest price at the expense of quality, and thus complicating efforts to change old mentalities. Still, socialization activities targeting public and private clients of PSCs have persisted, and representatives of the private security industry remain optimistic that, under constant pressure from them and from

CoESS, the targets of their socialization efforts will eventually change their definition of what counts as valuable/appropriate criteria for selecting private security providers.[46]

Old Habits Die Hard: Competing Logics of Security Provision in Eastern Europe

The campaign to change the logic of public procurement illustrates a broader challenge linked to the provision and governance of security in Eastern Europe. Thus, in Eastern Europe, recent processes of professionalization of private security and the accompanying revalorization of different forms of capital—though extremely important—have not completely eliminated the old ways of doing things. Rather, the situation that those countries face today is one in which the implementation of new norms and rules of the game is complicated by the persistence of old habits, and in which "old" forms of capital (which were particularly valuable in the early years of post-communist transition) continue to be influential, at least in some locations and areas of security governance and provision. The result is the perpetuation of a situation of flux and continued rearticulation of the field of security, as actors that are seeking to further professionalize the field and further integrate their polities into European and global structures coexist and compete—but in some instances also cooperate—with players who continue to mobilize (and seek to maintain the value of) rules of the game and forms of capital associated with the "old days" of early post-communist transition.

Before going any further it is important to note that this chapter does not claim to provide a comprehensive account of all the instances of cooperation and competition between actors that embrace different logics of security provision. Such an account would not be possible, particularly in light of the fact that information about illicit security provision practices remains incomplete. To further complicate matters, alliances (as well as instances of competition) among some of those actors can shift or break down very quickly. Consequently, any attempt to fully map the field of security could do no more than capture an incomplete, static, and possibly misleading snapshot of a rapidly evolving set of practices of security. Under these circumstances, what this section seeks to do is to demonstrate that both cooperation and competition occur in the new security environment, and to use some prominent examples to illustrate the coexistence of these different logics.

Let us start with the persistence of "old ways" of doing things in the former Yugoslavia. We noted in Chapter 3 that in the late 2000s Bosnia experienced a process of partial professionalization of security, in which internationalization and the addition of new actors led to the revalorization of forms of material and non-material capital that had previously been undervalued in Bosnia. This included professional training for PSCs, modern technologies, and the move toward security practices that are more consistent with respect for human rights and the rule of law—as opposed to illegal practices, such as racketeering.

Yet, even those developments did not translate into a complete transformation of the role of private security in Bosnia. Rather, what we seem to be witnessing is a persisting struggle over the rules of the game and the valorization of different types of capital in Bosnia's field of security. In that struggle, there are areas of security provision in which new, Western-style forms of capital and rules of the game of security provision prevail, but there are also areas in which the Western-style professionalization of security provision has been far slower and plagued with difficulties. Most notably, in practices of protection of large Western corporations and foreign embassies, forms of capital that are valued by private security companies in the West have also come to be valued by Bosnian-based PSCs. In that area, the rules of the game governing security provision have moved a lot closer to the rules of security provision that are expected to prevail in established liberal democracies, and the security professionals that possess "old" forms of capital have been significantly weakened.[47]

By contrast, there are areas in which old forms of capital and rules of the game remain quite influential. These include practices of protection of public sites/companies, as well as the provision of security to many local politicians and businesses, especially in rural areas. In a situation in which police forces continue to be cash-strapped and thus unable to perform all the security functions expected of them, and in which the court system remains inefficient and corrupt, there continues to be strong demand for PSCs that are perceived as "able to get things done" even if that involves the threat or use of illegal coercion.[48] Senior EU and NATO officials based in Sarajevo have also expressed concern that neither international institutions nor Bosnian authorities have the human and material resources that would be needed to monitor all PSCs operating in the country.[49] This is particularly problematic, they argue, in a situation in which there are strong suspicions that several PSCs—particularly those operating outside of Sarajevo and closely linked to particular ethnic groups—have been hiring individuals with close ties to the criminal world, who continue to be involved in dubious activities. Some of these PSCs are large and well armed, benefit from the expertise and training of personnel that were involved in the fighting in the late 1990s, and operate in what continues to be a lax environment, in which it is unclear for what purpose they are being used. This, it should be noted, concerns not only private clients but also public institutions. For instance, it is alleged that over 100 PSCs with strong political connections work for public companies and one of their *de facto* functions is illegal intelligence collection.[50] Thus, there now seems to be large-scale reliance on PSCs for purposes of illegal surveillance of various individuals and companies—without any form of accountability or transparency. Another concern expressed by international officials and Bosnian security experts is that, in the event of an incident (particularly one with an interethnic dimension) these companies could quickly intervene on the side of the ethnic groups to which they are tied, thereby making the situation far worse.

As regards Serbia, we noted above that after more than a decade of transition, the Law on Private Security was finally passed on November 26, 2013, and came into force on December 6, 2013. The adoption of the new law represents a significant step forward in the process of implementing in the field of security liberal-democratic norms of transparency, accountability, and respect for human rights. Thus, by introducing a system of licensing and by defining the boundaries of acceptable behavior by PSCs (including limits on their ability to exercise violence), the new laws hold the potential to eliminate some of the gravest abuses that have marked the process of security privatization until now. However, it is still too early to predict the final outcome of this transformation. Delays in the implementation of the 2013 law—and certain ambiguities inscribed in its provisions—mean that it is impossible to assess its full, eventual impact. As Petrović and Milošević have argued, however, what is beyond doubt is that some of the smaller PSCs operating in Serbia will need to close down because they will not be able to meet the new statutory requirements (Petrović and Milošević 2015: 104). Arguably, this raises the danger that at least some of the PSCs that are no longer viable will try to offer their services on the gray or black market.

Similar to the situation in Bosnia, Serbia seems to be witnessing the coexistence of different rules of the game in different areas of security provision. Multinational corporations and international banks, as well as national companies that seek to be internationally competitive, value—and hire—PSCs that respect Western norms and standards of professionalism, and are committed to a logic of care of the community in which they operate. Yet, the situation remains more ambivalent in other areas. Particularly problematic seem to be security arrangements that concern public actors, where some of the old ways of doing things are hard to change. Furthermore, the potential for corruption and even criminal behavior on the part of private security remains significant, not least because police officers who also work for PSCs privilege those companies and, it is alleged, warn them in advance about—and protect them from—public investigations into their practices.[51] Given that the Law on Private Security defines the Ministry of Interior as the supervisor of the private security industry, some Serbian analysts point out, there is the unavoidable question of who controls the controller? There is obviously a direct conflict of interest involved in this situation, and for this reason the activity of private security should be automatically incompatible with a service in the branch of public security (CEAS 2014: 77). In other words, in an ironic reversal of the logics conventionally attributed to the public and private domains of activity, it would appear that both in Serbia and in Bosnia practices aimed at protecting global private businesses often come closer to principles associated with the public good than practices enacted in the name of securing public sites/ entities, in which the profit of specific individuals sometimes prevails over other considerations.

In order to resolve these problems, it is necessary to establish a clear division of responsibilities, jurisdiction, and activities between public security and private security, namely clearly define what activities are incompatible with conducting duties of public security. Linked to this, the system of public procurements in the private security sector remains deeply problematic, despite the numerous initiatives and public warnings from Serbian and foreign security experts. This problem has not yet been addressed—either through the recent Law on Private Security or in other pieces of legislation. Consequently, many contracts are reportedly still awarded to private security providers that offer the lowest cost, regardless of the credibility and competence of their offer. Furthermore, in some instances there has been intense competition among several private security providers that were offering to secure critical infrastructure installations at unsustainably, artificially low prices. In those cases, the winner was the company that was not only willing to offer such an artificially low price but also had powerful political connections.[52] Indeed, several Serbian security experts have claimed that the majority of private security contracts with public companies are based on political links. In the absence of those links, a PSC is not likely to secure the contract, even if it possesses superior material capabilities and has more expertise and experience than its politically connected rivals. In other words, in those instances forms of non-material capital associated with the early days of transition continue to be more valued than forms of material and cultural capital valued in the Western world. Not surprisingly, this drastically limits the effectiveness of efforts to professionalize private security in Serbia (CEAS 2014: 77–9). The country is thus facing a "paradoxical situation of state institutions, in practice, valuing the profits of the owners of private security companies over the opportunity to legally receive the best quality service for the money they have at their disposal. Hence the state robs itself through political corruption" (Petrović and Milošević 2015: 98).

According to several security experts as well as senior G4S and Securitas employees, as late as 2015 the delays in the adoption and implementation of legislation in the private security sector, as well as the flaws that persist in the legislation that does get adopted, were, at least in part, the expression of the persistence of the old habitus. The survival of old ways of doing things allegedly made it easier for political actors and members of the public to tolerate and reproduce a situation that would be deemed unacceptable in an established liberal democracy. What this means is that further efforts to professionalize the field will need to include not only legislative reforms, but also, more broadly, a further transformation at the level of habitus, changing the ways in which both elites and the public think about private security, leading them to regard as illegitimate—and, hence, oppose—some of the practices that still prevail in the field of security.

In this context, it is interesting to note that some Serbian security experts as well as representatives of multinational PSCs operating in Serbia have argued that the best chance for further progress in this area is that of systematic socialization of Serbians into new conceptual and practical dispositions as part of the process of European integration.[53] Indeed, there have been calls for the EU to exercise more pressure and more guidance on Serbia in order to promote further professionalization of private security and, more broadly, deeper reform in the security sector. In this view, the EU should define the reform of the security system as an important part of the integration policy toward Serbia in the pre-accession process. In this context, Serbia should be pressured by the EU "to approach [the reform of the security system] strategically and consistently, with efficient use of available tools and means, especially by means of political criteria, and through chapters 23 and 31. Since the joint security and defense policy has been for the most part left under the responsibility of other member states, the initiative for such new approach must come from them." Also, in progress reports for Serbia, the EU should "systematically monitor the condition of the security system, dynamics and deficiencies of the reform." It should also "give recommendations for further reforms with the use of imperative language" (CEAS 2014: 82). However, at present it is not yet clear how much pressure the EU will apply in this area, and to what extent it will participate in efforts to socialize Serbian elites and security professionals into new ways of thinking about—and acting in— private security.

In fact, the cases of Bulgaria and Romania demonstrate that even East European states that are now members of the EU are still facing problems linked to the persistence of old perceptions (and forms of capital) in the security field. Old ways of thinking and acting remain particularly influential in the public sector. In Romania, for instance, it is revealing that, in an effort to enhance their position in the field of security, even some of the global PSCs have sought to combine their material capital and global experience/expertise with forms of capital inherited from Romania's "old days," and still valued in that country—especially in relations with public companies. What is more problematic is that at least in some instances those connections were linked to practices that departed from the global PSC's commitment to apply its high standards of professionalism in Romania and everywhere else where it was operating. A case in point is G4S, which came to Romania by acquiring a Romanian PSC, Valahia, whose owner, Liviu Tarsea, had strong links to the communist security services and post-communist political elites.[54] Until 2006, the owner of Valahia continued to work for G4S in Romania, and used his connections to secure for that company lucrative contracts with the state. Even after the departure of Tarsea the company continued to include in its management team individuals with powerful political connections, and systematically mobilized them for the benefit of the company. For example, through those connections G4S was able to secure—on artificially advantageous terms—overpriced contracts with the Romanian Postal Services (Posta Romana). Some of those contracts were only cancelled in 2013, when the National Agency for the Regulation and Monitoring of Public Procurement accused the director of Posta Romana of acting in collusion with G4S to maintain artificially high prices, to the detriment of Romanian taxpayers, and a Romanian Court of Appeal declared the contract void.[55] In a similar vein, in 2013 G4S joined forces with a Romanian PSC with strong political connections, Axis, and used those connections to secure five lucrative contracts to guard some of the busiest highways in the southern part of the country. As in the case of the Postal Service, the ability of G4S to obtain these contracts was apparently linked to its political contacts, and its willingness to offer very low prices.[56] Ironically, then, in this instance G4S appears to have acted in a manner that is directly opposed to what it was preaching in its official discourse, in which—as noted above—it was criticizing the practice of selecting PSCs on the basis of the lowest price, at the expense of quality-based criteria.

These instances can be seen as illustrative examples of a broader set of problems, which stem from a (still inadequate) legislative framework and the fact that even the legislation that is already in place is often not applied (or is applied in a flawed manner). As the 2014 report by the FSS President, Gabriel Badea, reveals, in spite of the progress made since the 1990s through the adoption of new legislation and institutional arrangements, the relationship between PSCs and Romania's public authorities remains problematic (Badea 2014).[57] To begin with, in Romania there continues to be a police-heavy regulatory regime governing the private security industry, leaving little if any power in the hands of other bodies (Badea 2014: 43). For instance, in addition to issuing or revoking licenses to PSCs, the police are also involved in the compulsory training of PSC employees, and provide consultancy to the private security industry. Predictably, one of the consequences of this situation is that there is inadequate involvement of civil society or parliamentary actors in the monitoring and governance of the private security industry, increasing the danger of corruption of police officers. In a similar vein, the disproportionally powerful position occupied by the police in the field of security in Romania means that they have little incentive to engage in systematic consultations with representatives of the private security industry, relying instead on personal contacts with specific PSC managers/directors.

To make matters worse, the police lack the administrative capacity that they would need in order to perform all the regulatory functions stipulated by Romanian laws. This tends to lead to selective enforcement of the "rules of the game," based on personal and political connections (Badea 2014: 71–7). In what could be seen as an instantiation of the Orwellian formula "all are equal, but some are more equal than others," those PSCs that have strong political connections tend not to be pursued by the police when they break the law. This problematic relationship between the police and private security is fuelled, to a significant extent, by a weakness in the Romanian legislation which has been attributed by several security experts to the fact that so many powerful political players have an interest in maintaining some links to the private security industry to the extent that they are reluctant to adopt legislation/take steps to address that problem. For instance, in Romania (as in Bulgaria) the legislation still allows police officers to enter PSCs right after retirement, further complicating the relationship between the police as regulator of—and participant in—private security (Badea 2014: 61). There is anecdotal evidence, for instance, that in several instances the police were reluctant to hold Romanian PSCs accountable for their violations of the laws governing the private security industry because they were anticipating joining those companies after retirement, and did not want to diminish their chances of being hired by those companies.[58]

In Bulgaria, too, in spite of recent legislative and institutional reforms, and for all the moves toward increased professionalization of the industry (in contrast to the situation that prevailed in the 1990s), the situation of PSCs and their relationship to public authorities continues to reflect a series of problems. Those problems reveal the fact that in some areas of security provision old ways of doing things persist, and actors that possess "old-style" forms of capital are still powerful. In particular, the owners and managers of many PSCs remain well connected to the political class, leading to unfair competition in public tenders. Thus, "there are no specific measures in the PSC legal regime preventing conflicts of interest and corruption, especially in connection with contracts for guarding important state-owned infrastructure" (Dzhekova and Rusev 2015: 51). At the same time, similar to the situation in Romania, in Bulgaria there continues to be a police-heavy regulatory regime governing PSCs, which means that the police still retain excessive power in this domain—thereby increasing the risk of corruption of the police, and making it more difficult for civil society actors or even other branches of the state to supervise security providers (Badea 2014; Dzhekova and Rusev 2015). Furthermore, in a situation in which at least until 2013 the Ministry of Interior provided its own commercial security services, it faced a serious conflict of interest since it was occupying the mutually incompatible positions of regulator/enforcer of rules and player in the security field (Badea 2014: 59; Dzhekova and Rusev 2015: 44).

Similar to Romania and the countries of the Western Balkans, in Bulgaria, too, there is evidence that the old forms of non-material capital—associated with the early, violent years of post-communist transition—continued to be valued at least in some aspects and areas of security provision—especially involving some public institutions. For instance, in recent years the Bulgarian ministries of interior and defense have started to work more systematically with PSCs in protecting their property, including sensitive sites such as munitions depots. The problem, however, is that for the most part those contracts are awarded on the basis of a combination of personal connections and the lowest price. As a consequence, the quality of security provided at these sites has left a great deal to be desired—resulting, for instance, in a series of incidents, including damaging explosions at some of those depots.[59] While those incidents led to renewed calls for a systematic fight against corruption in the field of security, during the period of time covered in this book there was no evidence that Bulgaria had either the resources or the political will to implement an anticorruption program that would effectively address those problems.

This chapter has shed light on the fluidity and complex mix of practices that have resulted from the growing Europeanization and globalization of the field of security in Bulgaria, Romania, Serbia, and Bosnia. As we have seen, those practices have challenged and weakened—but not completely defeated—attitudes and practices inherited from a deeply problematic past. By examining practices of security provision that result from the intersections of international actors and factors with national players and local dynamics, the chapter has sought to give the readers a better sense of what "glocalization" looks like in specific settings, at particular moments in time. The new political economy of security provision that has resulted from these intersections compels us to rethink conventional categories and divides between public/private and security/economics/politics. It also raises complex normative questions and challenges regarding the reconstitution and uses of public power in the name of protecting citizens and their property. It is to a discussion of some of those questions and challenges that we turn in the final chapter of the book.

Notes

1. This was confirmed in interviews with more than two dozen directors, managers, and deputy managers of global and local PSCs, security analysts, government officials, and investigative journalists in each of the four countries examined in

this book, between 2011 and 2014 (interviews conducted in Sofia, Bucharest, Belgrade, Sarajevo, and Brussels).

2. Given their complexity and fluidity, it would be impossible to provide a comprehensive, detailed account of all the activities, alliances, and contestations among those involved in security provision in contemporary Eastern Europe. Instead, the focus in this chapter is on shedding light on some key examples of cooperation and competition among those actors.

3. This section is based on the author's interviews with members of the management teams of five leading PSCs in each of the countries included in this project. In each case, global PSCs (G4S and Securitas) were among those top five companies. The study also included interviews with members of the management teams of two dominant foreign banks in the region (Raiffeisen Bank and Société Générale). They all stressed that they depended heavily on foreign PSCs for at least some of their security needs (particularly the transport of cash/valuables and cash processing). This was especially due to the fact that the police and local PSCs in Eastern Europe were not seen as able to provide global standards of security for financial institutions. On this, see also Petrović and Milošević 2015.

4. The first quotation comes from an interview with a member of the management team of the Belgrade branch of Securitas, while the second quotation is from an interview with his counterpart in Sarajevo. Interviews conducted by the author on June 17, 2013 in Belgrade and June 24, 2013 in Sarajevo.

5. Interview conducted by the author, June 28, 2013, Bucharest.

6. Interview conducted by the author, June 17, 2013, Belgrade.

7. Interview conducted by the author, March 12, 2014, Sarajevo.

8. This is similar to developments in Africa, as highlighted by Abrahamsen and Williams (2011: 108–14).

9. These were leitmotifs that surfaced in interviews with representatives of leading PSCs from Bulgaria, Romania, Bosnia, and Serbia (see note 1 above).

10. On the emerging PSC interest in cyber security, see also Badea 2015. While this is still a new, less-developed service provided by the private security industry, it is expected to grow significantly in the coming years. In this area, too, PSCs portray their services as proof of their ability to provide vital support to the state and, in some instances, to act where the state is unable or unwilling to act in an efficient manner.

11. More information about FSS, which brings under its umbrella three private security organizations—Patronatului Serviciilor de Securitate, or PATROSEC (the Organization of Security Services Employers), Asociatia Romana a Industriei de Securitate (Romanian Association of the Security Industry), and Asociatia Romane pentru Tehnica de Securitate (Romanian Association of Security Technology)—can be found on the FSS website: http://www.fss.org.ro/acasa.

12. This paragraph relies on information obtained in the course of interviews with a member of the FSS Governing Board and a member of the management team of PATROSEC, Bucharest, June 28, 2013 and March 18, 2014. See also the contribution by the President of FSS, Gabriel Badea, to the 2014 *CoESS White Paper on Cohesion* (Badea 2014).

13. Interview with a former member of the management team of BGS, March 20, 2014, Bucharest.
14. Interview as in note 13. These ideas were also stressed by employees of leading PSCs (G4S, Securitas, and BGS) in interviews with the author, Bucharest, June 2013 and March 2014.
15. Interviews with employees of leading PSCs (G4S, Securitas, and BGS), Bucharest, June 28, 2013 and March 20–3, 2014. The same images of PSCs are disseminated via the websites of these organizations: http://www.g4s.ro/ro-RO; http://www.bgs.ro; http://www.securitas.com.ro/ro/.
16. See G4S's own characterization of their profile and work in Romania at: http://www.g4s.ro/ro-RO.
17. As in note 16.
18. This description can be found on the BGS website: http://www.bgs.ro.
19. The National Association of Industrial Security Companies (NAFTSO), established in 2001, incorporates both global PSCs and national companies that seek recognition as legitimate companies, in contrast to the lawless private security providers of the 1990s. NAFTSO is a recognized representative employers organization of the private security sector in Bulgaria as well as a member of CoESS.
20. Interviews with NAFTSO representatives, June 20, 2012. This view of PSCs as performing an important role in aiding public authorities was also echoed by two representatives of the Bulgarian Security Police, June 19, 2012, Sofia.
21. Interview conducted in Sofia, June 28, 2012.
22. Interviews with members of the management team of three PSCs (two international and a Serbian PSC) represented in NCPSC.
23. Interview with representative of NCPSC, Belgrade, June 18, 2013.
24. These values/norms are at the heart of Securitas's and G4S's descriptions of their roles in Serbia. See https://www.securitas.co.rs/; and http://www.g4s.rs/.
25. G4S Serbia, "About Us," at: http://www.g4s.rs/.
26. As in note 25.
27. See Private Investors Council, Serbia 2014: 169–71.
28. Interview conducted by the author in Belgrade, June 17, 2013.
29. Interviews with a Bosnian security expert affiliated with the Sarajevo Centre for Security Studies, June 27, 2013. This view was echoed by an investigative reporter and a member of the EU Delegation to Bosnia (interviews March 11–12, 2014, Sarajevo).
30. Interview with a senior member of the management team of Securitas in Bosnia, June 27, 2013.
31. This section is based on an analysis of the websites of the main international PSCs (G4S and Securitas) operating in these countries, as well as one leading national company in Bulgaria, Romania, Serbia, and Bosnia. The national companies that I have selected occupy prominent positions in the security markets of their countries, are members of recognized professional associations, perform multiple types of security services, and have contracts with both public and private clients. They are: BGS in Romania (https://bgs.ro/en/divizia-de-securitate/compania/); Burgas in Bulgaria

(www.3ssot-bs.com/en.html); Dobergard in Serbia (http://www.dobergard.co.rs/EN%20about%20us.htm); and Gamma AA Security in Bosnia (http://gama-aa.ba/).

32. This situation was observed by the author during field research in all four countries; it applies in particular with respect to low-ranking employees working for local PSCs and guarding small businesses and/or less visible public sites. On the lack of sufficient equipment experienced by some PSC employees, see also Badea 2015.

33. See, for instance, the activity reports provided by G4S Bulgaria (http://www.g4s.bg/bg-bg/) (last accessed July 23, 2017) and G4S Romania (http://www.g4s.ro/). See also Securitas's description of its activities in Romania (http://www.securitas.com.ro/ro/), Serbia (http://www.securitas.co.rs/), and Bosnia (http://www.securitas.ba/bs-Latn-BA/).

34. I borrow the term "bubbles of governance" from Wakefield 2005.

35. Here, I draw on the work on Erik Ringmar. See, in particular, his analysis of the ways in which imagination and embodiment come together in specific performances. As Ringmar puts it, "actors are real only as they are imagined. Practices of various kinds—newspaper reading, educational pilgrimages—play a role here, but only as vehicles of imagination" (Ringmar 2017).

36. The first statement comes from a Securitas member in Bosnia, the second one from a BGS (leading Romanian PSC) member, the third one from a G4S member in Bulgaria, and the final one from a G4S member in Serbia. These themes were echoed in interviews conducted between 2012 and 2014 with members of managerial teams of G4S, Securitas, as well as leading national PSCs in all four countries.

37. Interview with a former member of the management team of G4S, Bucharest, March 22, 2014. On relations between the private security industry and the Romanian police see also Badea 2013, 2014, 2015.

38. Interview with NAFTSO representative, Sofia, June 14, 2012.

39. Telephone interview with representative of the NCPSC, June 1, 2014. The same ideas have been stressed in Private Investors Council, Serbia 2014: 169–71. See also Petrović and Milošević's discussion of the ways in which the private security industry has been trying to dilute the resistance of the Ministry of Interior to the establishment of a public–private partnership in the field of security (Petrović and Milošević 2015: 99).

40. Interview with a CoESS representative, March 4, 2014, Brussels.

41. Interviews with two NATO and three EU officials, Sarajevo, March 10–17, 2014. Reportedly, Bosnians requested the support of international officials, especially by asking them to insist in dialogue with local officials on the importance of professionalization of private security.

42. This view was confirmed in all the interviews conducted with representatives of legitimate PSCs and their associations in all four countries between June 2011 and July 2014.

43. The same concerns were expressed by a NAFTSO representative in an interview with the author on June 18, 2012.

44. Interview with representative of NCPSC, Belgrade, June 18, 2013.

45. The manual, titled *Buying Quality Private Security Services*, is aimed at explaining to public and private buyers the meaning and benefits of quality private security

providers. Its explicit ambition is to provide the buyer with the necessary arguments for which private security services should be based on best value, including social criteria relevant to the sector. It shows the key importance of defining, identifying, searching, and selecting best value for private security services. For more details, see: http://www.securebestvalue.org/wp-content/uploads/2014/11/Best-Value-Manual_Final.pdf.

46. This was confirmed in interviews with more than two dozen directors, managers, and deputy managers of global and local PSCs affiliated with professional associations in each of the four countries examined in this book, between May 2011 and June 2014 (interviews conducted in Sofia, Bucharest, Belgrade, Sarajevo, and Brussels).

47. Interviews with a senior member of the management team of the Bosnian branch of Securitas, June 28, 2013, and with two Bosnian experts affiliated with the Atlantic Initiative, Sarajevo, March 11, 2014.

48. Interviews as in note 47. Reports also indicate a persisting distrust in the police's ability and willingness to provide security to Bosnia's citizens. Thus, in 2014 it is reported that only about 40 percent of Bosnia's citizens expressed trust in the police (Bertelsmann Stiftung 2014).

49. Interviews with two NATO and three EU officials, Sarajevo, March 10–17, 2014.

50. Interviews as in note 49.

51. Interviews with two Serbian security analysts affiliated with the Belgrade Centre for Security Policy and two investigative journalists, Belgrade, June 17–20, 2013.

52. Interviews as in note 51.

53. Interviews as in note 51. It is also noteworthy that the Center for Euro-Atlantic Studies (CEAS) put forward a set of recommendations in a 2014 study titled *The Missing Link* that was realized within the joint CEAS–DPC project "Reform of the security system, military neutrality and EU integrations in Serbia—How the EU should best use its influence to advocate sustainable reform" supported by the Balkan Fund for Democracy of the German Marshall Fund of the United States of America.

54. Interviews with two Romanian investigative journalists, June 1–2, 2011, Bucharest.

55. Interviews with an independent security analyst and an investigative journalist, Bucharest, March 21, 2014.

56. Interviews as in note 55.

57. These ideas were also stressed by two former members of G4S's management team in interviews with the author, March 20, 2014.

58. Interviews with a representative of FSS and an independent security expert, Bucharest, March 21, 2014.

59. Interview with a senior Bulgarian security expert (former government official) affiliated with the Centre for the Study of Democracy, June 15, 2012, Sofia.

6

Normative Dilemmas and Challenges of Security Commercialization

In thinking about the commercialization of security, it is easy to fall into the trap of a comfortable dichotomy: depending on one's intellectual and political inclinations, this can be seen as either a development to be applauded because it brings an important area in the life of a polity closer to the logic of market efficiency, or, conversely, a deplorable phenomenon, which threatens to undermine social order and justice in any society by subordinating the provision of a key public good to the harsh logic of profit-seeking. Yet, a closer analysis of the impact of commercialization on practices of security provision reveals that any normative dichotomy would be simplistic and misleading. The proliferation of private security companies and, more broadly, the growing role of the commercial logic in the field of security have been, in many ways, mixed blessings.

In recent years, PSCs have become a very visible, regular presence not only in the protection of private clients but also in situations requiring crowd management, the protection of critical infrastructure, and, more broadly, the establishment and maintenance of safe spaces in East European polities. Through those practices, one could argue, the private security industry plays an essentially constructive role. It does so by helping to enact the state, extending the ability of the police and other public agencies to carry out their functions, particularly in situations or places where, due to limited resources or various forms of partiality, the state would otherwise be almost absent. In a similar vein, by virtue of their ability to offer—and be seen as offering—global standards of security provision, PSCs help to create the conditions under which international corporations (particularly foreign banks) are willing to operate in Eastern Europe. In a normative environment marked by the prominence of liberal ideas of globalization, free trade, and foreign investment, the private security industry can thus claim, and has systematically claimed, to be actively engaged in securing the economic well-being of former communist polities—thereby also protecting the interests of the public in a very broad sense. What is involved here is a series of tangible benefits at the level of society—enhancing the ability of the state to provide security, but also facilitating the influx of much-needed foreign capital and thus supporting economic growth. There have also been direct benefits to the lives of many individuals. Most obviously, the private security industry has enabled people and businesses to escape the situation of insecurity associated with weak, often corrupt state institutions, and to find a multitude of security solutions tailored to their needs. Interestingly, the benefits associated with the private security industry in Eastern Europe do not end there. To take just one example: in each of the East European polities examined in this book the growing presence of global banks that are protected by private security companies has facilitated access to credit for individuals and small companies that would otherwise have struggled to secure sufficient funding for, say, mortgages or business investments.

There is yet another way in which the private security industry can claim to participate in advancing the interests of the public: by helping to empower civil society in interactions with branches/agencies of the state that have been slow in advancing reforms. In several instances, representatives of the private security industry have forged alliances with security experts, NGOs, and a series of local politicians to push for the professionalization of the field of security, seeking to correct some of the abuses of the early years of post-communism. To give just an example: it will be recalled that in Serbia, representatives of the private security industry, in alliance with a variety of public/private actors, spent years advocating the adoption of comprehensive legislation aimed at clarifying the role of PSCs, formally defining their relationships to public authorities, and delegitimizing private security providers that engage in criminal activities. Following the adoption of the law on private security, a series of PSCs have continued to push for greater regulation of their sector through the adoption of secondary legislation which would clarify aspects that were left unaddressed by the 2013 law.

Furthermore, in the context of Europeanization and globalization, private security providers have drawn on global and European norms and standards of behavior and have used the emerging European political space to mobilize transnationally and lobby not only for a more prominent role of PSCs in contemporary practices of security governance and provision, but also for more rights for their employees. In particular, acting within the framework of CoESS (Confederation for European Security Services), representatives of global and national PSCs have invoked global norms of market rationality and risk-management and have systematically argued for greater involvement of the private security industry in practices of identifying and addressing prevailing risks in Europe, and for the recognition of PSCs as privileged partners of public authorities in the twenty-first century. At the same time, in the context of debates over the meaning of European integration and harmonization in the field of security, private security representatives have contested the dominant logic of security provision in the age of commercialization.

This has become particularly significant in the context of criticisms of the excesses of the neo-liberal logic that have been raised by the global financial crisis of 2007–8. Through their campaigns on public procurement, PSCs have joined forces with unions to invoke EU values and norms, including respect for socio-economic rights of individuals and protection of the environment to push back against the neo-liberal logic upheld by public authorities. More specifically, at the European level as well as in national arenas they have mobilized and have advocated a definition of public procurement of security services in Europe that includes more protections for security employees and more respect for environmental standards. Ironically, through those campaigns, global and national private security companies have cast themselves as actors that were more committed to the promotion of the rights and well-being of European publics than public authorities themselves. This has occurred in a situation in which the latter have supported a neo-liberal definition of public procurement, focusing almost exclusively on the lowest price—apparently, with little regard for the impact of that approach on labor and environmental standards.

This systematic involvement of the private security industry in practices of security provision and governance, however, should not lead us to assume that private security participation in efforts to transform the field of security is an unmitigated blessing, or that there is universal agreement over definitions of the desirable role and mandates of PSCs. On the contrary, many questions, debates, and contestations persist regarding the extent and ways in which PSCs should be involved in security provision, at both the national and the European level. At the heart of many of these debates are precisely the kinds of normative questions and concerns discussed in this chapter. These include questions about patterns of inequality among those who can and those who cannot afford to hire reliable PSCs, as well as questions about the dynamics, limits, and implications of partnerships between states and the private security industry. What is no longer contested, however—by either public authorities or private actors—is the idea that the private security industry will necessarily exercise an important role in the field of security. Indeed, in the age of security commercialization, it has come to seem normal to mix two logics—public good provision and profit-seeking—that used to be associated with distinct (public and private) spheres. Furthermore, this combination of logics has also made possible a situation in which some branches of the state now even offer commercial security services, in competition with the private sector.

In many ways, the normative dilemmas and challenges associated with the growing role of private security are linked to an ambivalence that is at the heart of the liberal vision of the state. As discussed in Chapter 2, the idea of security as a public good—to be provided by the state in a uniform manner, regardless of the socio-economic status or any other differences among citizens—was at the heart of the evolution of modern capitalism. The provision of security as a key public good continues to be a core ingredient in the institutional power of the state. Public support for the police and other state security agencies is based on the recognition that those forces serve the general interest, as opposed to advancing private agendas and protecting only particular segments of the population. Simultaneously, the modern liberal state—in contrast to communist regimes—is committed to respecting the right of its citizens to hold private property. Indeed, the ability to protect both public security and the integrity of private property is central to the legitimacy of the liberal state. Consequently, if the state were to be seen to promote private property and private interests at the expense of public security, its authority could easily and significantly be weakened.[1]

In the context of processes of liberalization and European integration, the private security industry has effectively used a discourse that casts PSCs as legitimate and effective participants in the practices of security provision precisely by virtue of their ability to resolve the liberal ambivalence in a constructive way, thereby promoting security as both a public and a private good. As a corollary to this, in discourses articulated by the private security industry, PSCs are depicted as actors that play an active part not simply in security provision but, more broadly, in promoting liberalism in former communist countries. The image of the private security industry, however, could be easily disrupted and compromised if PSCs were to be seen as endangering or marginalizing the promotion of the public good for the sake of protecting the private interests of their clients. And the analysis developed in this book reveals that, in recent years, this public/private tension has repeatedly manifested itself in the practices enacted by both global and national PSCs. Furthermore, in some instances, the growing reliance on the private security companies for performing functions of protection traditionally associated with the state has facilitated the reproduction of forms of capital and structures of power inherited from the corrupt processes of post-communist transitions.

Accountable Security Providers?

One of the most significant sets of challenges and dilemmas generated by the commercialization of security concerns the (re)distribution of power among different branches of the state, and the impact of this development on the accountability of security providers. Particularly problematic are those situations in which, by extending the capacity of the state to perform key security functions, PSCs have also empowered executive branches at the expense of legislatures and civil society organizations, and have enabled state agencies and officials to escape regular procedures designed to ensure accountability. These problems are not unique to Eastern Europe; indeed, in various ways and degrees they have affected many societies around the world.[2] What is particular about their presence in countries of the former Soviet bloc, however, is both that they have been shaped by, and, in turn, that they have affected the dynamics of post-communist transition. In other words, security commercialization—widely perceived as an important aspect of constructing liberalism in Eastern Europe—has, in some respects, significantly complicated the process of building effective liberal-democratic institutions.

There is already a significant literature that examines challenges of accountability generated by the proliferation of private security providers (Avant 2005, 2006; Krahmann 2007; Percy 2007; Leander 2010; Abrahamsen and Williams 2011; Abrahamsen and Leander 2015). This ability to escape accountability procedures has been particularly problematic in the case of private security actors involved in military activities. In particular, as Deborah Avant has cogently argued, the very flexibility that makes PSCs so beneficial, reducing the political as well as financial costs of sending/maintaining forces overseas, also entails significant political risks. Above all, the ability of governments to employ private security redistributes power within the state, empowering the executive over the legislature, reducing transparency, and enhancing the ability of commercially interested actors to impact policy (Avant 2005, 2006). Such reductions in transparency limit in problematic ways the ability of citizens to hold politicians accountable for their actions.

Although the provision of non-military security in societies outside of conflict zones is arguably less complicated from a normative point of view, it still raises significant challenges and problems of accountability. With PSC involvement in non-military activities outside of conflict zones, questions and problems of redistribution of power within the state, and challenges of accountability can be significant. Consider, for instance, post-conflict environments such as Bosnia, where the presence of unaccountable private security companies could pose significant dangers—potentially enhancing the risk of instability in that fragile country. As demonstrated in this book, PSCs and their political supporters in Bosnia have effectively used the discourse depicting the private security industry as an agent of public power to legitimize the rapid growth of that industry in the aftermath of the Yugoslav wars. As a result, their presence in the security landscape is so strong that today everyone takes them for granted—and even efforts to correct their abuses involve proposals for reforms to improve their behavior, not to outlaw them altogether. Both private and public Bosnian actors rely on the private security industry on a daily basis, and some PSCs have played constructive roles by helping to professionalize the security sector and extending the ability of cash-strapped authorities to perform their functions.

Yet, there is also a darker side of the use of PSCs to extend the power of the state. Thus, the proliferation of the private security industry has led to a situation in which some PSCs effectively operate as quasi-agencies of the state, performing important services to key individuals within the state. The problem, however, is that some of those services are not subject to the normal scrutiny procedures that are supposed to operate in a modern democracy. Consequently, they help to perpetuate attitudes and forms of behavior that are associated with the anti-democratic, violent Yugoslav past, undermining domestic and international efforts to transcend that past and (re)build Bosnia on the basis of liberal-democratic norms. For instance, as noted in Chapter 5, security experts, NGOs, as well as EU and NATO officials based in Sarajevo have expressed concern that there is no agency—either Bosnian or international—with sufficient resources to effectively monitor all the PSCs operating in the country. To make matters worse, some of the PSCs that escape the control of national and international authorities—particularly those operating outside Sarajevo—are closely connected to particular ethnic groups, appear to be powerful and well armed, and operate in an environment in which it is unclear what kinds of activities they carry out. The concern that is widely shared by Bosnian NGO representatives as well as EU and NATO officials is that various politicians and individuals close to them (including those with links to the Yugoslav conflicts) use PSCs to illegally collect intelligence about their adversaries, especially leaders of other ethnic groups.[3]

Furthermore, there is a suspicion that PSCs take advantage of the fact that they are not operating within strong structures of accountability to collect and hold serious quantities of small weapons. In a situation in which tensions persist among the different ethnic groups in Bosnia (especially outside of Sarajevo), the fear expressed by international officials is that in the event of a violent incident, some of these PSCs could quickly intervene on the side of one or another of the ethnic groups, and thus destabilize the fragile post-conflict state. In other words, private security actors could become a direct threat to the stability of the state, and could substantially undermine the ability of public institutions to protect Bosnian citizens. The solution recommended by EU and NATO officials based in Bosnia is to create a stronger, coherent regime for governing private security across Bosnia, so as to make it impossible for the private security industry to take advantage of the multiple divides within the country to operate as virtually independent, unchecked actors. Yet, in a situation in which tensions persist among (and sometimes within) the key ethnic groups and their parties in Bosnia, and in which the presence and involvement of international actors is no longer strong enough to effect substantial change, it is difficult to see how this type of reform might come about.

More broadly, the Bosnian situation illustrates a difficult normative dilemma concerning the appropriate level of international involvement in post-conflict societies. Thus, the most rapid way to secure further reform in the field of security—including a more effective regime to govern PSCs—may well be to reassert a stronger form of international intervention. Indeed, there are reports that the pace of reform in Bosnia slowed down considerably after 2007, when the international community, having shifted its attention to other regions, started to diminish its pressure on Bosnian political actors (Brady 2012). Yet, even if the international community had the political will to apply more pressure for reform—and there are no indications that it does— it is almost certain that any move in the direction of greater international (re)involvement in governing Bosnia would generate strong opposition from many Bosnian and international political actors. Indeed, for many—both in Bosnia and abroad—any efforts by the international community to reassert stronger control over the direction of Bosnian politics would probably be seen as the expression of a morally and politically unacceptable neo-colonial logic.[4]

The most productive course of action would be for the international community to avoid direct forms of intervention and instead work more systematically with Bosnian political actors and especially civil society groups who support democratic reforms. Collaboration with pro-reform Bosnians would need to include providing them with material resources and symbolic support to help their campaigns to hold political elites accountable and to seek to push forward democratic reforms. The EU could play a particularly helpful role in this area, but only if it is able and willing to keep alive the promise of closer integration—and the possibility of future Bosnian membership in the Union. For all their deep and multifaceted disagreements, many Bosnian political actors continue to believe that membership in the EU would be the safest way for their country to transcend its difficult past and emerge as a modern, functioning democratic polity. Given Bosnia's numerous and profound problems, it is clear that the process of acceding to the EU would be a long and arduous one. It is also clear that even a successful integration of Bosnia into the EU would not automatically translate into a resolution of all of that country's issues and challenges. As the Central and East European polities that are now EU members demonstrate, complex challenges of democratization and liberalization persist long after the official accession date. Nevertheless, keeping alive the prospect of eventual accession to the EU—and in the meantime continuing to build stronger economic, political, and cultural ties between Brussels and Sarajevo—would enable the EU to retain a reasonable degree of influence over Bosnia's politicians. That influence, if combined with sustained pressure from a well-organized set of Bosnian civil society actors, would hold the potential to reinvigorate the process of reform in the former Yugoslav republic.

While the political situation of Bosnia—and thus the challenges involved in ensuring the accountability of PSCs—can be seen as unique, the danger of privileging the executive at the expense of legislatures and reproducing unaccountable practices is also present in other East European polities. In Serbia, for instance, the adoption of the Law on Private Security and the Law on Private Detectives in 2013, followed by the Law on Weapons and Ammunition in early 2015, marks a significant step in the right direction, after so many years in which there was no comprehensive law governing private security. As Petrović and Milošević (2015) show, the Law on Private Security has introduced important measures aimed at defining, regulating, and professionalizing the private security industry. Importantly, the law also seeks to regulate the powers available to private security employees and private investigators, and to define procedures for overseeing the activities of those actors. Yet, the recent legislation also contains some problematic gaps and ambiguities, which are likely to complicate efforts to promote accountability in the field of security. In particular, the Private Security Law does not clarify how the Ministry of Interior will control private security companies, and does not establish clear procedures for holding the Ministry accountable for its performance of this control function. Furthermore, the 2013 law does not establish a licensing procedure that would compel entrepreneurs to reveal their pecuniary liabilities to the state, and does not establish clear security checks for PSC owners—thus making it more difficult to ensure that private security companies do not have links to organized crime (Petrović and Milošević 2015).

More surprisingly, problems of accountability also affect EU member states like Bulgaria and Romania. Similar to the case of former Yugoslav polities, some of these extensions of the state can be seen as constructive ways of enabling public authorities to perform important functions in a context marked by limited resources. As government representatives now acknowledge, in the absence of PSCs the state would have a limited ability to provide protection to its citizens and their businesses—particularly outside of the large cities. In other words, it is only with the support of the private security industry that the state can perform—and, importantly, be seen to be performing—functions of protection that are widely regarded as key attributes of sovereignty. As we have seen, the image that government officials seek to project is that of public agencies using PSCs as "junior partners," fully under the control of the state. This image is designed to reinforce the legitimacy of the state, portraying it as fully in control of—even if operating in collaboration with—private actors.

The private security industry, we noted in previous chapters, now participates in formulating collective norms and agendas, as well as helping to enforce those norms. In recent years, there have been a number of initiatives designed to enhance cooperation between the police and PSCs in assessing risks, identifying threats, and formulating solutions to those risks and threats. Proponents of those initiatives—on the public as well as private side—stress their merits, focusing in particular on the fact that, in an age of limited governmental/EU resources, the mobilization of material and non-material resources held by PSCs (ranging from specialized, modern technologies of protection to expertise, experience, and information controlled by the private security industry) can significantly enhance the ability of public agencies to identify and respond to potential risks at an early stage. Yet, significant challenges persist. In Romania, for example, we saw that during the period of time covered in this book the regulation of the private security industry remained firmly in the hands of the police, with the legislature and civil society actors largely unable to monitor or affect developments in this area (Badea 2014: 43). One of the key problems is that, in addition to issuing or revoking licenses to PSCs, the police are also involved in the compulsory training of PSC employees, and provide consultancy to the private security industry. Predictably, one of the consequences of this situation is an increase in the danger of corruption of police officers, thereby complicating Romania's efforts to transcend one of its key obstacles to good governance: corruption.

Similar to the situation in Romania, during the period of time covered in this book in Bulgaria there has continued to be a police-heavy regulatory regime governing PSCs, which means that the police still retain excessive power in this domain—thereby increasing the risk of corruption of the police, and making it more difficult for civil society actors or even other branches of the state to supervise and hold accountable security providers (Badea 2014: 43). Also similar to the situation in Romania, in Bulgaria police officers have continued to be allowed to work for PSCs right after retirement. All this means that the police have continued to have strong incentives to apply regulations in a selective manner, privileging companies that are likely to hire policemen once they retire. Furthermore, particularly until 2013 the Ministry of Interior (MoI) continued to be a major provider of commercial security, operating its own department for technical security services (SOD), with territorial units and specialized monitoring centers at regional police establishments (Dzhekova and Rusev 2015: 44). By 2012, the MoI had become the most powerful security services provider in Bulgaria (Dzhekova and Rusev 2015: 44). This, of course, placed it in a serious conflict of interest since it was occupying the mutually incompatible positions of regulator/enforcer of rules, and player in the security field (Badea 2014: 59). The situation improved in 2013, when, under pressure from professional private security associations—who argued that the conflict of interest was incompatible with European law—the MoI decided to close down its SOD unit (Dzhekova and Rusev 2015: 44). Nevertheless, Bulgaria continues to have two state-owned security companies that are active in the field, competing with private PSCs—although the position of those state companies is much weaker than the SOD once was (Dzhekova and Rusev 2015: 44). More broadly, there continue to be some gray areas that enable the unsupervised perpetuation of key security services. For instance, the provision of private investigative services is not covered by any regulation, and detective agencies are reported to operate in breach of personal data protection laws (Dzhekova and Rusev 2015: 53). Allegedly, at least some detective agencies have continued to take advantage of this situation of legal ambiguity to act as unaccountable quasi-agencies of the state, providing powerful individuals within the state with illegally obtained intelligence about their rivals and political enemies.[5]

To address these problems and limitations, it would be helpful to adopt new legislation that ensures that no state agency can play multiple, mutually incompatible roles, that no security agency can operate with impunity due to the absence of regulation, and that the other branches of the state—particularly legislatures—have enough power to hold the executive accountable for its actions in the field of security. During the period of time covered in this book, however, this did not seem to be a major priority for parliamentarians from Bulgaria and Romania. Furthermore, even if the right legislation were to be adopted, it is not clear that it would be consistently and effectively implemented—particularly as long as in both countries the police continue to have allies with substantial political influence.

Redefining the Relationship between the State and Civil Society

The commercialization of security via the proliferation of PSCs and their constitution as agents of public power and, simultaneously, the inscription of the commercial logic in key state institutions has also led to a redefinition of the relationship between the state and civil society—in ways that can be deeply problematic. In important ways, the normative concerns linked to the commercialization of security reflect broader tensions and difficult questions concerning the moral limits of markets in liberal societies. Those tensions and questions have been at the heart of some of the most influential contemporary political theory works. Consider, for instance, Michael Walzer's famous work on *Spheres of Justice* (1983). According to Walzer, a key concept that should guide the quest for good principles of governance is that of distributive justice, which involves an art of differentiation aimed at ensuring that in each sphere

169

of society the distribution of goods is carried out based on criteria appropriate to that sphere. The danger, in his view, is that money has a tendency to invade every other sphere and override their specific distributive criteria (Walzer 1983; Loader et al. 2014). When this happens, money can generate a form of market tyranny. Under these circumstances, justice requires that we define the boundaries of many and block or control certain exchanges so as to set limits on "the dominance of wealth" (Walzer 1983: 100). The aim, in this context, is to prevent the harms experienced in the realm of money from cascading outwards in ways that damage life and "social standing" (Loader et al. 2014: 473). Applying this argument to the sphere of security, the challenge becomes to put limits on the ways in which money can undermine the provision of this public good and can endanger its promise of equality.[6]

Two issues associated with the expansion of the logic of the market in the field of security are especially significant. First, there is the danger of weakening social cohesion within the state via the establishment of exclusive communities of protection. Second, there is the question of the redefinition of the public (and of public engagement): what is involved here is a process of turning citizens into partners who are systematically recruited to aid the state and its private security partners. One of the consequences of this development is that it has become difficult for individuals to act as agents of a powerful, independent civil society, with the power to hold public agencies accountable.

In discussing the challenge of maintaining social cohesion in the face of the logic of commercialism, it is useful to start from the argument put forward by Loader and Walker, who point out that a common sense of security is essential in the life of a political community. Members of the community are united, in part, by a structure of feeling that involves a perception of security as mutual; thus, the provision of security to all (as a key public good) is at the heart of a viable social order. In essence, public security plays a civilizing role; in its absence, social cohesion can be severely undermined and the political community itself can come under threat. For this reason, while various private actors may have certain roles to play within a pluralized structure of security provision, it is important that this be an "anchored pluralism," having the state and public authorities at its center as a way to avoid undermining social stability (Loader and Walker 2007).

There are, however, instances in which it is not easy to achieve the anchored pluralism advocated by Loader and Walker. As we have seen, in countries where public authorities in charge of security provision are too weak, partial, or perceived as corrupt they may not be recognized by their citizens as agents of the public good. Consequently, "public security" provision may come to be seen as a source of oppression or danger, leading citizens and businesses to rely for their protection on private security providers—including global corporations. This suggests that the ideal model of the state–sovereignty–security triad is, in some countries, little more than a distant aspiration, as different relationships between security, society, and structures of feeling are created and reproduced. In societies emerging from conflict, this can be even more complicated. For example, as noted in previous chapters, even decades after the start of the Yugoslav wars, in Bosnia as well as Serbia trust in the police remains limited. As long as this situation persists, individuals and businesses will continue to rely on private security companies for their protection.

Yet, this situation comes with its own dangers—most notably the creation of exclusive communities of protection, in which access to what has long been considered a key public good—security—is not guaranteed in equal measure to all citizens.[7] Rather, access to security depends on the extent to which individuals and businesses are able and willing to play the role of paying customers. In such cases, concentric circles of protection have effectively replaced the image of the horizontal communities traditionally associated with modern states and based on the assumption that all the members of the horizontal community are entitled to equal protection from the state. In a situation marked by the growing prominence of concentric circles of protection, there are clear discrepancies between inner circles (containing individuals and businesses who can afford to pay for the protection provided by top private security providers), and the outer circles of individuals who have to rely on the—often inefficient, sometimes corrupt—police services. As a corollary to this, there is the danger that, if the expansion of practices of private security accelerates in the future, it could contribute to the phenomenon of "secession of elites" (Lasch 1996; Loader et al. 2014).[8] The concern here is that rich individuals and groups come to rely on market-provided forms of protection to such a degree that they are no longer able to appreciate the direct value of public police provision. Linked to this, they can start to resent "paying twice" for their security: once to the private security companies they employ, and again to the state for a type of service that, as they see it, plays little if any part in the everyday practices of protection. In other words, the expansion of the market logic in the field of security operates in ways that could come to undermine the ability of the state to collect (via taxes) the resources that it needs to fulfill its democratic commitment of providing equal protection for all (Low 2003; Loader et al. 2014).

To further compound the problem, as part of their constitution as agents of public power, PSCs have been empowered to not simply respond to threats against their clients, but also to participate in practices of risk-management, in which they seek to prevent the unfolding of a dangerous scenario rather than react to a form of aggression or even a clear and present danger. It will be recalled that the legislation adopted in several East European polities in recent years empowers PSCs to set up admission regimes on the private or public properties they protect, in which they "filter" out individuals regarded as risky. In a situation in which the criteria used to define "risky" individuals remain vague, there has been a tendency on the part of many PSCs to identify as risky and exclude from the spaces they protect individuals selected on the basis of their socio-economic status or ethnic identity, rather than because of the acts they may have committed. Thus, there are strong indications that in Bulgaria and Romania as well as Serbia and Bosnia private security providers have used their powers to set up regimes of admission designed to "filter out" from the spaces they protect—including public places—the homeless, the visibly poor, and members of particular communities (especially the Roma).[9]

The situation is additionally complicated by the fact that, as we have seen, some state institutions offer commercial security services, and often devote more resources to their commercial operations than to their provision of security as a public good. Linked to this, the rise to prominence of the neo-liberal logic has also translated into a responsibilization of individuals and communities, leading to a situation in which—through both recently adopted legislation and everyday practices of the police and other public agencies—individuals and businesses are encouraged and expected to rely on private providers for their security. As a corollary to this, victims of crime are often perceived as being at least partly responsible for their plight—having failed to invest sufficiently in private security arrangements.

To put the discussion in a broader perspective, this shift to a responsibilization of individuals and communities associated with the neo-liberal logic entails a redefinition of the relationship between the state and civil society: the public is instrumentalized and mobilized as a partner of security provision. At first glance, one might get the impression that the citizens and residents of Eastern European polities have benefited from a massive process of empowerment in the field of security, as a result of legislative and institutional reforms adopted in recent years. After all, the protection of individuals and their private property is now at the heart of security agendas of post-communist polities, and several forums have emerged as part of state-sponsored processes of involving various non-state actors in consultations on how to better formulate and implement strategies aimed at protecting the public from a wide array of risks. In other words, at first glance what seems to be involved here is a vision of good governance that places heavy emphasis on the public good, and on creating conditions for a vibrant, liberal public sphere, in which citizens are able to debate, criticize, and if necessary alter practices of security provision.

Yet, a closer look at these recent reforms and initiatives reveals that in the area of security provision, to a large extent the concept of public involvement is less about democratic accountability and more about increasing the effectiveness of police activities. This entails harnessing the energies of civil society actors as partners of the police and other state security agencies—and as such as actors that have duties to participate in practices of provision of the public good. Thus, at least in part the mobilization of citizens and communities through a process of responsibilization amounts to a transfer of the burden of preventing and fighting crime, while making certain forms of behavior acceptable and identifying others as unacceptable. As we have seen, some of the key pieces of legislation adopted in recent years in East European societies include provisions aimed at delegating to citizens and businesses the duty of managing contemporary security risks. The responsibilization of individuals and companies has also been encouraged by external actors like the EU in the face of transversal issues like organized crime and terrorism.[10]

The result is a form of security governance defined by Niklas Rose as "governing through community," which combines the individualism of neoliberal political discourses with more left-wing ideals of empowerment and active citizenship.[11] By articulating a discourse that stresses multiple, often ill-defined risks, the governments of former communist polities have created a potentially endless duty on the part of citizens and communities to support all the policies and practices deemed by the government as necessary to ensure the protection of the population. Consequently, there is a risk of perceiving those who do not choose to hire private security as individuals/businesses that do not understand their own responsibilities.[12] What is compromised, meanwhile, is the ability of non-state actors to take distance from current security policies and practices, engage in a critical assessment of those policies, and have access to institutions and procedures that enable them to correct whatever problems they might identify.

There is another way in which citizen empowerment has been narrowed and made dependent on the market mechanism. In principle, the existence of a large array of private security actors can be seen as a source of power to citizens, who can now hold public agencies accountable, by behaving as "clients" who have the option of resorting to a different security provider, if they are not happy with the services provided by the state or by a particular PSC. Yet, this choice is not available—or at least not in equal measure—to all citizens and businesses. Rather, their ability to hold the police and other security agencies accountable largely depends on their economic status. The option of resorting to reputable, reliable private security providers is not readily available to the more vulnerable members of society, be they citizens or businesses. This situation was made worse by the global economic crisis of 2007–9, whose effects lingered in Eastern Europe for a long time. Thus, having suffered massive losses because of the crisis, many small businesses—and even some of the larger companies—became less able and willing to pay for private security services (Petrović and Milošević 2015: 87).[13]

The developments examined above illustrate the complexities involved in governing and providing security in a situation in which conventional boundaries between domestic/international, public/private, and security/economics are increasingly blurred. As if this situation was not complicated enough, the security environment continues to be affected by a darker side of security commercialization in the context of the Europeanization and globalization of East European polities. In particular, there is a problematic persistence of some links between legitimate security providers and illicit actors. These links make it harder to ensure that the field of security is governed by the liberal-democratic norms on which EU polities (as well as polities seeking integration into the Union) are expected to be founded.

The Illicit Security Professionals: The Dark Side of Europeanization and Globalization

As discussed in Chapter 3, the Europeanization and globalization of security in those polities has also had an illicit dimension, and elements of that dimension persist today—although in a more subtle manner than in the early years of post-communist transition. As criminologists from Eastern Europe have explained, while some of the most violent and obvious aspects of the links between PSCs and organized crime have been largely transcended as a result of the legislative and institutional changes introduced in the 2000s, illicit transnational security professionals have found new, more subtle, and less violent ways of operating in and through Eastern Europe (CSD 2012). More broadly, over the last decade, in most Eastern European polities organized crime has undergone a significant transformation, involving a decline in violence and growing attempts by organized crime to regulate illegal markets and settle accounts by other means. The conversion of criminal capital into legitimate business structures has led to greater demand and potential for corruption. On the one hand, corruption has been used to regulate criminal markets via corrupted law enforcement. On the other hand, corruption has also been used to settle business conflicts (via leverage in the judiciary) and to take control of additional economic resources, especially through manipulation of public procurement (CSD 2012: 17).

It is also interesting to note that, particularly in the cases of Bulgaria and Romania, accession to the EU in 2007 has opened a range of new opportunities for criminals, including tax crimes, which prompted part of the criminal networks to shift their focus toward new illegal activities. Their ability to move freely throughout Europe has greatly facilitated the operations of organized criminal groups, and made them attractive to transnational crime groups seeking access to Western Europe—for instance for illicit drugs but also the smuggling of human beings. Those forms of trafficking, as it is well known, grew exponentially in response to the persisting conflicts in countries like Syria and Iraq, prompting the largest influx of refugees in Europe. And, while it would be an exaggeration to claim that most PSCs are involved in all these types of criminal activities, there is credible evidence that a series of individuals connected to the private security industry have been influential participants in some of those networks and crimes—not least because of their "skills set" and experience (such as that of violent forms of protection of their clients' "cargos," and ability to help enforce "contracts" outside of the judicial system). This is yet another illustration of the ways in which the activities of PSCs complicate assessments of the private security industry and contribute to contradictory tensions in the field of security. Thus, PSC practices that have played productive roles in facilitating the insertion of East European states into legitimate European and global institutional structures and economic flows occur in parallel to the problematic involvement of some security actors in nurturing the illicit side of Europeanization and globalization, and in so doing contributing to the reproduction of insecurity to individuals and societies.

What seems to be involved here is the emergence and reproduction of illicit networks of security professionals that exist in parallel to the legitimate, transnational networks of security professionals, often empowered by the same processes of Europeanization, globalization, and blurring of boundaries between the public/private arenas. Furthermore, there appear to be at least some situations—and specific nodal points—in which the illicit and legitimate networks intersect, as some security professionals that are affiliated with legitimate PSCs also seem to have become involved in some illegal activities. To make matters even more complicated and problematic, there are reports that suggest that several of the individuals through which illicit and legitimate networks of security professionals intersect are public officials, including, sometimes, influential political actors. For instance, there is anecdotal evidence that members of a Bosnian PSC from Republika Srpska that is connected to a Bosnian Serb politician have been involved in smuggling into Western Europe small arms that were inherited from the Yugoslav wars of the 1990s.[14] This is of particular concern not only to pro-reform, pro-Western political actors in Bosnia but also to politicians and security experts from the EU, who fear that some of those weapons may fall into the hands of violent extremists affiliated with IS. In a similar vein, there are concerns that employees or former employees of a Bulgarian PSC have used their material as well as non-material capital (skills, expertise, political connections, but also small weapons) to set up or support rings/networks used to smuggle refugees fleeing conflicts in Syria and Afghanistan, as well as migrants from Africa into

Western Europe.[15] At the very least, this suggests that difficult questions need to be raised about the extent to which—and circumstances under which—security providers, including actors who operate within state structures, are committed to the provision of the public good.

Not surprisingly, reports about the links between private security and transnational organized crime vary and sometimes conflict with one another. Some security experts and EU/NATO officials based in Eastern Europe estimate that, particularly in Bosnia, more than 50 percent of the domestic private security industry has some links to transnational organized crime. Others argue that such figures are exaggerated, and that the illicit dimension of security privatization does not affect more than 30 percent of PSCs even in the Western Balkans. Yet others (particularly government officials from East European states) tend to insist that only a small percentage of PSCs have any links to transnational criminals.[16] While it remains difficult to accurately "quantify" its presence and connections with individuals associated with PSCs, what is interesting is that there is widespread agreement among security analysts, investigative journalists, international officials, and even many local practitioners that such links do exist. This is particularly significant in a situation in which academics and practitioners alike insist that transnational crime is one of the most important security challenges in the twenty-first century. Understanding the nature of these links, and finding ways to weaken and eventually eliminate them, should become a priority for security professionals and political actors at the national, regional, and global levels.

To further complicate matters, in many instances the illicit transnationalization of security professionals is hard to capture due to the fact that there is a virtual continuum between the legal economy, the gray economy, and organized crime—which often has a transnational connection (Andreas 2011; Gounev and Ruggiero 2012; Jakobi 2013). The resurgence of the gray economy since 2007 has contributed to a situation in which many businesses try to cut costs by resorting to unlawful techniques and practices (Petrović and Milošević 2015; Dzhekova and Rusev 2015). In Bulgaria, for instance, there is a complex, problematic continuum between the legitimate economy, the gray economy, and organized crime. As a study published by Bulgaria's Centre for the Study of Democracy (CSD) stresses, "High level corporate criminals known as the 'oligarchs' operate not only in Bulgaria but in most of Eastern Europe. Behind their legitimate corporate façade, oligarchs may be directly involved in criminal activities (VAT or excisable goods fraud, etc.) and rely heavily on illicit lobbying and corruption in their usual business practices. During the 1990s and the early 2000s, political corruption facilitated the rise of such economic conglomerates, initially via rigged privatisation deals, and later continued to exploit public resources through rigged public procurement tenders" (CSD 2012: 16).

Unlike Western Europe and the US, in Bulgaria white-collar criminals appear to be directly linked to various other forms of organized crime. According to the CSD, there are two major threats emerging from this situation: "The first is related to the inability of law enforcement and the judiciary to reach the top levels of organized crime, as these largely reside in the legal economy and have political leverage. As a result, whenever law enforcement institutions effectively crack down on low-level criminal structures these are immediately re-established by the structures at the higher levels. The second important threat is related to the persistent public and media perception that some large Bulgarian economic entities are involved in organized crime. This perception is often exploited by political parties who tacitly favour some and publicly denounce other oligarchs thus seeking populist effects" (CSD 2012: 16–17). This constellation of organized crime/the gray economy/legitimate businesses and organizations has facilitated the continued involvement of Bulgarian actors in transnational organized crime. Thus, Bulgaria has been—and continues to be—a transit country for various forms of illicit trafficking, and the role of Bulgarian organized crime groups is shaped by the geographic location of the country. For instance, with respect to drug trafficking, Bulgaria is on the Balkan route for smuggling heroin from Afghanistan to Western Europe and for smuggling synthetic drugs from Europe toward the Middle East. Bulgarians are also involved in transnational organized crime networks that are trafficking cocaine from South America toward Europe (CSD 2012: 27).

There is credible evidence that some of the Bulgarian players involved in these illicit forms of trafficking have links to the private security industry. For example, there is evidence that a Bulgarian PSC, whose owner is a former member of Bulgaria's anti-terrorist squad, systematically used his connections to set up and improve the position of his firm in both the legal and illegal markets.[17] What was involved in that case was that the PSC owner was able to cast his institutional background—and, specifically, his skills, knowledge, and experience with the anti-terrorist squad—as relevant cultural capital, and on this basis to enhance its symbolic capital in the field of security in contemporary Bulgaria. His key strategy seems to have been to argue that, in a situation in which crime was still a risk to Bulgarian entrepreneurs and businesses, and in which the judicial system remained slow and inefficient, individuals and corporations that wanted to do business in Bulgaria needed the protection of someone who "knew the system," had enough expertise and knowledge to warn and protect clients against various potential risks, could deal in an efficient manner with the authorities in case those individuals/businesses had any trouble, and could help to enforce contracts in a situation in which Bulgarian institutions were too weak and corrupt to do so. That PSC owner was able to attract not only Bulgarian but also Israeli capital, building a thriving private security business that he subsequently expanded to include a prosperous taxi business. In addition to these legitimate businesses, however—and using the capital gained through them—the PSC in question reportedly became involved in illegal trafficking, coming to control a significant proportion of the prostitution market and also acquiring a powerful position in the drug trafficking market.

More broadly, there are credible reports that a series of former extortionists turned oligarchs who are currently the owners or managers of PSCs continue to thrive by being involved in what some security analysts have described as a "closed business model."[18] For instance, particularly outside of Sofia, even in the 2010s it would seem that there were Bulgarian PSCs that drew on capital acquired in dubious circumstances in the 1990s, as well as funding that was apparently provided by Russian oligarchs, to provide insurance services as well as security to Bulgaria's Central Coop Bank. They then worked to promote that bank to the detriment of other (especially foreign) banks in various locations. The situation seems to have been particularly problematic at some Black Sea resorts, where certain hotels owned by Bulgarian companies combined private security and insurance, and where tourists had no choice but to conduct all their transactions at the Central Coop Bank—the only bank allowed to operate in those resorts.

As regards Romania, there is less information available about the role and power of transnational organized crime and its links to PSCs. Nevertheless, there is some credible evidence that those links do exist, although possibly on a smaller scale. As in the case of Bulgaria, Romania witnessed the emergence of a complex set of connections between criminal networks, the gray economy, and legitimate businesses with strong political connections, in a situation in which corruption in the government and even in the justice system provided fertile ground for criminal organizations to steal public money, and loopholes in the Romanian legislation—particularly in the early to mid-2000s—enabled criminals to walk free if they were caught.[19] In essence, Romania, like Bulgaria and other East European countries, has witnessed the emergence of powerful, transnational networks of insecurity professionals that mobilize forms of capital which are highly valued by organized criminal groups (e.g. knowledge of how the administrative and judicial systems work and how to manipulate them, political connections, as well as more technical skills—such as surveillance, and in some cases ability to apply intimidation and coercion to "enforce" illegal contracts) to gain more power in a fluid security environment. In that environment, contrary to the official Romanian discourse, Western-style liberal democratic norms do not always apply. And, as in the case of Bulgaria, it would be wrong to depict these networks of insecurity professionals as completely separate from, and controlled by, the official security professionals, since there are, reportedly, some powerful points of intersection between them. Indeed, it has been suggested that the illicit security professionals would not be able to operate (or at least not prosper) without some degree of support from a series of public officials. Some judges and prosecutors have argued that money and politically connected lawyers have helped a series of prominent drug dealers stay out of jail. The problem was reportedly compounded by the fact that, for a long time, many judges did not view drug trafficking and other forms of illicit trade as significant social threats, preferring instead to focus on other forms of crime.[20]

Similar to what happened in Bulgaria—Romania's involvement in transnational organized crime seems to be shaped by its geographic position and the fact that it is now a member of the EU, giving its citizens and businesses easier access to Western Europe. Consequently, Romania has emerged as a transit country for various types of illicit trafficking, including smuggling heroin from Afghanistan to Western Europe, and trafficking cocaine from Latin America toward Europe. In several instances, Romanian prosecutors and police officers that had spent months if not years working to identify and dismantle transnational drug trafficking networks operating on Romanian soil were, in effect, undermined by corrupt magistrates. In a series of notable cases in the 2000s police officers arrested several Romanian and foreign nationals involved in powerful drug trafficking rings, but Romanian magistrates decided that the traffickers were not a social threat and released them on unconditional bail, pending further investigation. Not surprisingly, many of those individuals subsequently left the country, using fake travel documents.

It would seem that it was when foreign government agencies, particularly the US Drug Enforcement Administration (DEA), became concerned about the transnational illicit trafficking going on on Romanian soil that authorities in Bucharest started to take the fight against these networks of organized criminals more seriously. Under pressure from the EU and the US government, and by working in collaboration with the US DEA, starting in 2007 the Romanian police arrested a series of individuals belonging to transnational networks involved in money laundering, drug trafficking, and cigarette smuggling that were operating in Russia, Moldova, Poland, Germany, Italy, Romania, Spain, the US, and Hong Kong, and confiscated drugs and illicit goods worth millions of dollars. Even in those cases, however, it is reported that the most influential members of the illicit networks were freed or only held in custody for a few days (OCCRP 2009). It is impossible to say with any degree of precision to what extent and in what ways PSCs were involved in all these illicit practices. Nevertheless, there are credible reports that several Romanian PSCs (particularly those operating on the Black Sea Coast, several of which had links to local politicians and/or businessmen) have participated in the protection and transport of illicitly obtained goods, as well as in human smuggling—particularly the smuggling of young women and girls coming from the Republic of Moldova and being trafficked into prostitution in

Western Europe. More recently, Romanians involved in transnational criminal groups have also participated in the smuggling of refugees from Syria, Iraq, and Afghanistan into Western Europe—for instance, by driving trucks and vans containing refugees from Hungary into Austria.[21]

Transnational organized crime seems to have an even stronger presence in the Western Balkans, including Bosnia and Serbia—not least because of the difficult legacy of the violent conflicts of the 1990s. The sanctions and embargoes of the 1990s, though lifted, continued to have a powerful impact on Bosnia and Serbia in the 2000s and beyond. According to several Belgrade and Sarajevo-based analysts, the problem is that political authorities (including Western officials and members of the international administration in Bosnia) paid insufficient attention to the criminalizing consequences of those developments. For instance, according to some estimates, approximately 50 percent of Bosnia's economy was black market by 2003 (Brady 2012). In the 2000s, the underground networks that had emerged in the former Yugoslavia during the wars turned into criminal networks with strong political connections, which were involved in massive smuggling, tax evasion, and trafficking in women and stolen cars (Brady 2012: 18). In the early 2000s, UN officials and EU representatives reported increases of organized criminal groups from the Western Balkans; those were said to be tightly interwoven into political structures, the police, the judiciary, and the secret service, and were also part of wider and looser networks. Balkan organized criminal groups started to become prominent in major EU countries, and began to form loose alliances with Russian and Italian mafia groups in trafficking counterfeit dollars, arms, and migrants. Linked to this, the 2000s also saw a re-emergence of the southern branch on the Balkan drug route. This era also saw a significant shift in the Colombian cocaine trafficking route into Europe, shifting from Spain to the Western Balkans (Brady 2012: 20). This new kind of transnational mafia brought together criminal groups from various countries, generating what the DEA has called a "Balkan Holy Alliance."[22]

One of the gravest concerns expressed by international officials based in Bosnia and Serbia is that insecurity professionals—including individuals affiliated with some PSCs—from the Balkans continue to be involved in the illegal sale and transnational supply of weapons.[23] The trade in weapons appeared to be very well structured and organized, with the Spanish and other Western intelligence services arguing that the IRA and ETA have been buying weapons from arms groups based in the Republika Srpska and indirectly from Serbia, which apparently originated from the former Yugoslav army (Brady 2012). In addition, there are reports that some of the most prominent organized criminal groups operating in Western Europe and further afield acquire weapons from the Balkans-based networks. Amnesty International has also claimed that weapons have been trafficked from Serbia and Bosnia into Liberia and the Congo (Brady 2012: 22).

Alarmed by those developments, the international administration in Bosnia sought to take action by imposing a tougher Criminal Code and procedural laws, and placing pressure on the Parliament of Bosnia to take up the fight against organized crime (Brady 2012). The problem, however, is that, as noted above, the international pressure started to diminish—and, with this, the Bosnian authorities' commitment started to dwindle—after 2006, when the international community's attention started to focus on other "problem" zones, particularly in the Middle East. Under these circumstances, and in a situation in which, as we have seen, the political system in Bosnia continues to be deeply divided, in recent years the commitment of Bosnian actors to the application of the Criminal Code and related legislation appears to have weakened, leaving illicit actors more room to maneuver.[24]

Another challenge involved in fighting this type of crime is that today, the Western Balkans appear to have followed the "lead" of countries like Bulgaria and Romania in the emergence of a continuum linking legitimate businesses (often with strong political connections), the gray economy, and organized crime. Thus, over the past few years both Bosnia and Serbia appear to have witnessed an increase in corruption, financial crime, and cybercrime (Brady 2012: 32). Public procurement, privatization, and tender processes were all highlighted in relation to the growth in corrupt behavior, prompting security experts to argue that corruption and white-collar crimes should be conceptualized as part of organized crime. It is reported that there have been multiple irregularities involving the abuse of public funds, the misuse of utility companies, procurement, and privatization that have empowered and enriched a series of politicians and their allies in business and the gray economy, including owners/managers of PSCs. Incidents such as the illegal transfer of property into private hands, buying off convictions, police involvement in drugs trafficking and allegedly human trafficking as well, and the issuing of unsecured loans to alleged drugs dealers are reported to have been regular occurrences in Bosnia and, to a lesser extent, in Serbia.[25] It is also worth mentioning that in Serbia there is a strong presence of the "black market security" (involving individuals who are not employed by any registered PSC) in the protection of bars, cafes, and nightclubs. Criminal groups operate with relative impunity in this sector, in a situation in which the Serbian Police have failed to impose order on them—not least because policemen are among those who moonlight in nightclubs and bars, and their colleagues are apparently reluctant to investigate fellow policemen (Petrović and Milošević 2015). In Bosnia, efforts to crack down on organized crime seem to have targeted low-to medium-level criminals, often failing to touch the most powerful individuals within the transnational networks operating on their soil. This, it is believed, is because such a move would reveal the complexity and depth of links between top-level organized criminals and political actors in that country.[26] All these cases are potent reminders of the fact that all the reforms and positive transformations that have occurred in recent years in the East European countries have not succeeded in completely eliminating the violent assemblages that include public as well as private actors engaged in illicit practices of insecurity.

In a situation in which there is no neat, sharp divide between the licit and illicit spheres/domains of activity in East European polities, it will be particularly challenging to change this situation. Passing more stringent laws to penalize the involvement of individuals and groups (including security providers) in illicit activities would be a useful step, but it cannot be enough. Thus, as long as those engaged in illicit practices are able to mobilize connections with powerful actors within state institutions, they will likely be able to circumvent the applicable legislation. What is also needed, therefore, is to protect and strengthen the independence of judiciaries, and enhance their ability to hold accountable all those engaged in illegal activities, regardless of their connections with influential politicians. In addition, it would be helpful to strengthen the ability of independent actors from civil society (the media, NGOs, think tanks) to support the judiciary in its campaign against illegal activities, and to put greater pressure on the other state branches to end the collusion between licit/illicit activities and actors. International actors, particularly the EU, could also help by supporting those national and local agencies that do seek to disrupt and eventually end these practices that transcend the licit/illicit boundaries. This could be done both via continued financial and symbolic support for pro-reform, anti-corruption civil society actors, and by maintaining pressure on East European politicians that condone corruption and/or act to undermine the power of institutions designed to hold the executive power to account. Yet, this is not an uncontroversial proposal. As noted above, the involvement of the EU has come to be resented by some actors within Eastern Europe, who argue that EU monitoring or "guidance" is excessive and undermines the sovereign power of East European states. It is noteworthy, for instance, that the EU Verification Mechanism set up to monitor Bulgaria and Romania following their accession to the EU is subject to intense domestic debates and contestations between those civil society actors and members of the judiciary who see them as necessary mechanisms for the pursuit of reforms, and, on the other hand, politicians and groups (often nationalists) who regard them as unfairly intrusive mechanisms. The danger, at a time of growing Euroskepticism in many places in Europe, is that the maintenance of verification mechanisms and procedures might reinforce the anti-democratic, anti-reform political forces at the expense of liberal-democratic actors.

Concluding Thoughts

When, following the collapse of communist regimes, the societies of the former Eastern bloc embarked upon processes of reform, many analysts and policymakers assumed that the transitions would lead them, in a relatively linear manner, to the establishment of liberal-democratic norms and institutions. Repressive, authoritarian regimes would be replaced by democratic, accountable institutions in all domains of life, including in the provision of security. Yet, more than a quarter century after the start of anti-communist revolutions, practices of security provision remain more complicated, and in many ways more problematic, than anyone could have expected.

This is not to deny the importance of the reforms that have been conducted in recent years. As we have seen, in Eastern Europe a complex set of processes of security commercialization has translated into the emergence of new networks of security providers that transcend domestic/international, public/private, and security/economics boundaries. In particular, there has been a spectacular empowerment of private security companies, who are now a regular, taken-for-granted feature of the security landscape in Eastern Europe, performing a multitude of functions of protection that were conventionally attributed to the state. As part of a complex process of integration in European institutional structures, PSCs based in those polities have also become integrated in transnational networks of security professionals, playing an increasingly important role in the formulation and enactment of European security agendas.

As a result of all these developments, countries like Romania, Bulgaria, Bosnia, and Serbia are now experiencing novel normative challenges and dilemmas. In particular, they—like their West European counterparts, and many other countries around the world—have to face a situation in which one of the core ideas of modern political imagination, the idea of the state's monopoly of legitimate violence, is increasingly subject to challenges and contestations. In sharp contrast to the vision of the state as the unique provider of that key public good, security, the contemporary diversification of the field of security can appear as dangerously fragmenting. As a corollary to this, the growing power of the private security industry can be seen as an inherent source of polarization between those who can afford to pay for protection for themselves and their property, and those who cannot. Seen in this light, security commercialization can be regarded as a recipe for weakening social cohesion and undermining the legitimacy of the state.

These concerns are not without foundation. It is indisputable that security commercialization can accentuate socio-economic divisions in society, generate exclusionary dynamics, and, as we have seen, weaken and instrumentalize civil society. Yet, it would be misleading to assume that all aspects of security commercialization are necessarily a recipe for disaster. In countries and situations where the ability of the state to provide security is limited, or where its legitimacy is questioned, the provision of security by private actors can be a stabilizing factor. As we have seen, in the absence of the resources provided by PSCs, it would be very difficult for cash-strapped states in Eastern Europe to provide security in all the areas where citizens expect protection—from securing critical infrastructure and public buildings to guarding the private property of individuals. Furthermore, in many instances the presence and growing power of PSCs—particularly global security companies—has pushed governments to enact long-overdue reforms, has helped to professionalize the field of security, and has contributed to the integration of former communist countries into European and global economic and political circuits. In turn, that has opened new avenues for mobilization in pursuit of more socio-economic rights by some of the most vulnerable members of society, and has facilitated the influx of much-needed foreign capital into Eastern Europe. Those developments have had a series of important implications, contributing not only to the modernization and economic growth of host countries but also to the protection and well-being of ordinary citizens.

Yet, this situation is far from constituting an unmitigated blessing. At the same time as they contribute to the security and empowerment of the population—including some of its most vulnerable members—processes linked to the commercialization of security can also help to reproduce problematic structures of power and threaten to weaken key liberal-democratic norms, including accountability and respect for the rule of law. Problems associated with security commercialization are not unique to Eastern European societies. But in those societies they are made more acute by the fact that they occur against the background of—and help reinforce—a series of undemocratic attitudes and abusive power structures inherited from the communist past. Thus, ironically, the very processes of privatization that were expected to help countries like Romania, Bulgaria, Bosnia, and Serbia to transcend their difficult historical legacies have, in some ways, contributed to the reproduction of some aspects of those legacies. And, at the same time as security commercialization has contributed to the integration of those societies into legitimate European and global flows, it has also facilitated their insertion into illicit regional and global structures, including those linked to organized crime. Private security companies, as we have seen, have been at the heart of many of those contradictory processes. Critically, since their emergence in the 1990s PSCs have played the roles of actors linked to the incorporation of crime within the state and have helped to sustain the nexus between public authorities–business–transnational organized crime. At the same time, however, the private security industry has mobilized its substantial material and non-material sources of capital to help enact the state and provide key public goods in areas in which the state was absent or inefficient.

These developments raise difficult questions and normative challenges, and the complex interplays of global and local, public and private, and domestic and international in contemporary security arrangements make it difficult to draw definitive conclusions about the dynamics, consequences, and merits of new security arrangements in specific settings. Analyzing those arrangements—and deciding how to respond to them—requires challenging many of the categories through which modern political life has conventionally been understood, and demands that we find novel ways for conceptualizing the manner in which security provision is connected to social, economic, and political structures and dynamics that defy conventional boundaries among academic disciplines and different domains of activity. Normatively, it requires that we treat private security as not simply a matter of consensual market exchange, or an issue to be decided on the basis of instrumental cost/benefit analyses of how resources can most efficiently be used. Rather, the growth of security markets and the broader process of security commercialization need to be understood as contested practices of governance that are filled with power and play important roles in (re)constituting subjectivities and shaping societies in ways that may challenge our ability to protect key democratic principles and promises. These issues will require the attention—and innovative thinking—of scholars and practitioners for a long time.

Notes

1. For an excellent discussion on this theme, see Abrahamsen and Williams 2011: 112–16.
2. For accounts of normative problems linked to the proliferation and growing power of private security providers and arrangements in different regions, see, for example, Stenning 2000; van Steden and Sarre 2010a; van Steden and de Waard 2013; Westermeyer 2013; White 2010. Also relevant are Dupont et al. 2003; Garland 2001; Kempa et al. 2004; O'Malley and Palmer 1996.
3. Interview with a Bosnian security expert affiliated with the Sarajevo Centre for Security Studies, June 27, 2013. This view was echoed by an investigative reporter, a member of the EU Delegation, and a member of the NATO Mission to Bosnia (interviews March 10–12, 2014, Sarajevo). See also Brady 2012.
4. There is a long-standing debate among IR scholars and practitioners over the relative merits of liberal interventions in post-conflict situations. While some regard liberal peacebuilding as a desirable—if imperfect—form of international involvement in societies emerging from conflict, and focus their attention on ways in which the limits and risks of liberal interventionism might be mitigated, others have been very critical of what they regard as a neo-colonial type of practices conducted in the name

of (re)building states. In a rich literature, see, for instance, the critique put forward by David Chandler (1999), and the defence of liberal peacebuilding articulated by Roland Paris (2010). For a discussion of the challenges that international actors face in trying to formulate and implement exit strategies to conclude peacebuilding missions, see in particular Caplan 2012.

5. Telephone interviews with a Bulgarian investigative reporter and a member of the management team of G4S, May 27, 2014.

6. For another influential account of the dangers of market overreach, see Sandel's (2012) discussion of the ways in which the inflated power and reach of money can lead to deep inequality and corruption. Sandel worries that, in a situation marked by massive inequalities of income, some individuals are likely to be unfairly coerced into market exchanges in all areas of life, including education, health care, and political influence. Furthermore, he argues, market exchanges can have a corrupting effect on society. This occurs because, in addition to allocating goods, markets also promote certain attitudes toward the goods being exchanged, often undermining their meaning and value. Also relevant is Debra Satz's analysis of "noxious markets," whose operations undermine the conditions that people need if they are to relate to one another as equals. See Satz 2010.

7. Various aspects of this problem are discussed in the contributions to the Abrahamsen and Leander 2015 volume. See also Abrahamsen and Williams 2011.

8. For a broader discussion of the moral limitations of markets, see also Anderson 1990, Radin 1996, and Harcourt 2011.

9. Interviews with investigative journalists and members of security think tanks from Bulgaria, Romania, Serbia, and Bosnia, June 2012–June 2014, Sofia, Bucharest, Belgrade, and Sarajevo.

10. In recent years the EU has adopted a wide range of measures aimed at combating organized crime and particularly terrorism, and many of these entail enhanced responsibility for individuals and businesses to behave in ways that are seen by European policymakers as necessary for reducing security risks. For a recent example, see the *EU Directive on Combating Terrorism* (http://www.consilium.eur opa.eu/en/press/press-releases/2017/03/07-rules-to-prevent-new-forms-of-terrorism/). The Directive—like many other EU anti-terrorism initiatives—has been criticized by human rights groups on the grounds that its provisions place too much power in the hands of authorities at the expense of civil society, and could easily result in human rights violations. For a critical analysis of the Directive, see Human Rights Watch 2016.

11. This situation is similar to developments in several African countries, as discussed by Abrahamsen and Williams (2011: 185, 193). For a discussion of changes in the definition of the public and its instrumentalization in different contexts and different social fields, see also Best and Gheciu 2014.

12. For instance, in interviews with the author, two owners of small businesses from Romania, one from Bosnia and one from Bulgaria, complained that the police were putting pressure on them to buy more private security services (especially electronic protection) than they estimated was necessary. (Interviews in Bucharest, Sarajevo, and Sofia, June 2012–June 2014.)

13. Interviews conducted between May 2012 and May 2014 in Sofia, Bucharest, and Sarajevo with some twenty members of the managerial teams of PSCs in the other three countries examined in this book reveal that the global economic crisis had similar negative impacts in those countries.

14. This point came up in the author's interviews with an investigative reporter, a member of the EU Delegation to Bosnia, and a member of the NATO Mission to Bosnia (interviews March 10–12, 2014, Sarajevo).

15. Interviews with two investigative journalists in Sofia, June 18, 2012, and with a former employee of EUROPOL, Brussels, March 6, 2014.

16. This section relies on information provided in the course of the author's interviews with two security analysts from each of the countries examined in the project, five government officials in each of those states, as well as two investigative journalists from the Sarajevo-based OCCRP project, and three EU officials that had worked in Bosnia and had knowledge of developments in all other countries from the Balkans. While many government officials tried to portray links between security professionals and organized crime as a marginal, limited problem, all the other interviewees suggested that the problem was much larger—with some arguing that, in some form or other, it was touching more than 70 percent of the security providers.

17. Interviews with two senior analysts affiliated with CSD, Sofia, June 6–14, 2012.

18. Interviews as in note 17.

19. The information provided in this section is based on interviews with an investigative journalist and a former member of the management team of G4S, Bucharest, June 28, 2013. It echoes findings published in OCCRP 2009.

20. It should be noted that those judges and prosecutors were only willing to talk on condition of anonymity.

21. Interviews with an investigative journalist from Romania (Bucharest, March 22, 2014) and a former employee of EUROPOL (Brussels, March 6, 2014).

22. For an interesting discussion on this, see Albertini 2011.

23. Interviews with more than a dozen EU and NATO officials based in Sarajevo, Bosnia, June 27–8, 2013 and March 10–14, 2014.

24. Interviews as in note 23.

25. Interviews with two Serbian investigative reporters, June 17, 2013, and with a Bosnian investigative reporter as well as two Bosnian experts affiliated with the Atlantic Initiative, Sarajevo, March 10–12, 2014.

26. Interviews as in note 25.

Bibliography

Abrahamsen, Rita and Anna Leander, eds. 2015. *Routledge Handbook of Private Security Studies*. Abingdon: Routledge.

Abrahamsen, Rita and Michael C. Williams. 2006. Privatisation, Globalisation and the Politics of Protection in South Africa, in Jef Huysmans et al. (eds.). *The Politics of Protection: Sites of Insecurity and Political Agency*. London: Routledge.

Abrahamsen, Rita and Michael C. Williams. 2007. Securing the City: Private Security Companies and Non-state Authority in Global Governance. *International Relations*, 21(2): 237–53.

Abrahamsen, Rita and Michael C. Williams. 2008. Selling Security: Assessing the Impact of Military Privatization. *Review of International Political Economy*, 15(1): 131–46.

Abrahamsen, Rita and Michael C. Williams. 2011. *Security Beyond the State*. Cambridge: Cambridge University Press.

Acharya, Amitav. 2004. How Ideas Spread: Whose Norms Matter? Norm Localization and Institutional Change in Asian Regionalism. *International Organization*, 58: 239–75.

Acuto, Michele and Simon Curtis, eds. 2013. *Reassembling International Theory: Assemblage Thinking and International Relations*. Basingstoke: Palgrave.

Adler, Emanuel. 2005. *Communitarian International Relations: The Epistemic Foundations of International Relations*. London: Routledge.

Adler, Emanuel. 2010. Damned If You Do, Damned If You Don't: Performative Power and the Strategy of Conventional and Nuclear Defusing. *Security Studies*, 19(2): 199–229.

Adler, Emanuel and Vincent Pouliot. 2011. International Practices. *International Theory*, 3: 1–36.

Adler-Nissen, Rebecca. 2013. *Bourdieu in International Relations: Rethinking Key Concepts in IR*. New York: Routledge.

Ahić, Jasmin. 2009. *Systems of Private Security/Sistemi Privatne Sigurnosti*. Sarajevo: University of Sarajevo Press.

Albertini, Matteo. 2011. The Adriatic Connection: Mafia Links from Italy to the Western Balkans. *Balkanalysis.com*. Available at http://www.balkanalysis.com/serbia/2011/06/01/the-adriatic-connection-mafia-links-from-italy-to-the-western-balkans/.

Alexander, Jeffrey C. 2011. *Performance and Power*. Cambridge and Malden, MA: Polity Press.

Alexander, Jeffrey C., Bernhard Giesen, and Jason L. Mast. 2006. *Social Performance: Symbolic Action, Cultural Pragmatics, and Ritual*. Cambridge: Cambridge University Press.

Amoore, Louise. 2007. Vigilant Visualities: The Watchful Politics of the War on Terror. *Security Dialogue*, 38(2): 215–32.

Anderson, Benedict. 1983. *Imagined Communities: Reflections on the Origin and Spread of Nationalism*. London: Verso.

Anderson, Elizabeth. 1990. The Ethical Limitations of the Market. *Economics and Philosophy*, 6(2): 179–205.

Andreas, Peter. 2011. Illicit Globalization: Myths, Misconceptions, and Historical Lessons. *Political Science Quarterly*, 126(3): 403–23.

Andreas, Peter and Ethan Nadelmann. 2006. *Policing the Globe: Criminalization and Crime Control in International Relations*. Oxford: Oxford University Press.

Avant, Deborah. 2005. *The Market for Force: The Consequences of Privatizing Security*. Cambridge: Cambridge University Press.

Avant, Deborah. 2006. The Implications of Marketized Security for IR Theory: The Democratic Peace, Late State-Building, and the Nature and Frequency of Conflict. *Perspectives on Politics*, 4(3): 507–28.

Avant, Deborah. 2016. Pragmatic Networks and Transnational Governance of Private Military and Security Services. *International Studies Quarterly*, 60(2): 330–42.

Avant, Deborah, Martha Finnemore, and Susan Sell, eds. 2010. *Who Governs the Globe?* Cambridge: Cambridge University Press.

Avant, Deborah and Virginia Haufler. 2014. The Dynamics of "Private" Security Practices and their Public Consequences: Transnational Organizations in Historical Perspective, in Jacqueline Best and Alexandra Gheciu (eds.). *The Return of the Public in Global Governance*. Cambridge: Cambridge University Press.

Avant, Deborah and Virginia Haufler. 2018. Public–Private Interactions and Practices of Security, in Alexandra Gheciu and William Wohlforth (eds.). *The Oxford Handbook of International Security*. Oxford: Oxford University Press.

Ayling, Julie, Peter Grabosky, and Clifford Shearing. 2009. *Lengthening the Arm of the Law: Enhancing Police Resources in the Twenty-First Century*. Cambridge: Cambridge University Press.

Azinović, Vlado et al., eds. 2011. *Assessing the Potential for Renewed Ethnic Violence in Bosnia and Herzegovina: A Risk Analysis*. Sarajevo: Atlantic Initiative Democratization Policy Council.

Badea, Gabriel. 2013. Un fenomen cu care ne confruntam in ultima perioada este tupeul hotilor. [A New Phenomenon is the Nerve of Burglars] *Interview with Agerpress*. Bucharest, July 21, 2013. Available at http://www.agerpres.ro/social/2013/07/21/interviu-gabriel-badea-fss-un-fenomen-cu-care-ne-confruntam-in-ultima-perioada-este-tupeul-hotilor-au-fost-si-jafuri-de-60-de-secunde-13-54-52.

Badea, Gabriel. 2014. About Police Governance over the Private Security Industry, in CoESS (ed.). *CoESS White Paper on Cohesion*. Brussels: CoESS.

Badea, Gabriel. 2015. În pofida progresului tehnologic, resursa umană nu va fi eliminată din serviciile de securitate ["Despite Technical Progress, Human Resources Will Not Be Eliminated from Security Services"]. *Interview with Agerpress*. Bucharest, May 28, 2015. Available at http://www.agerpres.ro/economie/2015/05/28/interviu-gabriel-badea-fss-in-pofida-progresului-tehnologic-resursa-umana-nu-va-fi-eliminata-din-serviciile-de-securitate-trebuie-sa-asigure-acordul-fin–12-45-29.

Barnett, Michael N. and Raymond Duvall. 2005a. *Power in Global Governance*. Cambridge and New York: Cambridge University Press.

Barnett, Michael and Raymond Duvall. 2005b. Power in International Politics. *International Organization*, 59(1): 39–75.

Bauman, Zigmunt, Didier Bigo, Paul Esteves, Elspeth Guild, Vivienne Jabri, David Lyon, and R.B.J. Walker. 2014. After Snowden: Rethinking the Impact of Surveillance. *International Political Sociology*, 8(2): 121–44.

Bećirević, Edina and Maida Čehajić. 2013. Politics, Policing and Security Sector Reform in Post-war Bosnia and Herzegovina, in Tobias Flessenkemper and Damien Helly (eds.). *Ten Years After*. Paris: Institute for Security Studies.

Beck, Ulrich. 1992. From Industrial Society to the Risk Society: Questions of Survival, Social Structure and Ecological Enlightenment. *Theory, Culture & Society*, 9(1): 97–123.

Beck, Ulrich. 1999. *World Risk Society*. Cambridge: Polity Press.

Beck, Ulrich. 2002. The Terrorist Threat: World Risk Society Revisited. *Theory, Culture & Society*, 19(4): 39–56.

Beck, Ulrich. 2004. The Silence of Words: On Terror and War. *Security Dialogue*, 34: 255–67.

Bell, Catherine M. 1997. *Ritual: Perspectives and Dimensions*. New York: Oxford University Press.

Berndtsson, Joakim. 2012. Security Professionals for Hire: Exploring the Many Faces of Private Security Expertise. *Millennium—Journal of International Studies*, 40(2): 303–20.

Bertelsmann Stiftung, BTI. 2014. *Bosnia and Herzegovina Country Report*. Gütersloh: Bertelsmann Stiftung. Available at https://www.bti-project.org/fileadmin/files/BTI/Downloads/Reports/2014/pdf/BTI_2014_Bosnia_and_Herzegovina.pdf.

Best, Jacqueline and Alexandra Gheciu. 2014. *The Return of the Public in Global Governance*. Cambridge: Cambridge University Press.

Bigo, Didier. 2000. When Two Become One: Internal and External Securitisations in Europe, in Morten Kelstrup and Michael Williams (eds.). *International Relations Theory and the Politics of Europe Integration*. London: Routledge.

Bigo, Didier. 2005. La mondialisation de l'(in)sécurité? Réflexions sur le champ des professionnels de la gestion des inquiétudes et analytique de la transnationalisation des processus d'(in)sécurisation. *Cultures et Conflits*: 53–100.

Bigo, Didier. 2006. Security, Exception, Ban and Surveillance, in David Lyon (ed.). *Theorizing Surveillance: The Panopticon and Beyond*. London: Willan Publishing.

Bigo, Didier. 2007. Detention of Foreigners, States of Exception, and the Social Practices of Control of the Banopticton, in P.K. Rajaram and C. Grundy-Warr (eds.). *Borderscapes: Hidden Geographies and Politics at Territory's Edge*. Minneapolis: University of Minnesota Press.

Bigo, Didier, Philippe Bonditti, and Christian Olsson. 2010. *Europe's 21st Century Challenge*. London: Ashgate.

Bigo, Didier and Elspeth Guild. 2005. Policing at a Distance: Schengen Visa Policies, in Didier Bigo and Elspeth Guild (eds.). *Controlling Frontiers: Free Movement into and within Europe*. Farnham: Ashgate.

Bolkovac, Kathryn and Cari Lynn. 2011. *The Whistleblower*. New York: Palgrave Macmillan.

Born, Hans, Marina Caparini, and Eden Cole. 2006. Regulating Private Security Companies in Europe: Status and Prospects. *Draft Report, Prepared for the European*

Committee on Crime Problems, Council for Police Matters. Geneva: Centre for Democratic Control of Armed Forces.

Börzel, Tanja and Thomas Risse. 2005. Public–Private Partnerships: Effective and Legitimate Tools of Transnational Governance, in Edgar Grande and Louis Pauly (eds.). *Complex Sovereignty*. Toronto: University of Toronto Press.

Bourdieu, Pierre. 1977. *Outline of a Theory of Practice*. Cambridge: Cambridge University Press.

Bourdieu, Pierre. 1986. The Forms of Capital, in John Richardson (ed.). *Handbook of Theory and Research for the Sociology of Education*. New York: Greenwood.

Bourdieu, Pierre. 1990. *The Logic of Practice*, trans. Richard Nice. Stanford: Stanford University Press.

Bourdieu, Pierre. 1998. *Practical Reason*. Stanford: Stanford University Press.

Bourdieu, Pierre. 2002. Social Space and Symbolic Power, in Mark Haugaard (ed.). *Power: A Reader*. Manchester: Manchester University Press.

Bourdieu, Pierre and Richard Nice. 2000. *Pascalian Meditations*. Palo Alto, CA: Stanford University Press.

Bourdieu, Pierre and Loïc Wacquant. 1992. The Purpose of Reflexive Sociology (The Chicago Workshop), in Pierre Bourdieu and Loïc J.D. Wacquant (eds.). *An Invitation to Reflexive Sociology*. Chicago: University of Chicago Press.

Brady, Sheelagh. 2012. *Organized Crime in Bosnia and Herzegovina*. Sarajevo: Centre for Security Studies. Available at https://www.occrp.org/documents/OC_in_BH_ENG.pdf.

Brodeur, Jean-Paul. 1983. High Policing and Low Policing: Remarks about the Policing of Political Activities. *Social Problems*, 30(5): 507–21.

Brodeur, Jean-Paul. 2010. *The Policing Web*. Oxford: Oxford University Press.

Bureš, Oldřich. 2015. *Private Security Companies: Transforming Politics and Security in the Czech Republic*. Basingstoke: Palgrave Macmillan.

Button, Mark. 2007. Assessing the Regulation of Private Security across Europe. *European Journal of Criminology*, 4(1): 109–28.

Caparini, Marina and Otwin Marenin, eds. 2004. *Transforming Police in Central and Eastern Europe: Process and Progress*. Münster, Germany and Piscataway, NJ: Lit Verlag and Transaction Publishers.

Caparini, Marina and Otwin Marenin. 2005. Crime, Insecurity and Police Reform in Post-Socialist CEE. *The Journal of Power Institutions in Post-Soviet Societies*, 12(2): 37–46. Available at https://pipss.revues.org/330#bodyftn2.

Caplan, Richard. 2005. *International Governance of War-Torn Territories: Rule and Reconstruction*. Oxford: Oxford University Press.

Caplan, Richard. 2012. *Exit Strategies and State Building*. New York: Oxford University Press.

Carlson, Marvin A. 2004. *Performance: A Critical Introduction*. London and New York: Routledge.

Center for Euro-Atlantic Studies (CEAS). 2014. *The Missing Link: Security Sector Reform, "Military Neutrality" and EU Integration in Serbia*. Belgrade: Center for Euro-Atlantic Studies. Available at https://www.ceas-serbia.org/images/prilozi/CEAS-DPC-Study-Missing-Link-SSR-military-neutrality-Serbia-EU-integration.pdf.

Centre for the Study of Democracy (CSD). 2004. *Partners in Crime*. Sofia: Centre for the Study of Democracy.

Centre for the Study of Democracy (CSD). 2012. *Serious and Organised Crime Threat Assessment 2010–2011*. Sofia: Centre for the Study of Democracy.

Chandler, David. 1999. *Bosnia: Faking Democracy after Dayton*. London: Pluto.

Chandler, David. 2006. *Empire in Denial: The Politics of State-building*. London: Pluto.

Coker, Christopher. 2009. *War in an Age of Risk*. Cambridge: Polity Press.

Committee on the Internal Market and Consumer Protection & Committee on Employment and Social Affairs of the European Parliament. 2011. *Draft Report on the Proposal for a Directive of the European Parliament and of the Council on Public Procurement*. Brussels. Available at http://www.europarl.europa.eu/sides/getDoc.do?pubRef=-//EP//TEXT+REPORT+A7-2013-0007+0+DOC+XML+V0//EN.

Confederation of European Security Services (CoESS). 2010. *Critical Infrastructure Security and Protection*: *The Public-Private Opportunity*. White Paper. Brussels: CoESS. Available at: http://www.naftso.org/language/en/uploads/files/home__0/home__b12b429e50767e06715e1294ce238774.pdf.

CoESS. 2011. *Facts and Figures*. Brussels: CoESS.

CoESS. 2013a. *The Socio-Economic Added Value of Private Security Services in Europe*, 4th White Paper (Madrid: CoESS). Available at http://www.coess.org/download.php?down=Li9kb2N1bWVudHMvd3AtNC0yMDEzLXRoZS1zb2Npby1lY29ub21ppYy1hZGRlZC12YWx1ZS1vZi1wcml2YXRlLXNlY3VyaXR5LXNlcnZpY2VzLWluLWV1cm9wZS5wZGY.

CoESS. 2013b. *Facts and Figures*. Brussels: CoESS.

CoESS. 2014a. *Critical Infrastructure Private Guarding Company Requirements Checklist*. Available at http://docplayer.net/1426812-Critical-infrastructure-private-guarding-company-requirements-checklist.html.

CoESS. 2014b. *CoESS White Paper on Cohesion*. Brussels: CoESS.

CoESS/ESTA. 2005. *Joint CoESS/ESTA Position Paper on the Draft Directive on Services in the Internal Market*. Brussels: CoESS.

CoESS and l'Institut National des Hautes Etudes de Sécurité. 2008. *Private Security and Its Role in European Security* (White Paper). Brussels: CoESS.

CoESS/UNI-Europa, UNI-Europa/EFCI, and EFFAT/FERCO [CoESS et al.]. 2012. *Modernisation of EU Public Procurement Policy*. Brussels: UNI-Europa/CoESS, UNI-Europa/EFCI, and EFFAT/FERCO.

Cortell, Andrew and James Davis. 2005. When Norms Clash: International Norms, Domestic Practices, and Japan's Internalisation of the GATT/WTO. *Review of International Studies*, 31(1): 3–25.

Coulloudon, Virginie. 1997. The Criminalization of Russia's Political Elite. *East European Constitutional Review*, 6(4): 73–8.

de Clerck, Hilde. 2011. *CoESS Position on the European Commission Consultation on an Industrial Policy for the Security Industry*. Brussels: CoESS.

de Waard, Jaap. 1999. The Private Security Industry in International Perspective. *European Journal on Criminal Policy and Research*, 7(2): 143–74.

Dean, Mitchell. 1999. *Governmentality: Power and Rule in Modern Society*. London: Sage.

Denzin, Norman. 2008. *Symbolic Interactionism and Cultural Studies: The Politics of Interpretation*. San Francisco, CA: John Wiley & Sons.

DeWinter-Schmitt, Rebecca. 2015. Transnational Business Governance through Standards and Codes of Conduct, in Rita Abrahamsen and Anna Leander (eds.). *Routledge Handbook of Private Security Studies*. Abingdon: Routledge.

Dojčinović, Stevan. 2010. Serbia: Nobody's Policing the Security Guards, in *Organized Crime and Corruption Reporting Project: Security Chaos*. Available at https://reportingproject.net/security/index.php/serbia/serbia-nobodys-policing-the-security-guards.

Dorsey, James. 2010. Private Security Firms in the Balkans Harbour Corruption, Observers Say, *Deutsche Welle, 19.06.2010*. Available at http://www.dw.com/en/private-security-firms-in-the-balkans-harbor-corruption-observers-say/a-5684942.

Dunigan, Molly and Ulrich Petersohn, eds. 2015. *The Markets for Force: Privatization of Security across World Regions*. Philadelphia: University of Pennsylvania Press.

Dupont, Benoît. 2014. Private Security Regimes: Conceptualizing the Forces that Shape the Private Delivery of Security. *Theoretical Criminology*, 18(3): 263–81.

Dupont, Benoît, Peter Grabosky, and Clifford Shearing. 2003. The Governance of Security in Weak and Failing States. *Criminal Justice*, 3(4): 331–49.

Dzhekova, Rosita and Atanas Rusev. 2015. Bulgaria, in Franziska Klopfer and Nelleke van Amstel (eds.). *A Force for Good? Mapping the Private Security Landscape in Southeast Europe*. Geneva and Belgrade: Centre for the Democratic Control of Armed Forces.

EFCI (European Federation of Cleaning Industries) and UNI-Europa. 2014. *Joint Statement by the European Social Partners of the Cleaning Industry Regarding the Directive 2014/24/EU of the European Parliament and of the Council on Public Procurement*. Brussels: EFCI and UNI-Europa. Available at http://www.feni.be/fileadmin/feni_files/documents/newsletters/2015/NL01/2014-10-29_EFCI-UNI_Europa_Final_joint_statement_Public_procurement_reform_EN.pdf.

Eichler, Maya, ed. 2015. *Gender and Private Security in Global Politics*. New York: Oxford University Press.

Elbasani, Arolda. 2013. *Europeanization or Business as Usual?* London: Routledge/UACES.

Epstein, Charlotte. 2012. Stop Telling Us How to Behave: Socialization or Infantilization? *International Studies Perspectives*, 13(2): 135–45.

Epstein, Rachel. 2008. *In Pursuit of Liberalism: International Institutions in Postcommunist Europe*. Baltimore, MD: Johns Hopkins University Press.

Ericson, Richard and Kevin Haggerty. 1997. *Policing the Risk Society*. Toronto: University of Toronto Press.

European Commission. 2010. Communication from the Commission to the European Parliament, the Council, and the European Economic and Social Committee. *EU 2020: An Integrated Industrial Policy for the Globalisation Era: Putting Competitiveness and Sustainability at Centre Stage*, {SEC(2010) 1272}, COM(2010) 614. Brussels: European Commission. Available at http://eur-lex.europa.eu/legal-content/EN/TXT/?uri=CELEX%3A52010DC0614.

European Commission. 2011. *Guide to the Case Law of the European Court of Justice on Articles 49 et seq. TFEU*. Brussels: European Commission.

European Commission. 2012. Communication from the Commission to the European Parliament, the Council and the European Economic and Social Committee, Security

Industrial Policy. *Action Plan for an Innovative and Competitive Security Industry*. Brussels: European Commission. Available at http://www.statewatch.org/news/2012/jul/eu-com-security-industry-com-417-12.pdf.

European Council. 2003. *A Secure Europe in a Better World: European Security Strategy*. Available at https://europa.eu/globalstrategy/en/european-security-strategy-secure-europe-better-world.

Fine, Gary A. 1993. The Sad Demise, Mysterious Disappearance, and Glorious Triumph of Symbolic Interactionism. *Annual Review of Sociology*, 19(1): 61–87.

Finnemore, Martha and Kathryn Sikkink. 1998. International Norm Dynamics and Political Change. *International Organization*, 52(4): 887–917.

Flessenkemper, Tobias and Damien Helly, eds. 2013. *Ten Years After: Lessons from the EUPM in Bosnia and Herzegovina*. Paris: Institute for Security Studies.

Fligstein, Neil. 1990. *The Transformation of Corporate Control*. Cambridge, MA: Harvard University Press.

Fligstein, Neil. 1996. Markets as Politics: A Political-Cultural Approach to Market Institutions. *American Sociological Review*, 61: 656–73.

Fligstein, Neil. 2001. Social Skill and the Theory of Fields. *Sociological Theory*, 40: 397–405.

Fligstein, Neil and Doug McAdam. 2011. Toward a General Theory of Strategic Action Fields. *Sociological Theory*, 29(1): 1–26.

Fligstein, Neil and Doug McAdam. 2012. *A Theory of Fields*. New York: Oxford University Press.

Fligstein, Neil and Doug McAdam. 2014. The Field of Theory. *Contemporary Sociology: A Journal of Reviews*, 43(3): 315–18.

Flockhart, Trine. 2006. Complex Socialization: A Framework for the Study of State Socialization. *European Journal of International Relations*, 1(12): 89–118.

Fogel, David. 1994. *Policing in Central and Eastern Europe: Report on a Study Tour*. Helsinki: European Institute for Crime Prevention and Control.

Galeotti, Mark, ed. 2005. *Global Crime Today: The Changing Face of Organized Crime*. London: Routledge.

Ganev, Venelin. 2007. *Preying on the State: The Transformation of Bulgaria after 1989*. Ithaca, NY: Cornell University Press.

Ganev, Venelin. 2009. Postcommunist Political Capitalism: A Weberian Interpretation. *Comparative Studies in Society and History*, 51(3): 648–74.

Garland, David. 2001. *The Culture of Control: Crime and Social Order in Contemporary Society*. Oxford: Oxford University Press.

Gestri, Marco. 2012. The European Union and Private Military and Security Contractors: Existing Controls and Legal Bases for Further Regulation, in Christine Bakker and Mirko Sossai (eds.). *Multilevel Regulation of Military and Security Contractors: The Interplay between International, European and Domestic Norms*. Oxford and Portland, OR: Hart Publishing.

Gheciu, Alexandra. 2005. International Norms, Power and the Politics of International Administration: The Kosovo Case. *Geopolitics*, 10: 121–46.

Gheciu, Alexandra. 2008. *Securing Civilization? The EU, NATO, and the OSCE in the Post-9/11 World*. Oxford: Oxford University Press.

Gheciu, Alexandra. 2011. Divided Partners: The Challenges of NATO–NGO Cooperation in Peacebuilding Operations. *Global Governance*, 17(1): 95–113.

Gheciu, Alexandra. 2014. Constructing a New Culture of Security: Reconstituting Public Power in Post-Communist Europe, in Louis Pauly and Bruce Jentleson (eds.). *Power in a Complex Global System*. Abingdon and New York: Routledge.

Goffman, Erving. 1959. *The Presentation of Self in Everyday Life*. Garden City, NY: Double Day.

Goold, Benjamin and Lucia Zedner. 2006. *Crime and Security*. Aldershot and Burlington, VT: Ashgate.

Gould, Alex. 2017. Global Assemblages and Counter-piracy: Public and Private in Maritime Policing. *Policing and Society*, 27(4): 408–18.

Gounev, Philip. 2007. Bulgaria's Private Security Industry, in Alan Bryden and Marina Caparini (eds.). *Private Actors and Security Governance*. Geneva: Centre for Democratic Control of the Armed Forces.

Gounev, Philip and Vincenzo Ruggiero. 2012. *Corruption and Organized Crime in Europe: Illegal Partnerships*. London: Routledge.

Grabosky, Peter. 2007. Private Sponsorship of Public Policing. *Police Practice and Research*, 8(1): 5–16.

Grande, Edgar and Louis W. Pauly. 2005. *Complex Sovereignty: Reconstituting Political Authority in the Twenty-First Century*. Toronto: University of Toronto Press.

Guzzini, Stefano. 2013. Power, in Rebecca Adler-Nissen (ed.). *Bourdieu in International Relations*. London: Routledge.

G4S. 2011. *International Magazine*. London: G4S. Available at http://www.g4s.com/~/media/files/international%20magazine/2011%20issue%201/international%20maga zine%20issue%201%202011.ashx, last accessed June 2, 2017.

Haggerty, Kevin D. and Richard V. Ericson. 2000. The Surveillant Assemblage. *British Journal of Sociology*, 51(4): 605–22.

Hajer, Maarten A. 2009. *Authoritative Governance: Policy Making in the Age of Mediatization*. Oxford: Oxford University Press.

Hall, Rodney Bruce and Thomas J. Biersteker, eds. 2002. *The Emergence of Private Authority in Global Governance*. Cambridge and New York: Cambridge University Press.

Hall, Tim. 2013. Geographies of the Illicit. *Progress in Human Geography*, 37(3): 366–85.

Handleman, Stephen. 1994. *Comrade Criminal: The Theft of the Second Russian Revolution*. London: Michael Joseph.

Harcourt, Bernard E. 2011. *The Illusion of Free Markets: Punishment and the Myth of Natural Order*. Cambridge, MA: Harvard University Press.

Haufler, Virginia. 1997. *Dangerous Commerce: Insurance and the Management of International Risk*. Ithaca, NY: Cornell University Press.

Haufler, Virginia. 2007. The Private Sector and Governance in Post-Conflict Countries, in Derick Brinkerhoff (ed.). *Governance in Post-Conflict Societies*. London: Routledge.

Haufler, Virginia. 2010. Corporations in Zones of Conflict: Issues, Actors, and Institutions, in Deborah Avant, Martha Finnemore, and Susan Sell (eds.). *Who Governs the Globe?* Cambridge: Cambridge University Press.

Herbst, Kathrin. 2013. Searching for Legitimacy—Private Military and Security Companies (Pmscs) Overcoming Ingrained Stereotypes. *Security Journal*, 26(3): 280–93.

Hobbs, Dick. 2001. The Firm. *The British Journal of Criminology*, 41(4): 549–60.

Hoffmann Mark. 2010. Norms and Social Constructivism in International Relations, in Robert E. Denemark (ed.).The International Studies Encylopedia. Oxford: Blackwell Reference Online. Available at http://www.blackwellreference.com/public/book.html?id=g9781444336597_9781444336597.

Human Rights Watch. 2016. *EU Counterterrorism Directive Seriously Flawed*. Available at https://www.hrw.org/news/2016/11/30/eu-counterterrorism-directive-seriously-flawed.

ICoC. 2010. International Code of Conduct for Private Security Providers. Available at http://psm.du.edu/media/documents/regulations/global_instruments/multi_stake holder/icoc/icoc_eng.pdf.

Ignatieff, Michael. 2003. *Empire Lite: Nation Building in Bosnia, Kosovo, Afghanistan*. London: Vintage.

Jakobi, Anja. 2013. *Common Goods and Evils?: The Formation of Global Crime Governance*. Oxford: Oxford University Press.

Jakobi, Anja and Klaus Dieter Wolf, eds. 2013. *The Transnational Governance of Violence and Crime: Non-State Actors in Security*. New York: Palgrave Macmillan.

Jarstad, Anna K. and Roberto Belloni. 2012. Introducing Hybrid Peace Governance: Impact and Prospects of Liberal Peacebuilding. *Global Governance*, 18(1): 1–6.

Jeffrey, Alexander Sam. 2012. *The Improvised State: Sovereignty, Performance and Agency in Dayton Bosnia*. Malden, MA: Wiley & Sons.

Joachim, Jutta and Andrea Schneiker. 2014. All for One and One in All: Private Military Security Companies as Soldiers, Business Managers and Humanitarians. *Cambridge Review of International Affairs*, 27(2): 1–22.

Johnston, Les. 1992. *The Rebirth of Private Policing*. London and New York: Routledge.

Johnston, Les. 2000. Transnational Private Security: The Impact of Global Commercial Security, in J.W.E. Sheptycki (ed.). *Issues in Transnational Policing*. London: Routledge.

Johnston, Les. 2006. Transnational Security Governance, in Jennifer Wood and Benoît Dupont (eds.). *Democracy, Society and the Governance of Security*. Cambridge: Cambridge University Press.

Johnston, Les and Shearing, Clifford. 2003. *Governing Security: Explorations in Policing and Justice*. London: Routledge.

Jovanović, Ivana. 2013. Serbia Moves to Regulate Private Security Sector. *Southeast European Times*. Available at http://iissonline.net/serbia-moves-to-regulate-private-security-sector/.

Kadar, Andras, ed. 2001. *Police in Transition*. Budapest: Central European University Press.

Katz, Anton and Margaret Maffai. 2015. The Extension of International Human Rights Law to Private Military and Security Companies, in Rita Abrahamsen and Anna Leander (eds.). *Routledge Handbook of Private Security Studies*. Abingdon: Routledge.

Kempa, Michael, Ryan Carrier, Jennifer Wood, and Clifford Shearing. 1999. Reflections on the Evolving Concept of "Private Policing." *European Journal on Criminal Policy and Research*, 7(2): 197–223.

Kempa, Michael, Philip Stenning, and Jennifer Wood. 2004. Policing Communal Spaces: A Reconfiguration of the "Mass Private Property" Hypothesis. *British Journal of Criminology*, 44(4): 562–81.

Kirshenblatt-Gimblett, Barbara. 1999. Playing to the Senses: Food as a Performance Medium. *Performance Research*, 4(1): 1–30.

Klingen, Christoph et al. 2013. *Banking in Central and Eastern Europe and in Turkey: Challenges and Opportunities.* Luxembourg: European Investment Bank.

Klopfer, Franziska and Nelleke van Amstel, eds. 2015. *A Force for Good? Mapping the Private Security Landscape in Southeast Europe.* Geneva and Belgrade: Centre for the Democratic Control of Armed Forces.

Kontos, Alexis. 2004. "Private" Security Guards: Privatized Force and State Responsibility under International Human Rights Law. *Non-State Actors and International Law*, 4(3): 199–238.

Krahmann, Elke. 2003. Conceptualizing Security Governance. *Cooperation and Conflict*, 38(1): 5–26.

Krahmann, Elke. 2007. Regulating Military and Security Services in the European Union, in Alan Bryden and Marina Caparini (eds.). *Private Actors and Security Governance.* Geneva: Centre for Democratic Control of the Armed Forces.

Krahmann, Elke. 2010. *States, Citizens and the Privatization of Security.* Cambridge: Cambridge University Press.

Krahmann, Elke. 2011. Beck and Beyond: Selling Security in World Risk Society. *Review of International Studies*, 37(1): 349–72.

Krahmann, Elke. 2015. Regulation through Procurement Policies, in Rita Abrahamsen and Anna Leander (eds.). *Routledge Handbook of Private Security Studies.* Abingdon: Routledge.

Kržalić, Armin. 2009. *Private Security in Bosnia and Herzegovina.* Sarajevo: Centre for Security Studies.

Lamaison, Pierre. 1986. From Rules to Strategies: An Interview with Pierre Bourdieu. *Cultural Anthropology*, 1(1): 110–20.

Lasch, Christopher. 1996. *The Revolt of Elites and the Betrayal of Democracy.* New York: WW Norton.

Latour, Bruno. 1993. *We Have Never Been Modern.* Cambridge, MA: Harvard University Press.

Lawson, George and Robbie Shilliam. 2010. Sociology and International Relations: Legacies and Prospects. *Cambridge Review of International Affairs*, 23(1): 69–86.

Leander, Anna. 2004. The Power to Construct International Security: On the Significance of Private Military Companies. *Millennium: Journal of International Studies*, 33(3): 803–25.

Leander, Anna. 2005. The Market for Force and Public Security: The Destabilizing Consequences of Private Military Companies. *Journal of Peace Research*, 42(5): 605–22.

Leander, Anna. 2008. Thinking Tools, in Audie Klotz and Deepa Prakash (eds.). *Qualitative Methods in International Relations: A Pluralist Guide.* Basingstoke and New York: Palgrave Macmillan.

Leander, Anna. 2010. The Paradoxical Impunity of Private Military Companies: Authority and the Limits to Legal Accountability. *Security Dialogue*, 41(5): 467–90.

Leander, Anna. 2011. The Promises, Problems, and Potentials of a Bourdieu-Inspired Staging of International Relations. *International Political Sociology*, 5(3): 294–313.

Leander, Anna. 2013. *Commercialising Security in Europe*. London: Routledge.

Leander, Anna and R. Van Munster. 2007. Private Security Contractors in the Debate about Darfur: Reflecting and Reinforcing Neo-liberal Governmentality. *International Relations*, 21(2): 201–16.

Loader, Ian. 1999. Consumer Culture and the Commodification of Policing and Security. *Sociology*, 33(2): 373–92.

Loader, Ian. 2000. Plural Policing and Democratic Governance. *Social & Legal Studies*, 9(3): 323–45.

Loader, Ian. 2005. Police Inc.: An Enterprise with No Limited Responsibility? Security, Civil Governance and Public Good. *Criminologie*, 38(2): 157–72.

Loader, Ian, Benjamin Goold, and Angélica Thumala. 2014. The Moral Economy of Security. *Theoretical Criminology*, 18(4): 469–88.

Loader, Ian and Neil Walker. 2005. Necessary Virtues: The Legitimate Place of the State in the Production of Security, in J. Wood and B. Dupont (eds.). *Democracy, Society and the Governance of Security*. Cambridge: Cambridge University Press.

Loader, Ian and Neil Walker. 2007. *Civilizing Security*. Cambridge: Cambridge University Press.

Löfstrand, Cecilia, Bethan Loftus, and Ian Loader. 2016. Doing "Dirty Work": Stigma and Esteem in the Private Security Industry. *European Journal of Criminology*, 13(3): 297–314.

Los, Maria. 1998. "Virtual" Property and Post-Communist Globalization. *Demokratizatsiya*, 6(1): 77–86.

Los, Maria. 2003. Crime in Transition: The Post-Communist State, Markets and Crime. *Crime, Law and Social Change*, 40(2): 145–69.

Los, Maria and Andrzej Zybertowicz. 2000. *Privatizing the Police-state: The Case of Poland*. Basingstoke: Macmillan and New York: St. Martin's.

Low, Setha M. 2003. *Behind the Gates*. New York: Routledge.

Lyon, David. 2003. *Surveillance after September 11th*. London: Polity.

Mac Ginty, Roger. 2010. Hybrid Peace: The Interaction Between Top-Down and Bottom-Up Peace. *Security Dialogue*, 41(4): 391–412.

Macdonald, Terry. 2008. What's So Special about States? Liberal Legitimacy in a Globalising World. *Political Studies*, 56(3): 544–65.

Macdonald, Terry. 2010. Corporations and Global Justice: Rethinking "Public" and "Private" Responsibilities, in Kate Macdonald and Shelley Marshall (eds.). *Fairtrade, Corporate Accountability and Beyond*. Farnham: Ashgate Press.

Mandel, Robert. 2001. The Privatization of Security. *Armed Forces & Society*, 28(1): 129–51.

Mead, George H. 1913. The Social Self. *The Journal of Philosophy, Psychology and Scientific Methods*, 10(14): 374–80.

Mérand, Frédéric and Amelie Forget. 2013. Strategy, in Rebecca Adler-Nissen (ed.). *Bourdieu in International Relations: Rethinking Key Concepts in IR*. London: Routledge.

Mérand, Frédéric and Vincent Pouliot. 2008. Le monde de Pierre Bourdieu: Éléments pour une théorie sociale des Relations internationales. *Canadian Journal of Political Science* 41: 603–25.

Millar, Gearoid, Jaïr van der Lijn, and Willemijn Verkoren. 2013. Peacebuilding Plans and Local Reconfigurations: Frictions Between Imported Processes and Indigenous Practices. *Journal of International Relations and Development*, 20(2): 137–43.

NAFTSO (Bulgarian National Association of Security Companies). 2011. *Appeal on the Occasion of the 10th Anniversary of NAFTSO*. Sofia: NAFTSO.

Nikolov, Jovo. 1997. Organized Crime in Bulgaria. *East European Constitutional Review* 6(4): 80–4.

Noutcheva, Gergiana. 2009. Fake, Partial and Imposed Compliance: The Limits of the EU's Normative Power in the Western Balkans. *Journal of European Public Policy*, 16(7): 1065–84.

OCCRP. 2009. *Prosecuting Organized Crime in Romania*. Sarajevo: OCCRP. Available at https://reportingproject.net/security/.

O'Malley, Pat and Darren Palmer. 1996. Post-Keynesian Policing. *Economy and Society*, 25(2): 137–55.

O'Reilly, Conor. 2010. The Transnational Security Consultancy Industry. *Theoretical Criminology*, 14(2): 183–210.

Organized Crime and Corruption Reporting Project (OCCRP). 2010. *Security Chaos*. Sarajevo: OCCRP. Available at https://reportingproject.net/security/.

Page, Michael et al. 2005. *SALW and Private Security Companies in South Eastern Europe: A Cause or Effect of Insecurity?* Belgrade: SEESAC.

Pagon, Milan, ed. 1996. *Policing in Central and Eastern Europe: Comparing Firsthand Knowledge with Experience from the West*. Ljubljana: University Press.

Palan, Ronen. 2000. A World of their Making: An Evaluation of the Constructivist Critique in International Relations. *Review of International Studies*, 26(4): 575–98.

Paris, Roland. 2002. International Peacebuilding and the Mission Civilisatrice. *Review of International Studies*, 28(4): 637–56.

Paris, Roland. 2004. *At War's End: Building Peace after Civil Conflict*. Cambridge: Cambridge University Press.

Paris, Roland. 2010. Saving Liberal Peacebuilding. *Review of International Studies*, 36(2): 337–65.

Pascali, Umberto. 2001. KLA and Drugs: The "New Colombia of Europe" Grows in Balkans. *Executive Intelligence Review*. Available at http://www.larouchepub.com/other/2001/2824_kla_drugs.html.

Percy, Sarah. 2007. *Mercenaries: The History of a Norm in International Relations*. Oxford: Oxford University Press.

Percy, Sarah. 2015. Norms and Regulations, in Rita Abrahamsen and Anna Leander (eds.). *Routledge Handbook of Private Security Studies*. Abingdon: Routledge.

Perdan, Slobodan. 2008. Bosnia: SSR under International Tutelage, in Timothy Donais (ed.). *Local Ownership and Security Sector Reform*. Geneva: Centre for Democratic Control of the Armed Forces.

Permanent Representation of Spain to the EU. 2002. *Note Regarding the Network of Contact Points of Authorities with Responsibility for Private Security*. Document 7245/02, ENFOPOL 41. Available at http://www.statewatch.org/news/2002/apr/priv07245.pdf.

Petrović, Predrag. 2010. Reserved Domains as Obstacles to Adopting the Law on Private Security Sector. *Western Balkans Security Observer*, 18: 13–28.

Petrović, Predrag and Marko Milošević. 2015. Serbia, in Franziska Klopfer and Nelleke van Amstel (eds.). *A Force for Good? Mapping the Private Security Landscape in Southeast Europe*. Geneva and Belgrade: Centre for the Democratic Control of Armed Forces.

Pingeot, Lou. 2012. *Dangerous Partnership: Private Military and Security Companies and the UN*. New York: Global Policy Forum.

Prisacariu, Catalin. 2010. Romania: New System, Same Players, in *Organized Crime and Corruption Reporting Project*. Available at http://www.reportingproject.net/security/index.php/stories/7-romania.

Private Investors Council, Serbia. 2014. *White Book of the Foreign Investors Council: Private Security*. Belgrade: Private Investors Council.

Radin, Margaret Jane. 1996. *Contested Commodities*. Cambridge, MA: Harvard University Press.

Richmond, Oliver. 2006. The Problem of Peace: Understanding the "Liberal Peace." *Conflict, Security & Development*, 6(3): 291–314.

Richmond, Oliver. 2010. Resistance and the Post-Liberal Peace. *Millennium—Journal of International Studies*, 38(3): 665–92.

Ringmar, Erik. 2012. Performing International Systems: Two East-Asian Alternatives to the Westphalian Order. *International Organization*, 66(1): 1–25.

Ringmar, Erik. 2014. Recognition and the Origins of International Society. *Global Discourse*, 4(4): 446–58.

Ringmar, Erik. 2017. The Problem with Performativity: Comments on the Contributions. *Journal of International Relations and Development*, forthcoming. Available at http://portal.research.lu.se/portal/files/19809858/Erik_Ringmar_The_Problem_with_Performativity_Academia_version.pdf.

Ritzer, George. 2004. *The McDonaldization of Society*, Revised edn. London and Thousand Oaks, CA: Sage.

Robertson, Roland. 1992. *Globalization: Social Theory and Global Culture*. London: Sage Publications.

Robertson, Roland. 1995. Glocalization: Time–Space and Homogenity–Heterogeneity, in M. Featherstone, S. Lash, and R. Robertsen (eds.). *Global Modernities*. London and Thousand Oaks, CA: Sage.

Rowland, Richard and Timothy Coupe. 2014. Patrol Officers and Public Reassurance: A Comparative Evaluation of Police Officers, PCSOs, ACSOs and Private Security Guards. *Policing and Society*, 24(3): 265–84.

Ruzza, Stefano, Anja Jakobi and Charles Geisler (eds.). 2015. *Non-State Challenges in a Re-ordered World*. London: Routledge.

Sandel, Michael J. 2012. *What Money Can't Buy: The Moral Limits of Markets*. New York: Farrar, Straus and Giroux.

Sassen, Saskia. 2006. *Territory, Authority, Rights from Medieval to Global Assemblages*. Princeton, NJ: Princeton University Press.

Sassen, Saskia. 2008. Deciphering the Global: Its Spaces, Scales and Subjects. *Social Thought and Research*, 29: 3–18.

Satz, Debra. 2010. *Why Some Things Should Not Be for Sale: The Moral Limits of Markets*. New York: Oxford University Press.

Schechner, Richard. 2002. *Performance Studies: An Introduction*. London and New York: Routledge.

Schechner, Richard. 2015. *Performed Imaginaries*. Abingdon and New York: Routledge.

Schimmelfennig, Frank and Ulrich Sedelmeier. 2005. *The Europeanization of Central and Eastern Europe*. New York: Cornell University Press.

Seiberth, Corinna. 2014. *Private Military and Security Companies in International Law: A Challenge for Non-Binding Norms: The Montreux Document and the International Code of Conduct for Private Security Service Providers*. Cambridge: Intersentia.

Shearing, Clifford and Philip Stenning. 2015. The Privatization of Security: Implications for Democracy, in Rita Abrahamsen and Anna Leander (eds.). *Routledge Handbook of Private Security Studies*. Abingdon: Routledge.

Shearing, Clifford and Jennifer Wood. 2003a. Governing Security for Common Goods. *International Journal of the Sociology of Law*, 31(3): 205–25.

Shearing, Clifford and Jennifer Wood. 2003b. Nodal Governance, Democracy, and the New "Denizens." *Journal of Law and Society*, 30(3): 400–19.

Shelley, Louise. 1995. Post-Soviet Organized Crime. *European Journal on Criminal Policy and Research*, 3(4): 7–25.

Shelley, Louise. 1999. Post-Socialist Policing: Limitations on Institutional Change, in R.I. Mawby (ed.). *Policing Across the World: Issues for the Twenty-First Century*. London: UCL Press.

Singer, Peter. 2004. War, Profits, and the Vacuum of Law: Privatized Military Firms and International Law. *Columbia Journal of Transnational Law*, 42(2): 521–50.

Singer, Peter. 2008. *Corporate Warriors: The Rise of the Privatized Military Industry*. Ithaca, NY: Cornell University Press.

Sklansky, David A. 2006. Private Police and Democracy. *American Criminal Law Review*, 43(89): 89–105.

Sossai, Mirko. 2015. The Legal Framework for the Armed Forces and the Regulation of Private Security, in Rita Abrahamsen and Anna Leander (eds.). *Routledge Handbook of Private Security Studies*. Abingdon: Routledge.

South Eastern Europe Clearinghouse for the Control of Small Arms and Light Weapons. 2005. *SALW and Private Security Companies in South Eastern Europe: A Cause or Effect of Insecurity?* Belgrade: SEESAC.

Stenning, Philip C. 2000. Powers and Accountability of Private Police. *European Journal on Criminal Policy and Research*, 8(3): 325–52.

Swartz, David. 1997. *Culture and Power: The Sociology of Pierre Bourdieu*. Chicago: University of Chicago Press.

Swyngedouw, Erik. 1997. Neither Global nor Local: "Glocalization" and the Politics of Scale, in Kevin Cox (ed.). *Spaces of Globalization: Reasserting the Power of the Local*. New York and London: Guilford Press.

Swyngedouw, Erik. 2004. Globalisation or "Glocalisation"? Networks, Territories and Rescaling. *Cambridge Review of International Affairs*, 17(1): 25–48.

Tayler, Jeffrey. 2001. Russia is Finished. *The Atlantic Monthly*, 287(5): 35–52.

Thumala, Angélica, Benjamin Goold, and Ian Loader. 2011. A Tainted Trade? Moral Ambivalence and Legitimation Work in the Private Security Industry. *The British Journal of Sociology*, 62(2): 283–303.

Tilly, Charles. 1992. *Coercion, Capital, and European States, AD 990–1992*. Cambridge, MA: Blackwell.

Tzvetkova, Marina. 2008. Aspects of the Evolution of Extra-legal Protection in Bulgaria (1989–1999). *Trends in Organized Crime*, 11(4): 326–51.

Ugljesa, Zvekic. 1998. *Criminal Victimization in Countries in Transition*. Rome: UNICRI.

United States Institute of Peace (USIP). 2002. *Special Report: Lawless Rule vs. Rule of Law in the Balkans*. Washington, DC: USIP.

Vachudová, Milada. 2005. *Europe Undivided: Democracy, Leverage, and Integration after Communism*. Oxford: Oxford University Press.

Vaglenov, Stanimir. 2010. *Bulgaria: The Public, Violent Side of Private Security*. Sarajevo: OCCRP. Available at http://www.reportingproject.net/security/index.php/stories/5-bulgaria.

Valverde, Marina and Michael Mopas. 2006. Insecurity and the Dream of Targeted Governance, in William Walters (ed.). *Global Governmentality*. New York: Routledge.

van Steden, Ronald and J. de Waard. 2013. Acting like Chameleons: On the McDonaldization of Private Security. *Security Journal*, 26(3): 294–309.

van Steden, Ronald and R. Sarre. 2010a. The Tragic Quality of Contract Guards: A Discussion of the Reach and Theory of Private Security in the World Today. *The Journal of Criminal Justice Research*, 1(1): 1–19.

van Steden, Ronald and R. Sarre. 2010b. Private Policing in the Former Yugoslavia: A Menace to Society? *Journal of Criminal Justice and Security*, 12(4): 425–40.

Volkov, Vadim. 2002. *Violent Entrepreneurs: The Use of Force in the Making of Russian Capitalism*. Ithaca, NY: Cornell University Press.

Wakefield, Alison. 2003. *Selling Security: The Private Policing of Public Space*. Cullompton: Willan.

Wakefield, Alison. 2005. The Public Surveillance Functions of Private Security. *Surveillance and Society*, 2(4): 529–45.

Walzer, Michael. 1983. *Spheres of Justice: A Defense of Pluralism and Equality*. New York: Basic.

Weber, Max. 1994. *Political Writings*, ed. Peter Lassman and Ronald Speirs. Cambridge: Cambridge University Press.

Wedel, Janine. 2003. Clans, Cliques and Captured States: Rethinking "Transition" in Central and Eastern Europe and the Former Soviet Union. *Journal of International Development*, 15(4): 427–40.

Weldes, Jutta. 1999. *Constructing National Interests: The United States and the Cuban Missile Crisis*. Minneapolis, MN: University of Minnesota Press.

Wendt, Alex. 1992. Anarchy Is What States Make of It—the Social Construction of Power-Politics. *International Organization*, 2(46): 391–425.

Wendt, Alex. 1999. *Social Theory of International Politics*. Cambridge: Cambridge University Press.

Westermeyer, Gloria. 2013. *The Impact of Private Actors on Security Governance*. Wiesbaden: Springer Fachmedien.

White, Adam. 2010. *The Politics of Private Security: Regulation, Reform and Re-legitimation*. Basingstoke and New York: Palgrave Macmillan.

White, Adam. 2012. The New Political Economy of Private Security. *Theoretical Criminology*, 16(1): 85–101.

203

Wiener, Antje. 2007. Contested Meaning of Norms: A Research Framework. *Comparative European Politics*, 5: 1–17.

Williams, Michael C. 2007. *Culture and Security: Symbolic Power and the Politics of International Security*. New York: Routledge.

Williams, Michael C. 2012. The New Economy of Security. *Global Crime*, 13(4): 312–19.

Wilson, Eric. 2009. *Government of the Shadows: Parapolitics and Criminal Sovereignty*. London and New York: Pluto Press.

Windolf, Paul. 1998. Privatization and Elite Reproduction in Eastern Europe. *European Journal of Sociology*, 39(2): 335–76.

Wood, Jennifer and Benoît Dupont. 2006. *Democracy, Society, and the Governance of Security*. Cambridge: Cambridge University Press.

Wood, Jennifer and Clifford Shearing. 2006. *Imagining Security*. Cullompton: Willan.

Working Group on the Use of Mercenaries as a Means of Violating Human Rights. 2015. *Concept Note on a Possible Legally Binding Instrument for the Regulation of Private Military Security Companies*. Available at http://www.ohchr.org/Documents/HRBodies/HRCouncil/WGMilitary/Session4/WG_MercenariesCN_14April2015.pdf.

Young, Jock. 1999. *The Exclusive Society: Social Exclusion, Crime and Difference in Late Modernity*. Los Angeles and London: SAGE.

Zaum, Dominik. 2007. *The Sovereignty Paradox: The Norms and Politics of International Statebuilding*. Oxford: Oxford University Press.

Zedner, Lucia. 2006. Liquid Security. *Criminology & Criminal Justice*, 6(3): 267–88.

Index

Index